THE BORDERS OF PRIVILEGE

ARTICULATIONS STUDIES IN RACE, IMMIGRATION, AND CAPITALISM

EDITORS
Cedric de Leon
Pawan Dhingra

THE BORDERS OF PRIVILEGE

1.5-Generation Brazilian Migrants Navigating Power Without Papers

KARA B. CEBULKO

STANFORD UNIVERSITY PRESS
Stanford, California

Stanford University Press
Stanford, California

© 2025 Kara Beth Cebulko. All rights reserved.

No part of this book may be reproduced or transmitted in any form or by any means, electronic or mechanical, including photocopying and recording, or in any information storage or retrieval system, without the prior written permission of Stanford University Press.

Printed in the United States of America on acid-free, archival-quality paper

Library of Congress Cataloging-in-Publication Data

Names: Cebulko, Kara Beth, author.
Title: The borders of privilege : 1.5-generation Brazilian migrants navigating power without papers / Kara B. Cebulko.
Other titles: Articulations (Stanford, Calif.)
Description: Stanford, California : Stanford University Press, [2025] | Series: Articulations: studies in race, immigration, and capitalism | Includes bibliographical references and index.
Identifiers: LCCN 2024022276 (print) | LCCN 2024022277 (ebook) | ISBN 9781503637177 (cloth) | ISBN 9781503641532 (paperback) | ISBN 9781503641549 (ebook)
Subjects: LCSH: Brazilians—United States—Social conditions. | Brazilians—Race identity—United States. | Noncitizens—United States—Social conditions. | Immigrants—United States—Social conditions. | Illegal immigration—United States. | United States—Emigration and immigration—Social aspects.
Classification: LCC E184.B68 C43 2025 (print) | LCC E184.B68 (ebook) | DDC 305.86/98073—dc23/eng/20240604
LC record available at https://lccn.loc.gov/2024022276
LC ebook record available at https://lccn.loc.gov/2024022277

Cover design: Jason Anscomb
Cover art: Unsplash
Typeset by Newgen in 10/14.75 Minion Pro

CONTENTS

	List of Tables	vii
	Acknowledgments	ix
	Introduction	1
ONE	Deportability	40
	Navigating Power Without Papers in Everyday Interactions	
TWO	Transitions Out of High School	72
	Navigating Higher Education and Work	
THREE	Love Lives	102
	Romance and Marriage	
FOUR	Sense of Belonging	133
	American and Ethno-Racial Identities	
	Conclusion	163
	Appendix: Reflections on Methodology	175
	Notes	191
	References	201
	Index	221

TABLES

TABLE 0.1. Comparison of Race, Class, and Nation-State
            Building Contexts   16
TABLE 0.2. Descriptive Information for All Respondents in
            the Analysis   34
TABLE 4.1. (Non)American Identities of 1.5-Generation Brazilians 140

ACKNOWLEDGMENTS

I am forever grateful to the young people who shared their stories with me, some who did so over the course of nearly fifteen years. Without their stories, this book would not have been possible. I have been inspired by their resilience in the face of hostility and institutional discrimination as well as their critical honesty about the ways in which race and class shaped how Americans and government officials have treated them. Indeed, I'll never forget the way that Elisabete so vividly described the power of whiteness in US society, even as she dealt with obstacles and hardships most people in the US will never have to deal with. It truly was that first conversation with Elisabete so many years ago that paved the way for the specific story told in this book.

I have been fortunate to have this research financially supported by several institutions. In the early stages, funding from the National Science Foundation (Doctoral Dissertation Improvement Grant, Award Number 0727933) and Indiana University (Advanced Departmental Fellowships, Spring 2007 and Fall 2007) were vital to the completion of the project. Later, funding from a Committee on Aid for Faculty Research (CAFR) Grant at Providence College (510481) helped me to continue data collection and analysis.

This book also would not have been possible without the support and encouragement of mentors, colleagues, Brazilian community members, friends, and family members. Collectively, their intellectual, logistical, and emotional support, networking, critical insight, and friendship were invaluable in completing every stage of the research process. I must start with Leah VanWey, who took a chance on me when I was a quiet graduate student back in 2002. At the time, I felt in limbo, the way many young adults do. I was uncertain if a PhD in sociology was for me. But Leah gave me the opportunity to serve as her research assistant—encouraging me to study Portuguese and bringing me to Altamira, Brazil, as part of an interdisciplinary and international team of scholars. This partnership reinvigorated my commitment to a career in sociology. Her mentorship, including the quick, timely, and comprehensive feedback during the earliest years of this research, was truly invaluable. Donna Eder, Brian Powell, and Eliza Pavalko were also crucial members of my graduate committee, providing excellent feedback and support during the earliest years of this project.

Importantly, I also must thank the dynamic interdisciplinary and international team of scholars I joined through Leah. All of these people—including Eduardo S. Brondizio, Emilio F. Moran, Tony Cak, Scott Hetrick, Christine Chavez, Álvaro D'Antona, Paula Costa, Danilo Oliveira, Thais Tartalha, Vanessa Dotto, Maria Grings, Douglas Tyminiak, Simone Rodrigues, and Karoline Gonçalves—taught me the value of cross-cultural research, thinking collaboratively and from multiple perspectives, and the importance of a good joke when exhausted after a day of fieldwork. They also helped my Portuguese-language skills and critical thinking about migration and intergenerational dynamics. Indeed, it was thinking about the experiences of children of migrants in the Brazilian Amazon that planted the seeds for doing a project about the children of Brazilian immigrants' experiences in the US. Maria Fernanda (Mafer) d'Antona, who became one of my best friends when I was living in Bloomington, was my unofficial Portuguese language tutor. Every week, she made me Brazilian food as we talked for hours—about the weather, psychoanalysis, pregnancy, TV shows, American culture, Brazilian culture, and all things Bloomington, Indiana. It was Mafer who first gave me the idea to research the Brazilian community in Boston.

I also have to thank countless people I met in the Boston area, all of whom were vital to the completion of this project. Enrico Marcelli provided me with a place to live and brought me on to his research team to help canvass Brazilian neighborhoods in the summer of 2006. With his help, I made my first contacts with Brazilian community leaders and nonprofit staff members—contacts that became stronger and more extensive over the years. For confidentiality purposes for my respondents, I will not name the specific ways in which each of these individuals contributed to this research project. But I am indebted to Alexandra Barker, Marta Ferreira, Fernanda Garcia, Álvaro Lima, Fausto Mendes da Rocha, Heloisa Galvão, Joyce Padua, Helen Sinzker, Eduardo Siqueira, Natalícia Tracy, and Allesandra Pierotti for all of their invaluable assistance, generosity, and insight over the years. While some of these individuals played larger roles than others in this research, collectively, they let me learn from them and/or welcomed me into their circles, allowing me to tag along to cheer on the Brazilian men's national team in the 2006 World Cup, putting me in touch with 1.5-generation Brazilians who participated in this project, and/or helping me make sense of the dynamics I was observing and hearing. While my attempts to repay their support will never be enough, I am glad that I was able to use some of my fundraising skills to help financially support some organizations important to them and the larger immigrant communities in the Greater Boston area. Additionally, I thank Philip Granberry, Jessica Patti, Leslie Hu, Stephanie Park, and Jill and Bryan Marquard for providing me with logistical help and emotional support during the early stages of this research, including places to crash in Boston for the night.

I need to extend a special thanks to Helen Marrow, who met me for coffee in the summer of 2006 when I reached out to discuss her work with Brazilian youth. She invited me to be a part of Harvard University's Migration and Immigrant Incorporation (MII) Workshop in 2007–2008, an invaluable intellectual experience. She has been a supportive friend and colleague since that time. Alexis Silver has been instrumental to my journey as an academic and I am indebted to her for her friendship and critical feedback on early drafts of several chapters. Mintzi Auanda Martínez-Rivera, Christopher Chambers, Trina Vithayathil, Zophia Edwards, Orly Clergé, Sylvia Dominguez, Eric Hirsch, Abigail Brooks, and Charlotte O'Kelly all read and provided me with important feedback on various iterations of chapters in this manuscript. Meanwhile, conversations with the following scholars over the years—Joanna Dreby, Leah Schmalzbauer, Leisy J. Abrego, Esther Yoona Cho, Laura E. Enriquez, Roberto G. Gonzales, Caitlin Patler, Jake Watson, Tiffany Joseph, Tanya Golash-Boza, Daniela Pila, Allesandra Bazo Vienrich, Cecilia Menjívar, Mary Waters, Grace Yukich, Sarah Willen, Heide Castañeda, and Kevin Escudero—have inspired me to think more critically about the experiences of illegality. Additionally, conversations with Magali García-Pletsch, Rashawn

Ray, Pamela Braboy Jackson, Jenny Stuber, Judson Everett, Laura Hamilton, Cherise Harris, Niki Hotchkiss, Lisa Weber, and Stephanie McClure helped me to think more critically about race and social class and how these social locations shape young people's experiences in the US.

I also want to thank everyone in the Global Studies and Sociology and Anthropology Departments at Providence College that I have not already thanked—Eve Veliz-Moran, Brandon Martinez, Maureen Outlaw, Charlotte Roberts, Rhiannon Miller, Rahsaan Mahadeo, Todd Mele, Richard Greenleaf, Jim Tull, Nick Longo, Nuria Alonso García, Bilal Ibrahim, Ana Cláudia São Bernardo, and Maria Bose. I learn from all of you every day. Your collective respect for public sociology and teaching undergraduate students motivate and encourages me to be the best teacher-scholar I can be. Additionally, I must thank my current and former students at Providence College, who make my job such a rewarding one. A special thank-you to Deborah Lopez, Madison Cohen, and Christina Roca for your role as research assistants in our GST 495 course. I also thank Beth Papagolos, Vanessa Sullivan, Emily Meehan, and Katherine Lynch, all of whom have served as administrative assistants and/or administrative coordinators in Sociology or Global Studies over the past fifteen years. Your logistical support day in and day out is invaluable for the completion of faculty research and I am so grateful I got to work with each of you. I also want to thank Paula Dias, Nicole Kenny, and Sarah Trayers for your work in transcribing some of the interviews.

I am indebted to the anonymous reviewers who provided excellent feedback during this book process and to all the editors and design team members at Stanford University Press, who helped in the production process of this book. A special thanks to Marcela Maxfield, who has been so helpful, thoughtful, and direct as an editor. Cedric De Leon, one of the series editors, has believed in this book project from its infancy. I am grateful to both him and Pawan Dhingra for their support and insightful feedback at all stages of this process.

Finally, and certainly not least, I have to thank my friends and family for supporting me throughout this process. I thank my mom and dad for being my biggest cheerleaders on my educational and professional journeys. I thank my brothers—who listen to me talk about migration, race and/or immigration policies (even when they do want to!) whenever we are together. I thank Abbey Levenshus, whose daily phone calls on navigating academia and motherhood kept me going during this process. And I thank Heather Maly, Laura Gvozdas, Katie Spencer, Beth Walse, Kristi Gibbs, Christina Matteucci, and Michelle Lane for supporting me in countless ways over the past twenty years.

I dedicate this book to my husband and daughter—Brady and Libby Portaro. These two bore the brunt of my anxiety and my long hours of work. Every day, they inspire me to keep doing more for my family—to be present and to not forget that family time is important, even when work seems overwhelming. I love you both beyond words.

THE BORDERS OF PRIVILEGE

INTRODUCTION

"DACA is a crappy piece of duct tape," Elisabete, twenty-five, exclaimed over lunch at a bright Brazilian café back in 2015.[1] DACA, short for Deferred Action for Childhood Arrivals, is an Obama-era policy that provides temporary relief from deportation to young people like Elisabete—immigrants who came to the US as children but still do not have lawful status in the country.[2] While DACA had been celebrated in many political and media circles for bringing youth out of the shadows when it was announced in 2012, for Elisabete it has been a Band-Aid that fails to fix the overarching problem, which is the absence of full legal membership in society. The precarity of DACA has been underscored in recent years as Republicans have attacked the program, throwing its future into legal jeopardy. Indeed, as of this writing in winter 2024, a federal judge in Texas had ruled the program unconstitutional, likely setting up another Supreme Court decision.[3]

But even before the program was in legal jeopardy, Elisabete was frustrated with DACA. On the one hand, it provided her with a work permit and Social Security number. In so doing, DACA has allowed her to reap the benefits of her investment in higher education, opening up work opportunities in the corporate world. But on the other hand, DACA has always been temporary and uncertain, as it does not provide a pathway to citizenship.[4] Furthermore, when we met up that day, DACA had not allowed Elisabete to reunite with her husband, Keith, a British citizen of Asian descent. According to Elisabete, Keith never had trouble securing a visa to the United States—until DACA. The couple met as high schoolers when he was visiting the States, fell in love, and were married in the US years later. But soon after Elisabete "outed herself to the government" when she applied for DACA, Keith was denied a student visa, despite being accepted into a prestigious graduate program. Elisabete told me that immigration officials suspected that his "student" reasons for coming to the United States were fraudulent because of his marriage to Elisabete.

In many ways, Elisabete's story is similar to the story of the over 800,000 DACA beneficiaries—a tale of immigrants living their lives in a gray area of legal limbo as they face legal uncertainty and severe limits to full membership in society. Like most of her DACA peers, illegality became more salient for Elisabete during the transition to adulthood, as she faced countless barriers to education and work (Cebulko 2013; Gonzales 2011; Silver 2012). A strong student in high school, she discovered during the college application process that she was ineligible for federal financial aid. Because she also lived in Massachusetts, undocumented immigrants like her were also barred from in-state tuition.[5] Thus, legally in Massachusetts, undocumented students had to pay out-of-state tuition without the help of federal grants or loans to go to college. Elisabete resigned herself to enrolling in—and commuting to—the state school in her hometown, the school she claimed her like-minded, high-achieving high school classmates deemed the place that "failures" attended. In a testament to her own hard work and resilience, she managed to graduate from this state school in three years. But after graduation, Elisabete discovered that without a work permit, she was blocked from legally working in a job commensurate with her education. Instead, Elisabete began nannying during the day and working as a janitor at night.

Because of these frustrations, we might think that legal status is the most salient identity in Elisabete's life. Roberto Gonzales, one of the most prolific immigration scholars, has persuasively argued that legal status becomes a "master status" overpowering all other social identities during the transition to adulthood for 1.5-generation immigrants. Yet the negative impacts of illegality are only part of Elisabete's story. A more complete and nuanced picture of her life experiences—and her own understanding of them—suggests that the master status frame does not adequately capture her lived experiences. Indeed, Elisabete does not fit the stereotypical, racialized image that most

Americans imagine undocumented immigrants to be. As Leo Chavez (2013) argues, Americans conflate illegality with "looking Mexican," which they associate with having indigenous features, including brown skin, short stature, and dark black hair (Ortiz and Telles 2012). But with her light skin, light brown hair, and high cheekbones, Elisabete looks white. And whiteness is so essential to Elisabete's identity that she told me that if a genie offered her the option to come back to earth as nonwhite with legal status, she'd continue to choose being white and undocumented. "Us white girls, we have a lot of privilege," she said matter-of-factly. Thus legal status by itself is insufficient for understanding Elisabete's life experiences. Instead, as I demonstrate in this book, we need to capture how illegality articulates with social class and race to shape Elisabete and other 1.5-generation Brazilians' experiences in the United States.

The importance of whiteness to Elisabete's identity emerged before I even met her in person. Before our first interview, Elisabete told me I could spot her by looking for the "American-looking white girl." When I met her for a second interview at a casual dining café tucked in-between hip coffee shops, bars, and little boutiques, she consciously presented herself in racialized, gendered, and class-specific ways—this time as a corporate woman, wearing a black pencil skirt, Ray-Ban sunglasses, and a Kate Spade purse, signaling membership in upper-middle-class, white American society. As she told me over dinner, none of her coworkers at her corporate firm thought that she was undocumented, and often pejoratively referred to immigrants as "illegal aliens" in front of her.

Elisabete was particularly conscious of how her whiteness has allowed her to escape negative interactions with the criminal justice system. During college, she was driving without a driver's license, as DACA had not yet been passed. One day she hit a bicyclist—a US citizen—with her car. As the police approached the scene of the accident, Elisabete felt sick to her stomach. She did not have a license to present to him. But in stark contrast to systemic police brutality toward Black Americans, the police officer did not even get angry with her. Instead he told her to go home to retrieve her license and he would meet her there. Elisabete's anxiety doubled over—she had just inadvertently invited the police officer to her home. But when he showed up, and she admitted she did not have a license due to her undocumented status, he did not turn her over to Immigration and Customs Enforcement (ICE). Instead he gave her a ticket. He told her to show up in court and assured her she would face no penalty in court beyond a fine. And he was right.

Elisabete understood her good fortune to be related to her whiteness, not luck. "My face would have been all over the news if I hadn't been white," she told me. She is not wrong that race and racial assumptions likely played a role in the minimal consequences she faced. As Chavez (2013) has shown, politicians and the mass media have helped create the "Latino Threat Narrative"—a story of undeserving, criminal, undocumented brown people harming innocent white American citizens. But Elisabete is highly educated, speaks English without a (Brazilian) accent, and looks white.

Importantly, it is not just whiteness that has profoundly shaped her life in beneficial ways—so has her Brazilian middle-class roots. For Elisabete, going to college, despite the obstacles she faced due to her legal status, was never a question. Indeed, it was an expectation in her Brazilian middle-class family. In Brazil, they had lived in a gated community with a pool and security. Her dad had graduated from high school and been a pricing analyst. Although he experienced downward mobility in the United States, working as a janitor due to his undocumented status, Elisabete knew that his sacrifices would be worth it when she, his daughter, achieved a better life. And she was not going to let her family or herself down, as she was determined to repay her parents' sacrifices, fulfilling what sociologist Robert C. Smith (2005) refers to as "the immigrant bargain."[6] Her ability to overcome the barriers to college as an undocumented immigrant, even if she did have to downgrade her choice of school, is certainly a function of her own hard work and resilience. However, it was also a function of her family's Brazilian social class, as their pre-migration wealth provided a financial safety net in the US. For example, even though her parents worked as undocumented laborers in the US, their pre-migration wealth helped her pay tuition for college, without the assistance of federal grants or loans. While other undocumented youth around the country feel pressure to work instead of go to school in order to help support their low-income families (Gonzales 2016), Elisabete was able to work and go to school. She did not need to work full-time to support her family's daily expenses.

Still, her powerful racial and (Brazilian) social class positions relative to most of her undocumented peers does not mean that Elisabete identifies as American. In Elisabete's case, she does not even identify as a hyphenated Brazilian-American. "You [America] don't deserve me. You don't get to screw me over and then have the privilege of having me [identify as American] in your census." Whiteness, which has been—and continues to be—so important for inclusion in American society, has not led to formal legal citizenship for Elisabete. And due to this legal exclusion from full membership, including the political, social and civil dimensions of citizenship (Marshall 1950), she does not feel a sense of belonging as American. Furthermore, Elisabete does not racially identify as white in the US, despite passing as white and feeling very Americanized. Nor, however, did she identify as Latino/a/x. Instead she refused to ethno-racially categorize herself altogether, a phenomenon that Julie Dowling (2014) has found to be true for other Latin American groups.

How can we understand Elisabete's experiences? I argue that we cannot understand Elisabete's story—and the stories of other 1.5-generation Brazilians who migrated as part of the first large wave of Brazilian migrants to Massachusetts—without situating their lived experiences in an articulation framework that accounts for the interlocking systems of stratification that shape their lives *and* considers how race, class, and (il)legality join together in specific spaces in particular historical moments (Clarno and Vally 2023; Hall 1980). In other words, we must think about how race, class, and legal status in the US are connected to global histories of domination and oppression *and* how those global histories of structural domination travel across spatial borders and play out in specific historical conjunctures. Elisabete's Brazilian middle-class roots and whiteness are no historical accident, as race and class are deeply intertwined in Brazil, a legacy of Portuguese colonization and (after independence) Brazil's own racial projects in nation-state building (FitzGerald and Cook-Martín 2014; Hernández 2012; Loveman 2014; dos Santos 2002; Telles 2004). In part, Brazilian middle-class families like Elisabete's sought economic opportunities through migration, hoping to maintain their families' place in the global racial-economic hierarchy (Cebulko 2013). Importantly, Elisabete and other 1.5-generation Brazilians' privileged economic and racial positions in Brazil have impacted both how they were able to *migrate* (on tourist visas) and *integrate* in the US (as discussed throughout this book). At the same time, the wholesale transfer of racial and economic privilege across borders is disrupted by increasingly hostile US laws and policies that make the lives of undocumented immigrants more difficult and precarious.

For Elisabete and many other 1.5-generation Brazilians I met, navigating their everyday lives in this hostile anti-immigrant context involves presenting themselves as white. I argue that these constructions of whiteness are a form of what Angela García (2019) calls "legal passing," which ultimately allows them to avoid the deleterious impacts of a racialized immigration status (Asad and Clair 2018). While being undocumented is not a visible trait, illegality is racialized and conflated with certain physical traits (and nationalities, languages, and low-status job) such that it makes sense to talk about "racialized legal status' or "racialized illegality" *and* to attend to the ways that race and illegality intersect to impact immigrants' lives (Asad and Clair 2018; García 2017; Herrera 2016; Menjívar 2021; Patler 2014). To be clear, not all 1.5-generation Brazilians are as unambiguously white as Elisabete. Indeed, at times—depending on who they are with, what they are wearing, and what language they are speaking—many white-passing 1.5-generation Brazilians are racialized as nonwhite, most often as Latino/a/x. (I use white-passing rather than white for two reasons. First, as explored in Chapter 4, many 1.5-generation Brazilians do not racially identify as white in the United States. This was true for Elisabete. Indeed, while she was almost always perceived as white and accrued some of the wages of whiteness, there were limits to its privileges for her. Second, as mentioned here and in other places in the book, many 1.5-generation Brazilians who can present as white also have experiences being racialized by others as Latino/a/x.) Thus, constructing whiteness serves as a "protective mechanism" from the deleterious impacts of racialized illegality (Enriquez and Millán 2019) and sometimes involves distancing themselves away from Latino/a/xs (Cebulko 2021). In these ways, we can see both how the interlocking structures of white supremacy and capitalism shape their experiences of illegality *and* how immigrants' everyday practices and identities sustain these very structures of domination and oppression.

POWER WITHOUT PAPERS

This book examines the ways in which social locations, namely race, class, and legal status, rooted in interlocking systems of domination and oppression, articulate together to shape the lived experiences of Elisabete and other children of Brazilian immigrants in the 1980s, '90s, and early 2000s.[7] I ask the following: How does power—especially power in racial and class hierarchies—join together with (il)legality to shape their lived experiences? How do Brazilians navigate these interlocking systems that privilege them in some ways in the United States and marginalize them in others? And what do their experiences of privilege and marginalization reveal to us about how systems of power and oppression travel across borders and play out in particular historical conjunctures?

I introduce the concept "power without papers" to capture how power—along race and social class lines in particular—hangs together with illegality to shape where 1.5-generation Brazilians live, their public interactions, their school and work experiences, who they date and marry, and their sense of belonging and identities. Analytically, power without papers builds on scholarship that calls for attention to racialized experiences of illegality (Asad and Clair 2018; García 2017; Herrera 2016; Menjívar 2021; Patler 2014) and to situate these experiences in interlocking systems of domination and oppression (Collins 1990; Crenshaw 1991; Du Bois 1935, 1965; Hall 1980; Robinson 2000). In this way, power without papers challenges scholars to not only extend the master status framework, but to move beyond the canonical literature on immigrant assimilation. As Tiffany Joseph, Tanya Golash-Boza, and Orly Clergé remind us, our dominant assimilation theories do not critically account for the interlocking systems of white supremacy and capitalism nor the logics of anti-Blackness and anti-indigeneity that undergird them (Clergé 2014, 2019; Joseph and Golash-Boza 2021). For example, early assimilation frameworks assumed immigrants and their children would inevitably become more like the dominant white mainstream society (Alba 1985; Gans 1979).[8] Meanwhile, the segmented assimilation framework—which largely examines the experiences of the post-1965 wave of immigrants and their children from Latin America, Africa, and Asia—argues that not all immigrants will achieve upward mobility to a dominant white middle class and instead theorizes that many Black and brown immigrant children will adopt the norms and values of a Black and brown underclass, leading to "downward assimilation" (Portes and Rumbaut 2001; Portes and Zhou 1993). But while segmented assimilation argues that race matters for immigrant incorporation, it does not account for the role of structural racism in creating and perpetuating the ethno-racial hierarchy immigrants and their children confront (Joseph and Golash-Boza 2021). Furthermore, it ignores the class, nationality, and cultural heterogeneity of Black and brown America, and assumes that adopting "Black and brown" values and norms will lead to negative outcomes for immigrant children (Clergé 2014, 2019).

In contrast to these dominant assimilation frameworks, power without papers situates the experiences of 1.5-generation Brazilians in a global, historical system of racial capitalism and pays attention to the specific work that race is doing for capitalism in particular historical conjunctures (Clarno and Vally 2023; Hall 1980). Scholars and activists in the Black Radical Tradition have underscored the constitutive roles that colonialism, imperialism, and racism play in capitalism, the world's dominant economic system (Cox 1948; Du Bois 1899, 1935; Robinson 2000). This tradition has brought to the forefront how capitalism has always been interconnected with racism, as European settlers—and their descendants—accumulated wealth by exploiting people who are racialized as nonwhite, especially Blacks, while extracting resources from colonized lands and removing or enslaving the indigenous populations that were present. Importantly, power without papers also builds off the work of Jamaican-born sociologist Stuart Hall, who pushes us to consider how race and class hang together in particular spaces at specific historical conjunctures.[9] That is, a power-without-papers lens not only considers how race, class and (il)legality are rooted in *global* systems of domination and oppression, but examines how they articulate together as 1.5-generation Brazilians came of age in the late 1990s and 2000s in Massachusetts and navigated early and mid-adulthood in the 2000s and 2010s. This time period is important, as it has been characterized by decades of neoliberal policies rooted in a free-market ideology—including free trade, tax cuts, the shrinking of the welfare state, and the growth of the policing and military apparatus—that have transformed the racial economy in important ways (see Golash-Boza 2015).[10]

Specifically then, a power-without-papers lens illuminates how power and marginalization work together by situating 1.5-generation Brazilians' experiences in global systems that play out in context-specific ways at particular conjunctures. Thus, Elisabete and her peers are born into a global racialized economic hierarchy where whiteness, although defined in different ways in Brazil and the United States, brings status, power, and material benefits. Their families, who primarily saw themselves as white in Brazil and came from middle-class backgrounds in the wealthiest regions of that country (the south/southeast), fled that context in no small part because of an economic crisis—one exacerbated by neoliberal policies dictated by international creditors—that jeopardized their lifestyles and status.[11] While Brazilian middle-class families in the 1980s and '90s largely lacked the necessary familial connections in the US to facilitate legal migration, their class positions allowed them to enter the US on tourist visas and overstay, bypassing the more dangerous route to the US through Mexico (Braga and Jouët-Pastré 2008; Margolis 1994; Martes 2011). But remaining in the US—and working and going to school without the "right papers"—made them "undocumented," a racialized and stigmatized status in the US (Asad and Clair 2018; Chavez 2013; Menjívar 2021). Importantly, as visa overstayers, they face fewer barriers to adjusting their status in the US than their peers who entered without inspection (Cebulko 2016, 2018; Gomberg-Muñoz 2016; López 2021). And yet the negative impacts of being undocumented become more severe for those who are unable to adjust their status before adulthood, especially as the US has implemented a more hostile immigration enforcement apparatus (De Genova 2002; Golash-Boza 2011).

The hostile immigrant enforcement policies that 1.5-generation Brazilians and other immigrants have confronted are part of broader neoliberal agenda that has been transforming the US racial economy since the 1970s (Golash-Boza 2015). As the US moved from an economy based on industrial production to an economy based on financial investment, blue-collar manufacturing jobs in the US—jobs that had previously provided middle-class wages and benefits—were automated or moved overseas under free-trade agreements (Harvey 2003). Increasingly, the US became a bifurcated *service* economy, with good-paying service jobs that require a college degree on one end and low-wage service jobs that do not require a college degree on the other. Some factory jobs remained, but they are less regulated, more dangerous, and do not pay well (Golash-Boza 2015; Muñoz 2011). As Tanya Golash-Boza (2015) argues, in this neoliberal racial economy, capitalism has relied on the vulnerability of *racialized (un)documented immigrants*—a disposable workforce—to work in these low-wage and dangerous jobs (Golash-Boza 2015).

In this historical period of racial capitalism, middle-class Brazilians who migrated in the 1980s and '90s and overstayed tourist visas discovered that their Brazilian economic and racial privilege had limits in the US. As undocumented immigrants, they face legal obstacles to socioeconomic mobility and risks to deportation. Furthermore, they also discover that the logics of whiteness are different in the US than in Brazil. Indeed, many undocumented Brazilians—especially first-generation Brazilians (but also 1.5-generation Brazilians) find themselves racialized as Latino/a/x—not as white—when they are working in low-wage jobs and/or speaking Portuguese in public (Beserra 2005; Cebulko 2013).[12] But importantly, for 1.5-generation Brazilians like Elisabete, who are raised in the US and can speak English with no discernible Brazilian accent, constructing and presenting themselves as white is more possible for them than it is for their first-generation counterparts, underscoring the fluidity of race (Saperstein and Penner 2012). And these successful constructions of whiteness in the neoliberal racial economy serve, at least at times, as protection from the deleterious impacts of illegality.

To be clear, 1.5-generation Brazilians, like previous and current waves of immigrants, are active agents in constructing their identities and navigating everyday interactions and opportunities in the US racial economy (Bashi Treitler 2013; Brown 2011; Du Bois 1935; Roediger 1991). Indeed, many 1.5-generation Brazilians (and their family members) draw boundaries between themselves and other marginalized groups in the US, and do so in gendered ways, as they work toward accruing what W. E. B. Du Bois called the "psychological and public wages of whiteness."[13] According to Du Bois (1935), white ethnics who were exploited under capitalism and earned low wages in the 1800s and early 1900s still experienced public wages (including "public deference and title of courtesy" and access to "public functions, public parks" and "the best schools") and psychological wages (including a sense of confidence that they would be treated with respect in everyday public life), wages that prevented their solidarity with Blacks (700–701). I argue that undocumented white-passing Brazilians also work to earn the public and psychological wages of whiteness, even as their legal status may render them deportable and exploitable laborers under capitalism.

Though public and psychological wages of whiteness sometimes lead to material benefits, there are certainly limits to 1.5-generation Brazilians' abilities to "cash in" on them, especially if they are still undocumented as they age into adulthood. For example, in the case of Elisabete, whiteness did not bring citizenship or reunification with her husband at the time of our interviews. Passing as white also didn't bring about a collective racial identity as white nor a sense of belonging as American. In other words, Elisabete and other 1.5-generation white-passing, undocumented Brazilians experience something akin to what Du Bois (1935) called "double consciousness"—as they know that as undocumented immigrants from Latin America, white Americans perceive them as "problems."[14] Thus, analytically, power without papers makes clear both the everyday practices that sustain the structures of white supremacy, and the limits of whiteness for those who experience exclusion on the basis of illegality.

In the next section, I examine legal status as an important source of stratification. Then I turn to why we need an articulation perspective—one that accounts for how race, class, and illegality hang together. I then more explicitly situate these stories in the larger, global systems of domination and oppression that have created the interlocking racial, class, and legal status structures in Brazil and the US.

LEGAL STATUS AS A SOURCE OF STRATIFICATION

Elisabete's story among 1.5-generation immigrants is unique, but the challenges she faced are hardly exceptional. There are an estimated 98,000 undocumented immigrants who graduate from high school each year (Zong and Batalova 2019), and their stories of frustrations with blocked opportunities to higher education are well documented by scholars (Abrego 2006; Cebulko 2013; Gonzales 2011, 2016; Silver 2012, 2018b). Undocumented youth, including DACA beneficiaries, are barred from federal grants and loans that help pay for college. The financial barriers to college are particularly acute in states without in-state tuition policies or laws for undocumented youth, including Massachusetts at the time of my study (Cebulko and Silver 2016). Due to financial barriers to college—and in some states, outright legal barriers denying them access to public schools—some undocumented young persons are forced to significantly downgrade their college choices. Others forgo their college dreams altogether (Abrego 2006; Cebulko 2013; Gonzales 2016; Greenman and Hall 2013; Silver 2018b).

Because of the educational and other barriers that undocumented immigrants face, scholars argue that legal status is an important form of stratification in their lives (Abrego 2006; Cebulko 2014; Gonzales 2016; Greenman and Hall 2013; Massey 2007; Menjívar 2006). Like gender, race, and class, legal status is legally and socially constructed (De Genova 2002; Menjívar 2006; Ngai 2004). That is, illegality is not an inherent condition of human beings; rather, it is produced through laws, policies, and everyday practices of private citizens. In recent decades, the negative consequences of illegality—including arrest, detention, and deportation—have intensified as the state has aggressively pursued the expansion of enforcement mechanisms (Golash-Boza 2011, 2015). Sociologists Cecilia Menjívar and Leisy Abrego (2012) argue that contemporary immigration laws are a form of legal violence, creating social suffering and long-term harmful impacts for undocumented immigrants and their friends and families. Meanwhile, Laura Enriquez (2020) argues that these harsh immigrant laws impact not only undocumented immigrants, but the next generations. Thus she considers these anti-immigrant laws to be a form of multigenerational punishment.

Importantly, legal status is not binary, as there are gray areas of legal membership that straddle legality/illegality (Cebulko 2014; Menjívar 2006; Mountz et al. 2002). For example, DACA is a form of liminal legality, as beneficiaries have some protection from deportation and gain important "paperwork" but still experience precarity (Abrego and Lakhani 2015; Burciaga and Malone 2021; Cebulko 2014; Cebulko and Silver 2016; Hamilton, Patler, and Savinar 2021; Roth 2019). DACA beneficiaries receive Social Security numbers (for work purposes) and employment authorization, paperwork that not only provides opportunities to legally work but in some states can provide access to other benefits, such as driver's licenses and in-state tuition. Yet DACA is a form of liminal legality because it is temporary, does not provide guaranteed protection from deportation, and does not offer a pathway to citizenship. Nor is DACA the only form of liminal legality, as there are other legal dispensations that result in migrants confronting gray areas of legal uncertainty (see Cebulko 2013, 2014; Menjívar 2006). Of course, in this era of hostile anti-immigrant policies, even lawful permanent residents (green card holders) experience precarity as they are deportable (Cebulko 2014; Golash-Boza 2011). Yet green card holders have access to significant resources that DACA recipients and others in liminal legality do not—including, but not limited to, federal grants and loans that pay for college (Cebulko 2014).

For undocumented youth raised in the United States, legal status becomes increasingly salient as they transition to adulthood (Gonzales 2011; Silver 2012). At age eighteen, they officially begin accruing "unlawful presence" time in the United States, which significantly increases the threat of deportability for themselves (United States Citizenship and Immigration Services 2022). Due to laws passed in 1996, anyone who has accrued more than 180 days of unlawful presence and who leaves the US faces a three-year bar to reentry. Someone who has accrued more than 360 days of unlawful presence and leaves the US faces a ten-year bar to reentry (American Immigration Council 2016).[15] Thus the threat of deportation becomes increasingly consequential after age eighteen given the bars to reentry if one is deported.

Without lawful immigration status, 1.5-generation immigrants also find themselves increasingly excluded from the rituals and rights their peers take for granted as they age into adulthood (Gonzales 2011; Silver 2012). The Supreme Court's 1982 decision in *Plyler v. Doe* required public schools to educate undocumented youth in grades K–12. Thus undocumented youth go to school alongside their documented peers, socialized into American culture and schooling norms (Abrego 2006). But no federal law exists guaranteeing access to higher education. Instead, states set their own tuition and enrollment laws for their public institutions while private schools set theirs. This means that while undocumented youth grow up being socialized in American schools alongside their peers, they face great uncertainties after graduation (Abrego 2006) and without work permits are often forced to work in menial-wage jobs like their parents (Gonzales 2016).

Due to these overwhelming barriers to education, work, and other realms of their lives, some scholars define legal status as a "master status" that comes to overpower all other social locations (Gleeson and Gonzales 2012; Gonzales 2016; Gonzales and Burciaga 2018; Gonzales and Ruszczyk 2021). In his seminal work, *Lives in Limbo,* Gonzales argues that while an undocumented status "is less consequential in childhood," it "becomes a master status in adulthood," framing "their lives in such a way that years lived in the United States, acculturation to American norms and behavior, and educational attainment are all inconsequential to their everyday routines as undocumented immigrants" (15).

The master status concept has rightfully underscored the devastating impacts of the nation-state's power to legally exclude immigrant young persons, especially in ways that earlier assimilation scholarship on the children of post-1965 immigrants did not reveal (Kasinitz et al. 2008; Portes and Rumbaut 2001; Portes and Zhou 1993; Suárez-Orozco, Suárez-Orozco, and Todorova 2008; Zhou 1997). At the same time, Elisabete's own perspective draws our attention to how whiteness has been just as vital to her identity and ability to navigate life. This was especially pronounced when she told me she would continue to choose whiteness and illegality over nonwhiteness and lawful immigration status even after the election of Donald Trump as president in 2016. The point here is not just that she is more privileged among undocumented immigrants (although she is), but also that in a country built on white supremacy, her performance of whiteness matters significantly for her everyday experiences and opportunities, especially as an undocumented (and now DACAmented) woman in the United States in a historical moment in which Black and brown immigrants are detained and deported in record numbers. Thus Elisabete's experiences underscores the need for an approach that situates her experiences in a global racial economic system in which whiteness is valued in important material and nonmaterial ways, and in which whiteness is constantly being constructed by the state and the everyday practices of individuals across borders in particular historical conjunctures. That is, we need to understand how illegality is articulated in other systems of power.

THE ARTICULATION OF ILLEGALITY IN OTHER SYSTEMS OF POWER

Roberto Gonzales and Edelina Burciaga (2018) acknowledge that while an undocumented status is an "exemplar" master status, undocumented immigrants' lives are stratified by education and other factors. Other studies of 1.5-generation immigrants further demonstrate how race, class, and/or gender modulate experiences of illegality (Cebulko 2018; Cho 2017; Enriquez 2017, 2020; Patler 2014). Sociologist Laura Enriquez's (2017) work is particularly notable for imploring scholars to think about how race, class, and illegality intersect to shape educational pathways for low-income undocumented Mexicans and Central Americans who live and go to school in segregated, poorly funded schools. Meanwhile, sociologists Zulema Valdez and Tanya Golash-Boza (2020) argue that undocumented Latino/a/x college students in California assert an intersectional identity more than a singular undocumented identity, while Kevin Escudero (2020) has demonstrated how undocumented youth leverage an intersectional movement identity in their organizing work.

Scholars and activists in the Black Radical Tradition, intersectionality, and LatCrit have long pointed out the need for theoretical perspectives that better account for the relationship between multiple systems of power. The Black Radical Tradition demonstrates how capitalism and racism are mutually constitutive and have been central to nation-state projects around the world (Du Bois 1899, 1935; Robinson 2000). Meanwhile, intersectionality, born out of the work and activism of Black feminists and queer activists of color, is an analytical—and liberating—framework that explains Black women's experiences (Cohambee River Collective 1977; Collins 1990, 2015; Crenshaw 1991; Jordan-Zachery 2007). Analytically, intersectionality requires scholars to situate people's experiences, perspectives, and opportunities in interlocking systems of domination and oppression. That is, if we focus only on one aspect of a person's identity, we can obscure the ways in which multiple social locations operate together to impact their lives.

Kimberlé Crenshaw (1991) emphasizes the importance of understanding how immigration regimes, white supremacy, and patriarchy intersect to shape women's experiences in reporting violence. Immigrant women who face deportation if they report violence to police might stay in abusive, violent relationships in order to protect themselves from deportation. Moreover, poor immigrant women of color may not have access to the resources necessary for acquiring the documents that might grant them a visa waiver to remain in the United States when they do report abuse. Meanwhile, Mary Romero and other LatCrit scholars have importantly shown the ways in which race and class shape immigrant experiences with immigration enforcement as immigration officers target Latino/a/x working-class spaces (Golash-Boza 2015; Romero 2006; Romero and Serag 2005). More recent work, operating within the traditions of LatCrit and intersectionality, has pointed to the need for considering how race and legal status intersect together, arguing we should think about racialized illegality (García 2017; Herrera 2016; Patler 2014) or racialized legal status (Asad and Clair 2018).

This book is informed by all these traditions. But I extend them in two ways. First, I shift the focus from multiple forms of marginalization to examine how marginalization (illegality) works together alongside racial and class power to shape undocumented young persons' experiences in the US.[16] As Collins (1990) argues, we need to understand not only how multiple forms of marginalization operate, but how penalty and privilege work together in these interlocking systems of domination and oppression. Few persons, she observes, are "pure victims or oppressors." Rather, each "individual derives various amounts of penalty and privilege from the multiple systems of oppression which frame everyone's lives" (Collins 1990: 229).

Second, I merge these insights with Stuart Hall's (1980) emphasis on the articulation of race and class in specific historical conjunctures. As Hall (1980) argues, 'race is . . . the modality in which class is lived, the medium through which class relations are experienced" (341). Hall insists that race is never strictly ideological nor cultural, but rather is always articulated in everyday social and economic relations. For Hall, race cannot be reduced to other sets of social relations, but at the same time, race cannot be understood outside these very relations. Furthermore, Hall implores us to think how race and class join together in particular geopolitical spaces, embedded in local and global racialized social relations that are the result of centuries of domination by white Europeans over indigenous groups, Blacks, and other racialized subjects.

White supremacy has long undergirded the nation-state and capitalist development of both the United States and Brazil, shaping immigration and citizenship policies that define who can and cannot reap the benefits under racial capitalism. And this ongoing history matters for 1.5-generation Brazilians pre-migration lives *and* their experiences with migration, including their mode of entry (on tourist visas) and their incorporation in the US. Table 0.1 presents a comparison of these similarities and differences in racial histories and understandings between Brazil and the US—which are further explored below. These similarities and differences can help us to better understand 1.5-generation Brazilians' experiences of power without papers, especially as their Brazilian understandings of race and racial positioning come into tension with their experiences as undocumented immigrants in the American neoliberal racial economy (Joseph 2015).

TABLE 0.1. Comparison of Race, Class, and Nation-State Building Contexts

	BRAZIL	US
Prevailing Racial Ideology at Time of Brazilian Migration in 1980s and '90s	Racial Democracy	Color-blind Ideology Bootstrap Narrative
History of Interracial Marriage	Miscegenation encouraged since the time of Portuguese colonization	Laws prohibiting interracial marriages, in order to protect white racial purity, were not struck down in every state until 1967.
Children of Interracial Unions	Children of interracial unions could be white, depending on skin color.	Laws often ensured that children born to one nonwhite parent were not white.
Dominant Assumptions of Whiteness	More expansive than US More fluid than US "Mulatto escape hatch"—one can become white through marriage and having children.	Less expansive than Brazil Not fluid Emphasis on white racial purity; one drop of nonwhite blood made you not white.
Previous Waves of Southern Europeans and Whiteness	Southern Europeans recruited to whiten the nation at beginning of twentieth century. In some cases, passageways were paid, land provided.	Southern Europeans [and the Irish and Eastern Europeans] were threats, but "became white" through laws, policies, own strategic efforts.

TABLE O.1. *(continued)*

	BRAZIL	US
History of Slavery and Settler Colonialism	Colonized indigenous lands. Last country in Western Hemisphere to end slavery. Black and indigenous groups continue to be marginalized.	Colonized indigenous lands. Civil War ended slavery in US South; Jim Crow laws followed to ensure white dominance. Black and indigenous groups continue to be marginalized.
Anti-Blackness	Despite "racial democracy" discourse, anti-Blackness and systematic racial discrimination continue, including police brutality.	Color-blind ideology suggests racism toward Blacks has ended, but there is ongoing systematic racial discrimination in all aspects of society, including police brutality.
Race/Class Hierarchies	Whites are disproportionately represented among political and economic elites and middle-class. Blackness devalued in beauty, wages, housing, health care, schooling. The south and southeast of Brazil are regionally the whitest states and "most developed," especially in comparison to the northeast and Amazon. Large mixed-race population. Some research suggests that this group occupies the middle space in hierarchy, with darker-skinned individuals having the lowest levels of schooling and money.	Whites dominate economic and political elites and are disproportionately wealthier. Blackness devalued in beauty, wages, housing, health care, schooling. Often characterized as a Black/white binary, but this binary has never truly captured everyone's experiences with race in the US—especially for groups from Latin America and Asia.
Narratives of Who Are "Real" Brazilians/Americans?	"Real Brazilians" are multiracial.	"Real Americans" are white and middle-class [or wealthy]. Ancestors came from Europe, not Latin America.
Undocumented Workers	Bolivians, Haitians, and Venezuelans make up largest numbers of undocumented immigrants, work in harsh conditions, and experience racism. Their numbers have grown in the past two decades.	Undocumented immigrants are largely racialized as Latino/a/x and stigmatized and treated as disposable workers under neoliberal capitalism.

SITUATING "POWER WITHOUT PAPERS" IN RACE AND NATION-STATE BUILDING IN THE US AND BRAZIL

I am indebted to scholars in the Black Radical Tradition who have challenged traditional Marxist approaches, with their strict emphasis on class, to demonstrate the racial character of global capitalism (Cox 1948; Du Bois 1935; Robinson 2000). Cedric Robertson (2000) argues that today's modern world system of global racial capitalism evolved from a Western feudal system that racialized differences *and* was dependent on slavery, violence, genocide, and imperialism. Throughout the Americas, European colonizers built their wealth by enslaving Africans, committing genocide against indigenous populations, and exploiting other racialized groups. And as nation-states in the Americas declared (and fought) independence from their colonial powers, race was foundational to the nation-state building process, with whiteness providing access to citizenship, material opportunities, and nonmaterial benefits. In the case of many Latin American nations—including Brazil—building a "white" nation was also an attempt to project to the global community that their country was "modernizing" (Loveman 2014; Marx 1997). Given that nation-states do not exist in a vacuum, but in a global community, scholars David Cook-Martin and David Fitzgerald (2010) argue we must situate the internal factors leading to a nation-state's laws (and racism embedded in those laws) within "the broader global ideological currents" as well as the nation's "embeddedness in a system of bilateral and multilateral relationships" (11).

Racial Capitalism, Migration, and Nation-State Building in Brazil
For much of the twentieth century, Brazilian elites painted their nation, both at home and abroad, as a "racial democracy" where Europeans, Africans, and indigenous peoples lived in harmony, free of the racial discrimination and racial violence prevalent in the US. Brazilian political and social theorist Gilberto Freyre, who helped romanticize Brazil's history of slavery and develop the concept of "racial democracy" in Brazil, was profoundly shaped by the horrors of Jim Crow segregation he witnessed in the US (Andrews 1996). In the "Masters and the Slaves," Freyre (1986) argued that Brazil's history of miscegenation, or racial intermixing, was proof of racial democracy (Freyre 1986) where Brazilians (unlike Americans) lived in harmony. As we will see,

the myth of racial democracy was foundational to Brazilian state-making throughout the twentieth century. In practice, however, Brazil protected and advanced light-skin privilege through immigration and citizenship policies that would "whiten the nation" (FitzGerald and Cook-Martín 2014).

There is some evidence that the ideology of racial democracy is no longer hegemonic in Brazil (Telles 2004). In the first two decades of the twenty-first century, Brazil began reckoning with race and racial inequalities, especially in the implementation of affirmative action quotas in higher education (Bailey, Fialho, and Peria 2018). Yet, despite some reckoning, the past and present manifestations of white supremacy reverberate. There continue to be racial inequalities in housing, education, and health as well as ongoing and violent overpolicing of Afro-Brazilians (French 2013; Hernández 2012; Monk 2016; Ramos et al. 2022; Telles 2004; UNHR 2022). Whites are disproportionately represented among the nation's political and economic elite, while Blacks remain at the bottom of the social and economic hierarchy (Bailey, Loveman, and Muniz 2013; Hernández 2012; Lima and Prates 2019; Telles, Flores, and Urrea-Giraldo 2015). Meanwhile, immigrants from Bolivia, Haiti, and Venezuela make up the largest groups of undocumented immigrants, with those from Bolivia in particular racialized as indigenous (Castillo 2012; Fujita et al. 2019; Ikemura Amaral 2022). Thus in Brazil—as in the United States—race and class are deeply intertwined. This interconnection is not a historical accident, but rather the product of colonialism, global racial capitalism, and the Brazilian nation-state building process.

In the decades following Brazil's independence from Portugal in 1822, Brazilian political, economic, and intellectual elites feared that the demographic complexion of the nation was "too dark" to reach the kind of economic growth and global supremacy they desired. More than 5.2 million enslaved Africans had been forcibly brought to Brazil over the course of three centuries, such that Blacks and their descendants were the majority of the Brazilian population by the end of the 1700s (dos Santos 2002). The Portuguese, whose colonizers had primarily been men, had encouraged racial intermixing from the very beginning of colonization. Importantly, while Gilberto Freyre (1986) romanticized relations between Portuguese colonizers and indigenous and African women, feminist scholars remind us that Portuguese colonizers engaged in systematic racialized gendered violence against Black and indigenous women (Garraio 2019).

By 1872, the year of the first census—a project undertaken to signal Brazil's modernity to the global community—"whites" accounted for less than 40 percent of the nation's population (Loveman 2014).[17] With European scientific racism taking hold on the global stage, Brazilian political and economic elites were deeply anxious that the nonwhite racial complexion of the nation would inhibit progress and economic development (Andrews 1996). Thus Brazilian elites pursued a strategy of "whitening." As part of that strategy, Brazilian elites encouraged racial mixing, arguing that the inherent supremacy of white genes would whiten the nation over generations (dos Santos 2002). Importantly, then, while scientific racism led white US elites to argue *against* racial intermarriage for fear of "tainting" the purity of Anglo-Saxon whiteness, it led Brazilian elites to *encourage* racial mixing.

A second key part of the Brazilian strategy to whiten the nation was to encourage the migration of "free labor" from Europe. According to racist abolitionists like Joaquim Nabuco, encouraging free "white labor" would necessitate ending slavery (dos Santos 2002). Brazil would not end slavery until 1888, the last country in the Americas to do so. But even before slavery ended, the Brazilian federal government—and the government of São Paulo province—heavily recruited European immigrants, often subsidizing their transatlantic passage. Between 1851 and 1937, approximately 4.8 million Europeans migrated to Brazil, nearly 2.5 million of whom went to work, mostly on coffee plantations, in São Paulo province (Hernández 2012). But while Europeans were recruited, their passage often paid, the Brazilian government excluded Asian and African migration (FitzGerald and Cook-Martín 2014).[18]

Most European immigrants to Brazil in the late 1800s and early 1900s came from just three countries—Italy, Portugal, and Spain. Thus, while the US government was actively restricting these southern (and eastern) European groups (as they were stigmatized as poor and racially undesirable migrants), the Brazilian government largely welcomed Southern Europeans, with most settling in the southern and southeastern Brazilian states (Amaral and Fusco 2005; Hernández 2012; Hing 2004). Today, these southern and southeastern states are the wealthiest (and whitest) states in Brazil. And as we will see later in this chapter, it is from these southern and southeastern states that most Brazilian migrants to Massachusetts in the 1980s and '90s came (Lima and Siqueira 2007; Marcelli, Holmes, Estella, et al. 2008).

While mass migration from Europe to Brazil largely ended in the 1940s, the conflation of whiteness, progress, development, and modernity has continued into the present day. These interconnected race and class-based regional inequalities are reflected in contemporary Brazilian identities and discourses. For example, Brazilians from São Paulo embrace a "Paulista" identity that was constructed via exceptionalist narratives that elevated and linked whiteness, modernity, and development while framing most other Brazilians negatively, especially northeastern Brazilians (Weinstein 2015).[19] In Minas Gerais, the state that has sent the largest number of Brazilians to Massachusetts, a *mineiro* identity also signals connection to a historical past grounded in white supremacy and anti-Blackness (McDonald 2014:iv).[20]

Given this ongoing history, it is not surprising that whiteness brings power in contemporary Brazil—nor that whites are disproportionately wealthier than nonwhites. Yet the specific history of racial capitalism and nation-state building in Brazil has also led whiteness to be more expansive and fluid in Brazil than in the US. Due to the long history of miscegenation and the myth of racial democracy during the twentieth century, skin color has traditionally been more important than ancestry in determining whether one identifies as white. Indeed, while "one drop" of Black ancestry legally made someone Black in some US states, that has not been the case in Brazil. Degler (1986) argues that there has been a "mulatto escape hatch" in Brazil where any drop of non-Black ancestry allows someone to "opt out" of the stigma of a Black identity. While scholars debate the evidence for a mulatto-escape hatch (Loveman, Muniz and Bailey 2012; Sheriff 2001; Telles 2004), many Brazilians *believe* that race and class articulate in such a way that "money whitens." For example, Schwartzman (2007) finds that nonwhite parents with higher levels of education are more likely to classify their children as white than those nonwhite parents with lower levels of education. Meanwhile, other scholars find that money "whitens" individuals' own assessment of their race (Silva 1994) and how others perceive them (Telles 2002, 2004).

What is considered white in Brazil also changes across its geographic space, reflecting the regional dynamics and racialized history of the nation. For example, what is considered "white" in northern Brazil could be considered "brown" in southern Brazil, where more light-skinned Brazilians live.[21] Importantly, Ellis Monk (2016) argues that skin color, even more than race, is the strongest predictor of educational attainment and occupational status, underscoring how "color" (as measured by interviewers) and "race" (as measured by census categories) are analytically distinct concepts. Yet many Brazilians conflate race and color in their conversations (Monk 2016).

This racial context is important—as it frames the racial understandings that Brazilians bring with them to the US (Joseph 2015; McDonnell and Lourenço 2009). Specifically, their ideas about race and whiteness have been "informed by the prominence of social class, the idea of racial democracy, and the fluidity of racial identities" (McDonnell and Lourenço 2009:244). But once in the US, Brazilians are confronted with new understandings of race and racism, informed by the particularities of white supremacy and nation-state building in the US. Indeed, they soon find out that while whiteness is still powerful in the US, whiteness is less fluid and more exclusive (Sansone 2003; Winant 2004).

Racial Capitalism, Migration, and Nation-State Building in the United States

While the myth of racial democracy dominated Brazilian discourse for much of the twentieth century, US national discourse has perpetuated different racial myths. These myths include the myth of "color-blindness"—that Americans no longer "see color" and therefore race no longer matters (Bonilla-Silva 2017), and the myth of the "European bootstrap narrative," which suggests that poor Europeans from Ireland, Italy, and other European nations came to the US with nothing but worked hard (and without government assistance) to "make it" in America (Chomsky 2018). While the color-blindness myth ignores ongoing widespread racial disparities in housing, education, health care access, investigatory police stops, police killings, and incarceration (Bonilla-Silva 2017; Epp, Maynard-Moody, and Haider-Markel 2014; Gilbert and Ray 2016), the bootstrap myth conveniently leaves out how Europeans, since the nation's founding until the current moment, have benefited from "the wages of whiteness", which allowed them easier access to citizenship, government assistance for housing, and membership in labor unions—all of which helped them in achieving the "American Dream" (Alexander 2012; Brodkin 1998; Du Bois 1935; Fox 2012; Haney López 1996; Ignatiev 1995; Ngai 2004; Roediger 1991). Importantly, these European groups did not just passively benefit from "the wages of whiteness." Rather, as explored below, they worked hard to become white by fighting any connection to Blackness (Du Bois 1935; Roediger 1991).

Of course, it was never just Europeans coming to the US. And the stories of these other immigrant groups—including the Chinese, Mexicans, and Afro-Caribbeans—are stories of being denied access to citizenship, economic opportunities, and social membership. Indeed, the first naturalization laws in the US limited citizenship to free white men, underscoring that citizenship was, from its beginning, race-, class-, and gender-based. While Blacks gained access to citizenship after the Civil War, racial requirements for citizenship were not fully lifted until 1952. Furthermore, citizenship has never brought full social membership for Blacks, nor other nonwhites, underscoring how citizenship is stratified by race (Asad and Clair 2018; Chomsky 2014; Du Bois 1935; Fox 2012; Hing 2004).

Given the importance of whiteness for access to citizenship, land, and resources—and Blackness for sustaining the institution of slavery for the accumulation of white wealth—the American federal government and individual states were preoccupied with legally restricting nonwhites from migration and citizenship in the US *and* with legally defining who in the US could be considered "white" and who was "Black" (Haney López 1994; Omi and Winant 2014). From the 1880s onward, the US government—like other governments around the world—barred most migration from Asia and Africa. Nor was the US government subtle about its discrimination. In the 1880s, it passed the Chinese Exclusion Act, which would not be repealed until 1942. In contrast, Congress sought to limit but not altogether restrict southern and eastern European migrants through national origin quota laws (Hing 2004; Ngai 2004). But while these laws discriminated against undesirable and racialized European migrants, these laws did not *bar* these groups. Indeed, southern and eastern Europeans still had pathways to citizenship upon arrival, setting legal boundaries around whiteness (Ngai 2004).

It was not just Congress that shaped the legal constructions of whiteness; so did the courts (Ngai 2004; Haney López 1996). Sometimes the Supreme Court ruled that who was white was based on science (that is, scientific racism), and at other times in accordance with what the "common man" said whiteness was (Ngai 2004). Haney López (1996) demonstrates the arbitrary criteria the courts used to make racial decisions—sometimes using skin color, facial features, national origin, language, culture, ancestry, scientific opinion, or popular opinion. In other words, the legal constructions of race—which impacted people's access to citizenship, and thus the right to own land and to vote—were based on racist scientific and social logics.

Meanwhile, for Blacks in the US, racial discrimination and racial segregation were codified into law via Jim Crow laws in the American South after slavery ended. Almost as soon as the Thirteenth Amendment ratified the abolition of slavery, localities and states in the South passed ordinances that legally controlled where Blacks could live, how and where they traveled, and how and where they could work. These laws and codes also kept many Blacks from voting and gave whites the ability to seize Black children to become forced laborers. In stark contrast to Brazil, antimiscegenation laws in some US states made marriage and sexual relations between whites and Blacks illegal until these laws were finally ruled unconstitutional in 1967 in the Supreme Court case *Loving v. Virginia* (see Osuji 2019 for more details).[22]

In the American Southwest, similar laws—akin to Jim Crow laws in the South—targeted Mexican Americans. Per the terms of the Treaty of Guadalupe Hidalgo, which ended the Mexican-American War (a war that began when white American settlers invaded Mexican lands) in 1848, Mexicans who had been living in what is the present-day American Southwest were offered American citizenship. Due to the white racial requirement for citizenship at the time, Mexicans who stayed were considered *legally* white. But while legally white, Mexican Americans were seen as *socially* nonwhite and faced racial discrimination under Jim Crow–like laws and practices (Donato and Hanson 2012; Gutiérrez 1995). Still, from the end of the Mexican-American War until 1965, migration from Mexico was largely encouraged to fulfill capitalist labor needs. But while Mexicans were desired as temporary workers, they were not welcomed as potential immigrants deserving of full membership and rights (Chomsky 2014).

Thus, while both Black Americans (following the end of the Civil War) and Mexican Americans (who were living in the US at the end of the Mexican-American War) were granted access to citizenship, neither group has ever enjoyed full social membership or relief from racism that white citizens enjoyed. Importantly, however, overt racism fell out of favor in the 1960s.[23] In its place, new forms of structural racism emerged, racism that Bonilla-Silva (2017) has argued is seemingly "color-blind." Yet, in this "new Jim Crow era," these seemingly color-blind laws still rely on criminalizing Black and brown persons and incarcerating and/or deporting them on the supposed basis of "lawbreaking" rather than race, thereby "legitimizing" the state's discrimination against them (Alexander 2012; Chomsky 2014; Golash-Boza 2015).

Michelle Alexander (2012) argues that while previous racial caste systems (slavery, Jim Crow) maintained Blacks as an exploitable labor force, the "new Jim Crow" system—via laws incarcerating them and stripping them of rights and ability to work after prison—removes African Americans from the labor market in an economic era when their labor is deemed a "surplus." Meanwhile, Golash-Boza (2015) argues that deportability works in similar (and complementary) ways for Black and Latino/a/x immigrants in a neoliberal era of global racial capitalism. She demonstrates that in the contemporary era, immigrants from the Caribbean and Latin America, especially men, are criminalized on the basis of their race and "illegality"—thereby "legitimizing" the state's hostility toward them. At the same time, the nation-state maintains a racialized, disposable labor force—deporting them in mass numbers only when their labor is deemed a surplus (Golash-Boza 2015).[24]

The rise in deportation has also been coupled with the rise in the number of undocumented immigrants in the US since the 1960s. And we can also only understand this rise by situating it in the larger neoliberal restructuring taking place across the globe (which displaces migrants from their home contexts—see Golash-Boza 2015; Muñoz 2011) *and* changes in US immigration laws that reflect a move toward seemingly "color-blind" laws (Massey and Pren 2012) while still discriminating on the basis of race (Rosenberg 2022; Watson 2018). The Hart-Celler Act of 1965 officially removed the outright racist national-origin quotas and replaced them with an employment and family-based system that was supposed to reflect labor force needs and a commitment to family reunification. While the changes in laws did facilitate an increase in the number of immigrants from Asia, Africa, and Latin America (Massey and Pren 2012), the changes did not reflect the history of US imperialism, colonialism, and interference in other nations (Chomsky 2014; Massey and Pren 2012). Indeed, the Hart-Celler Act put into place the first ever *limits* on migration from the Western-hemisphere. Later, in the 1970s, per-country limits were added. In other words, the Hart-Celler Act artificially constrained migration that had once been legal, especially from neighboring Mexico, as the law ignored the structural and historical connections between the US and many of these other countries.

Today, in the American public imagination, "illegality" is conflated with Mexican migration (Chavez 2013). Meanwhile, "looking Mexican" is associated with "looking indigenous" (Ortiz and Telles 2012). As Chavez (2013) points out, however, many immigrants and their descendants from Latin America are seen as "potentially Mexican" and *as* economic, political, and cultural threats to American society (Chavez 2013). Thus, while the undocumented population is racially and geographically diverse, the conflation of illegality with Latino/a/x remains in the public imagination. Furthermore, the racialization of illegality is perpetuated through contemporary laws that regulate the ability for immigrants from Latin America to lawfully migrate and other US institutional practices (see Armenta 2017; Asad and Clair 2018; Massey 2012; Menjívar 2021).[25]

But importantly, the construction of race, class, and the nation has never just been an elite or top-down endeavor. In both Brazil and the US, everyday Brazilians and Americans have also worked to position themselves favorably in their nation's status hierarchies where whiteness was valued and Blackness and indigeneity are devalued (Bashi Treitler 2013; Osuji 2019; Roediger 1991; Twine 1998). In the next section, I examine the history of US ethno-racial projects and consider what this history means for thinking about "power without papers" in the present day.

NAVIGATING THE US RACIAL ECONOMY: THE POWER AND LIMITS OF WHITENESS IN THE US

As Chavez (2013) argues, before the "Latino threat," there was the "German threat" and the "Irish threat." In the 1700s, Benjamin Franklin notoriously worried that Germans could not acquire the "complexion" nor the "language" and culture of Anglo-Saxons. Centuries later, it was the Irish who were seen as racialized, impoverished others incapable of "assimilating." Over time, however, through laws and their own agency in navigating the pervasive anti-Blackness in the US, German and Irish immigrants and their descendants became white. Indeed, even when European groups faced anti-immigrant sentiment and poor wages in the labor market, they still enjoyed some benefits of whiteness (Du Bois 1935; Roediger 1991).

Writing in the 1930s, pioneering sociologist, historian, and activist W. E. B. Du Bois (1935) argues that white workers in the American South who were economically exploited by white capitalists in the US labor market still received the "public and psychological wages" of whiteness that "had great effect on the personal treatment and the deference shown them" as they were given courtesy titles, let into public parks, functions, and schools, and recruited to join the police forces to control Blacks (700–701). Furthermore, Du Bois demonstrates that poor white workers in the South would choose poverty rather than solidarity with Black workers because of the feelings of superiority that whiteness provided, or the "psychological wage of whiteness." Meanwhile, in the North, Du Bois (1899) argues, white ethnics helped strip Blacks in Philadelphia of voting rights and even joined mobs that killed Blacks.

Importantly, Vilna Bashi Treitler (2013) shows that it is not just white ethnics who have fought for racial uplift by racially distancing themselves from those at the "bottom" of the hierarchy, but other groups too. She demonstrates how Mexicans, Chinese, and Afro-Caribbeans have all worked for racial uplift by drawing boundaries away from Blackness (Bashi Treitler 2013). According to Bashi Treitler (2013), however, their "ethnic projects" for racial uplift have been less successful than those of European groups due to racism.

I take seriously these insights of Du Bois and Bashi Treitler in this book and argue that we must consider how undocumented, white-passing 1.5-generation Brazilians might strategically work to accrue and benefit from the wages of whiteness in this historical conjuncture. In other words, to truly understand the experiences of Elisabete and other 1.5-generation Brazilian immigrants, I contend that it is not enough to think about their experiences as undocumented (or DACAmented), which does make them vulnerable to deportation and labor market exploitation in this era of neoliberalism. Rather, we must also think about how they, even as undocumented immigrants, may benefit from whiteness. Furthermore, we must take seriously the role they might play in strategically navigating the global and US racial economy, which provides material and nonmaterial benefits for whiteness.

Part of my argument in this book is that 1.5-generation Brazilians who migrated in the 1980s and '90s work to position themselves favorably in the US ethno-racial hierarchy in order to avoid the deleterious impacts of illegality and to accrue the wages of whiteness.[26] But in so doing, I also contend that their middle-class Brazilian families migrated in the 1980s and '90s to recoup lost earnings due to economic troubles in Brazil and maintain their positions in the global racial economy. And while first-generation Brazilians who are undocumented in the US experience a downgrade in their socioeconomic and racial status in the US context as they speak Portuguese (which sounds like Spanish to most Americans), work in low-wage jobs, and are racialized as Latino/a/x (Braga and Jouët-Pastré 2008; Margolis 1994, 2007; Martes 2000), things are often different for their 1.5-generation Brazilian children who are socialized in American schools and often lose their accents over time. That is, 1.5-generation young Brazilians are more likely to be able to successfully use the American ethno-racial hierarchy to their advantage, just as past immigrant groups have done, by distancing themselves from racialized groups and constructing whiteness (Bashi Treitler 2013; Brodkin 1998; Ignatiev 1995; Roediger 1991). Because their whiteness is often not a given in the US context, however, 1.5-generation Brazilians often actively construct whiteness, in part by drawing boundaries between themselves and other racialized groups, especially Latino/a/xs. To be sure, in a national context in which being racialized as Latino/a/x depresses opportunities in the labor market and carries increased risk of detention and deportation, constructing whiteness is a form of self-preservation. But in the process, these same actions sustain the structures of white supremacy.

Ultimately, then, I argue that a power-without-paper lens is necessary to truly explain Elisabete and other Brazilians' experiences in the United States. Sometimes they will benefit from the wages of whiteness, as it does serve as a protection from arrest, detention, and deportation and help them avoid the most precarious jobs in the US economy. Yet being undocumented does limit their race and class privilege: they are still vulnerable to deportation, they still face barriers to socioeconomic mobility, and their experiences with illegality negatively impact their sense of belonging in the US. In these ways, there are limits to the wages of whiteness.

THE CASE OF POWER WITHOUT PAPERS: THE FIRST WAVE OF BRAZILIANS IN MASSACHUSETTS

When I arrived in Boston in the summer of 2006 to begin preliminary fieldwork and interviews, Brazilians were one of the largest immigrant groups in the state (second or third behind the Chinese and, perhaps, Dominican communities) and about 70 percent were undocumented (Marcelli, Holmes, Estella, et al. 2008). Brazilians began migrating to the state in large numbers in the 1980s and '90s following an economic collapse in Brazil (Goza 1994; Margolis 1994). While the dominant perspective has been that Brazil's increasing public deficits and debts caused the financial instability and crises in the 1980s, Dalto (2019) argues that this blame is misplaced, and points out how the financial interests of international creditors in the Global North drove the imposition of exchange rates devaluation, hikes in real interest rates, and neoliberal public investment cuts, all of which "generated recession and financially instability (notoriously inflation)" (Dalto 2019).

By far, the Brazilian state that has sent the most Brazilians to Massachusetts is Minas Gerais, especially the town of Governador Valadares (Joseph 2015; Lima and Siqueira 2007; Martes 2011). The first linkages between Boston and Minas date back to World War II, when American engineers from Boston helped build a railroad that linked Minas Gerais to coastal areas (Martes 2000). However, Brazilians have come from other southern and southeastern states too, the wealthier and whiter regions of the country (Lima and Siqueira 2007; Martes 2011). When they arrived in Massachusetts, they often settled in communities the Portuguese had settled (Siqueira and Jansen 2008) as the presence of the long-standing Portuguese community "offered immediate linguistic familiarity" (Braga and Jouët-Pastré 2008:5).

While Ana Cristina Braga Martes (2011) argues that there is no typical migrant to Massachusetts—her 2005 survey of 300 Brazilians in the Greater Boston area indicates that the majority came from southern and southeastern region and that their educational levels were higher than the typical Brazilian. Indeed, 62 percent had completed high school and some college back in Brazil (Martes 2011). Meanwhile, other studies have found that most Brazilians who came as part of the first wave thought of themselves as white in Brazil (Margolis 1994; McDonnell and Lourenço 2009) and are relatively light-skinned, at least in comparison to Dominicans, one of the other large immigrant groups in the Greater Boston area (Marcelli, Holmes, Estella, et al. 2008; Marcelli, Holmes, Troncoso, et al. 2008).

Most of the Brazilians who left during the crisis saw themselves as sojourners in the US, hoping to return to Brazil in a stronger position (Margolis 1994; Joseph 2015). Because they largely lacked the specific family connections and employment-based skills that would facilitate lawful migration, they primarily entered on tourist visas and overstayed (Braga and Jouët-Pastré 2008; Margolis 1994; Martes 2011). But as undocumented workers from Latin America in the US, many Brazilians who considered themselves middle-class and white in Brazil found that their class and racial positions in the US were much more contested. Indeed, scholars have shown that first-generation Brazilians—even those with lawful status—are often dismayed when they are racialized as Latino/a/x in the US (Beserra 2005; McDonnell and Lourenço 2009; Joseph 2015). Some assert new racial identities in an attempt to avoid an imposed Latino/a/x identity. For example, Maxine Margolis (1994) documents how "being Brazilian" goes from being a national identity to a racial identity in the US. Meanwhile, Helen Marrow (2003) finds that the Brazilian second generation—those born in the US—are more likely to identify as white—or Black—than as Latino/a/x.

Yet, while first-generation Brazilians are often racialized as Latino/a/x and are undocumented, there is evidence that they fare better than other immigrant groups from Latin America in the Boston area, including groups who are less likely to be undocumented. In 2007, an estimated 70 percent of Brazilians were undocumented, while only 8 percent of Dominicans were. And yet Brazilians outearned Dominicans (Marcelli, Holmes, Estella, et al. 2008; Marcelli, Holmes, Troncoso, et al. 2008). Meanwhile, a 2017 Boston report found that Brazilians had the highest standard of living of any group from Latin America (Boston Planning & Development Agency Research Division 2017). Only 11 percent of Brazilians lived below the census poverty line while approximately 43 percent had achieved a middle-class standard of living. Brazilians' higher relative economic position in the Boston area is not an accident, but rather is tied to racial and class characteristics of the early Brazilian migration stream to the US and the politics of race in the US racial economy.

Given the high rates of undocumented immigrants in the Brazilian community, and their higher relative economic position as compared to other immigrant groups from Latin America in the Greater Boston area, the first wave of Brazilian immigrants present a good case study for thinking about "power without papers." Furthermore, the state of Massachusetts is an important context for thinking about experiences of illegality. With some important exceptions (see Burciaga and Malone 2021; Gonzales and Ruiz 2014; Martinez and Ortega 2019; Roth 2019; Silver 2012: 2018b), most studies of 1.5-generation undocumented immigrants have focused on the California context (and, to a lesser extent, Texas), two states with vastly different contexts for undocumented immigrants. Despite Massachusetts's national reputation as a "progressive state," California and Texas (and many other states) have historically provided a more inclusive context for children of immigrants—especially in providing access to in-state tuition for higher education since the early 2000s (Gonzales 2016; Rincón 2008). Not only does in-state tuition dramatically reduce the cost of higher education for undocumented youth, but these tuition bills also provide a legitimizing identity for youth (Abrego 2011) and access to a support network of peers and allies. In contrast, in Massachusetts, there was no in-state tuition until August 2023, years after I had concluded my research. In 2007, the state did provide in-state tuition rates for those with work permits, but this policy was not well-known until after DACA was implemented in 2012. Furthermore, when I began my research in 2006, the in-state student-led undocumented organizing movement was just starting to take off. Thus the 1.5-generation Brazilian youth I met largely navigated a state context in which there was no guaranteed access to reduced tuition and no widely known organizing apparatus of young activists

HEARING AND OBSERVING THE STORIES OF 1.5-GENERATION BRAZILIANS: DATA AND METHODS

The stories in this book come primarily from in-depth interviews with 43 1.5-generation Brazilian immigrants in the Boston area who experienced illegality at some point in their lives.[27] I began fieldwork and interviews in 2006 and continued to stay in touch with some interview respondents for the next fifteen years. Indeed, 23 of these 43 respondents participated longitudinally—engaging in follow-up interviews and informal conversations to share how their lives changed over time. The longitudinal data provided valuable insight into how changes in the legal and political landscape—at the national, state, and local levels—were shaping their lives as they aged into their midtwenties and later, their thirties. Their stories—told to me over "cafezinhos" (coffee) in their homes, dinners at Brazilian churrascarias (steakhouses) and American restaurants, and in their favorite bookstores and suburban parks—were supplemented with fifteen years of noncontinuous fieldwork, including informal conversations with Brazilian community leaders, immigration lawyers, and Brazilian small business owners. In addition, during the first stage of the study (from 2006 to 2008), I conducted 16 formal in-depth interviews with other adult children of Brazilian immigrants, including 8 second-generation Brazilians (some of whom were romantic partners of undocumented respondents).[28] Given that these 16 respondents did not experience illegality while growing up in the Greater Boston area, they were excluded from the final sample for this book. Nevertheless, my conversations with these young adults led to a greater understanding of my respondents' experiences, as these 16 individuals often echoed my respondents' understandings of regional stereotypes in Brazil, race, and racism in the US and Brazil, and other US political, cultural, and legal dynamics shaping my respondents' lives.

When I began fieldwork in the summer of 2006, I worked closely with two Brazilian nonprofits in the area. One of them, Brazilians United (BU), was partnering with a Boston-based professor for an upcoming survey of Brazilian immigrants.[29] In the summer of 2006, I joined this collaborative research team to canvass census blocks with large numbers of Brazilians. Then, in the winter of 2007, I starting working for BU, planning their annual fundraising dinner. I spent my days soliciting donations from large and small donors in the Greater Boston area, many of whom were immigration lawyers, Brazilian business owners, or nonprofit directors and staff members. I also joined a newly formed committee focused explicitly on immigrant students' needs and rights in Massachusetts. The insight I gained from these observations and conversations in the larger Brazilian and immigrant communities helped me to not only ask better questions during formal interviews, but to situate the stories told to me in the local, state, national, and transnational contexts. Furthermore, my fieldwork often led to informal interactions with some respondents, given the ways in which my community work and networks intersected with their social and work lives.

After completing the initial wave of interviews between 2006 and 2008, I began a second round of formal interviews in 2011. Over the next two years, I deliberately sought out those respondents who had still been undocumented when they turned eighteen. This second wave of interviews coincided with the announcement *and* implementation of DACA, providing a window into how DACA was shaping their lives, especially in comparison to our earlier conversations. I completed additional interviews with some respondents between 2015 and 2019. These years overlapped with the announcement of Trump's candidacy and his presidential administration.

During the thirteen years that my research took place, the federal immigration context generally became increasingly hostile, even before the Trump years (Asad 2023; De Genova 2002; Golash-Boza 2015; Menjívar and Abrego 2012; Rosenberg 2022). Importantly, however, federal, state, and local laws and policies often move in contradictory directions and can change quickly and unpredictably, creating instability for undocumented young people as they navigate the transition to adulthood (Silver 2018b). Indeed, this was the case in Massachusetts, as politicians would sometimes sign agreements to enable state troopers to acts as immigration agents, even as local police in certain communities would not. And these federal, state and local context often changed quickly, creating confusion.[30]

Table 0.2 presents demographic information for all 43 respondents. Fourteen respondents were men and 29 were women.[31] More than half of respondents came from the state of Minas Gerais, while most other respondents came from the wealthier and whiter states in the south and southeast, including Rio de Janeiro, Santa Catarina, Espirito Santo, and São Paulo. This context is important, as many Brazilians I met during fieldwork and interviews expressed a sense of superiority over Brazilians from other parts of Brazil—especially the Amazon and the northeast—whose populations they racialized as "indigenous" or as "Black" and stigmatized as "backwards" and "undeveloped."[32]

Only one respondent described her family as "poor." This young woman's father had been a coal miner back in Brazil and she was the only respondent who entered without inspection via Mexico. Most respondents, however, indicated that their families had been middle-class (or lower-middle-class) in Brazil. Indeed, they often told me that they knew their families were better-off than many households in their Brazilian hometowns. They reported that at least one of their parents had completed high school and/or a post–high school degree, and many of their parents had been small business owners. Six respondents, however, said they were likely part of the upper middle class, describing their private schooling, gated housing communities, parents' college educations, and/or high-end family vacations.[33] Most of the 1.5-generation Brazilians I met also told me that they thought of themselves as white in Brazil. Indeed, only 2 of the 43 respondents said definitively that they would have been considered nonwhite in Brazil. This correlation between self-reported race and class for my respondents is not surprising given that scholars find that darker-skinned Brazilians have lower levels of schooling (Telles et al. 2015) and that "money whitens," such that Brazilians with higher levels of education are more likely to think of themselves (and their kids) as white (Schwartzman 2007).

TABLE O.2. Descriptive Information for All Respondents in the Analysis

	N = 43
Legal Status at Age 18	
Undocumented	22
Liminal Legality	10
Green Card	6
Citizen	5
Legal Status at Last Contact	
Undocumented	3
Liminal Legality	13
Green Card	16
Citizen	11
Race in US	
White-Passing	37
Nonwhite	6
Social Class in Brazil	
Upper-middle	6
Middle	36
Poor	1
Age of Migration	
0–5	13
6–10	16
11–15	14
Origin State and Region	
Minas Gerais (Southeast)	26
Rio de Janeiro (Southeast)	8
Santa Catarina (South)	5
Espirito Santo (Southeast)	1
São Paulo (Southeast)	1
Paraiba (Northeast)	1
Paraná (South)	1
Gender	
Women	29
Men	14

Discussions about illegality often emerged as respondents spoke about why they had not returned to Brazil and/or gone to college. All but one respondent had entered the US on a nonimmigrant visa and overstayed. For most respondents, this was a tourist visa.[34] When their families stayed in the US and violated the terms of those visas, they became "undocumented," subject to deportation and ineligible for the rights and benefits reserved for US citizens.[35] Importantly, my respondents' and their families' ability to enter the US on a tourist visa, rather than entering without inspection via Mexico, underscores their relatively privileged positions in Brazil's racial economy. The US government only grants tourist visas to those who can provide proof of financial assets.[36] Furthermore, coming to the US via plane requires being able to afford plane tickets.

While those who overstay visas are undocumented, they do have greater access to the (very) limited pathways to citizenship than those who illegally cross the US/Mexico border, underscoring the ways in which US immigration and citizenship laws play a role in reproducing class and racial inequality across borders (Aptekar and Hsin 2023; Cebulko 2018; Gomberg-Muñoz 2016; López 2021). Indeed, as we will see in this book, although Elisabete had not been able to secure an adjustment of status at the time of writing, many of her Brazilian peers did. As Table 0.2 demonstrates, while only 13 respondents were lawful permanent residents or citizens at the time they turned age eighteen, 27 were lawful permanent residents or citizens by the time of my last contact with them. One other respondent had moved legally to Canada with her white Canadian spouse. Furthermore, while 22 respondents were "fully" undocumented at age eighteen (and did not have a work permit or Social Security number), only 3 respondents were at the time of last contact (13 others were still in liminal legality). How was this possible? Some respondents had been able to adjust their status to lawful permanent resident through marriage to a US citizen, a process that is easier for those who overstayed a visa (see Chapter 3). But many respondents attempted to adjust their status through a different legal dispensation (one that also favors racially and class privileged immigrants), a process that often left them in legal limbo for years.

Indeed, during the first wave of interviews from 2006 to 2008—years before DACA was implemented in 2012—many Brazilians described being in a kind of liminal legality. They had work permits and Social Security numbers and a pending case for an adjustment in status, but did not have a guarantee of a green card. In most cases they had been in this situation for six or more years. Through discussions with them and immigration lawyers it became clear that one of their parents—usually their fathers—had been the beneficiary of an employment-based petition under Section 245i of the Immigration and Nationality Act, which was first introduced by Congress in 1994 and last extended under the Legal Immigration Family Equity (LIFE) Act in 2000. To be eligible under the extension provided by the LIFE Act, immigrants had to pay a fine and be the beneficiary of a visa petition of labor certification application filed on or before April 30, 2001.[37] Section 245i was important as it allowed unauthorized immigrants to adjust their statuses in the US, avoiding returning to Brazil to visit a consulate, thereby avoiding three- and ten-year bars to reentry put in place in 1996 (see Chapter 1). My respondents, who were under twenty-one years of age at the time their parents filed this paperwork, were listed as dependents to the primary beneficent (the parent). Often they received a Social Security number and employment authorization card while the adjustment-of-status application was pending.[38] During this time, they were not deportable on the basis of legal status, although they could be deported for criminal offenses.

In many cases, these processes dragged on for years but eventually resulted in a green card. In others, though, the parent's application—and thus theirs—was denied five or more years after application, leaving them without work permits and making the entire family vulnerable to deportation. Because respondents' legal statuses shifted over time (sometimes in different directions), Table 0.2 only includes legal status at two key junctures: the time they were eighteen, as scholars generally agree that illegality becomes more salient at this time in the life course (Cebulko 2013; Gonzales 2011; Silver 2012), and the time of last contact with me (in order to examine how many experienced shifts toward lawful permanent status).[39]

Thirty-seven of the 43 respondents were white-passing in the United States, while 6 respondents articulated that they were never seen as white in the United States due to their phenotypical appearance (dark brown skin and/or other physical features—curly hair and/or facial features). None of these respondents were consistently racialized as Black in the United States. Rather, 5 of the 6 reported that they were largely seen as Latino/a/x. One respondent, however, said that he was sometimes racialized as Latino, sometimes as Muslim (when flying on planes), and sometimes as Black (such as when wearing an American football jersey). While 8 respondents reported that they were almost always perceived as white in the United States, the other 29 reported that how they were seen in the US fluctuated and depended on how "tan they were," what they were wearing, how they styled their hair, who they were with, what language they were speaking, and/or what places and spaces they were occupying.[40]

ORGANIZATION OF THE BOOK

The rest of this book is divided into four chapters, followed by the conclusion. In Chapter 1, I examine how power without papers shapes 1.5-generation Brazilians' everyday lives and interactions, including in public spaces and with state authorities and officers. In this era of neoliberal racial capitalism, the risk of deportation for themselves increases after age eighteen as they begin to accrue "unlawful presence time" in the US. But despite their legal vulnerability, "legal passing" as white allows many 1.5-generation Brazilians to avoid some of the deleterious impacts of illegality and to accrue the public and psychological wages of whiteness. I examine the mechanisms that allow them to avail themselves of these wages, including the social meanings of whiteness in the US, white racial solidarity from other whites, and Brazilians' own boundary-work, a process in which they make claims to whiteness and draw distinctions between themselves and racialized others (see Lamont and Molnár 2002). Their boundary-work from racialized others in the US is shaped by their understandings of their families' own race and class positionalities in Brazil, their families' downward mobility in the US, and their own experiences with discrimination and exclusion in the US racial economy. Ultimately, I argue that whiteness serves as a protective mechanism against some of the stigma and risks that come with illegality. And yet negative impacts of illegality do remain, manifested in situational anxiety, the pain of a loved one's deportation, and, in the rare case, of their own deportation. Importantly, however, racial and class privilege continues to shape experiences of deportation back in Brazil.

In Chapters 2 and 3, I turn my attention to how 1.5-generation Brazilians navigate some of the most important life course rituals and transitions associated with young adulthood: education completion, labor force participation (Chapter 2), and romantic relationships, including marriage (Chapter 3).

Chapter 2 focuses on their experiences navigating higher education and work after they leave high school. In this chapter, we see how salient illegality is in shaping their educational and career ambitions. Those who are undocumented when they graduate from high school experience more involuntary delays and interruptions in pursuing college dreams and face a more restricted labor market than their peers with lawful immigration status, which causes anxiety, sadness, and anger. At the same time, the story of blocked mobility is nuanced. Indeed, coming from Brazilian middle-class families allows some 1.5-generation undocumented Brazilians to overcome the enormous financial barriers to college in the state of Massachusetts. For example, some families are able to help their children pay thousands of dollars out of pocket to go to college. Furthermore, while those who are undocumented face a restricted labor market, race, class, and gender shape *how* they navigate and experience this racialized and gendered labor market.

Chapter 3 examines how power without papers shapes respondents' romantic relationships, including dating and marriage. Marriage remains one of the most viable pathways to citizenship, a reality that looms large in undocumented 1.5-generation Brazilians' minds. But while (il)legality shapes all stages of romantic relationships, including feelings of desirability and plans for the future, many 1.5-generation Brazilians state that they could never strategically "marry for papers" as they deeply value romantic love relationships. Indeed, nationality and race, even more than citizenship status, shape whom they desire in a love match. Nearly all 1.5-generation Brazilians were in relationships with white Americans or light-skinned Brazilians, with some explicitly stating that they were not attracted to Black partners. For some, marriage to a white American is a strategy to "become white," demonstrating a very Brazilian understanding of race, where marriage has long been seen as a way to "change" race. Thus, while illegality leads them away from wanting to marry for papers, this chapter also reveals how family formation is a powerful site for the reproduction of racial inequalities.

Chapter 4 examines what these experiences mean for 1.5-generation Brazilians' sense of belonging in society, including their ethno-racial and national identities. In this chapter we see how illegality limits the wages of whiteness, presenting a major barrier to belonging. Being undocumented during the transition to adulthood led most 1.5-generation Brazilians to form a double consciousness—either identifying ambivalently as an American or eschewing an American identity altogether. One-and-a-half-generation Brazilians point to illegality as a *stigmatized and racialized* status that had excluded them from socioeconomic opportunities and undermined their sense of belonging. Furthermore, few of those who pass as white in the US actually identify as white in the US, citing their birthplaces in Latin America and their experiences as undocumented "others" in the US. In their minds, to be "white" in the US is to have citizenship, power, and money. Their lives as undocumented immigrants stand in contrast to these definitions of whiteness.

In the Conclusion, I examine what this Brazilian case means for scholars of migration and the implications for public policy and for coalition-building for social change. We often think of undocumented individuals as some of the most precarious members of society, and they are. Indeed, even for undocumented immigrants with racial and class privilege, we see how illegality penetrates the most intimate aspects of their lives, limits their socioeconomic opportunities, and undermines their sense of belonging. Yet, as the stories in this book make clear, the story of illegality is not uniform, and race and class privilege do shape their lives in profound ways, including providing protection from deportability and helping them to avoid the most stigmatized jobs in the labor market. Ultimately, then, 1.5-generation Brazilians' lived experiences suggest that we must take seriously how race, class, and (il)legality articulate together in particular spaces in specific historical conjunctures.

ONE DEPORTABILITY

Navigating Power Without Papers in Everyday Interactions

RICARDO'S STORY

> I was inside this car. [Border patrol] looked in, everybody there was white. I blended right in—you know what I mean? To him, it was just five white college kids who had played rugby . . . and they were going home. Had I looked distinctly, like, Guatemalan or something . . .—Ricardo

Denied legal recognition by the state, undocumented immigrants are targets for state-sanctioned forms of legal violence (Menjívar and Abrego 2012), including the threat of detention and deportation, which ensures a surplus of racialized, compliant workers who can be easily removed and replaced under neoliberal racial capitalism (Golash-Boza 2015).[1] Over the past few decades, these threats of deportation have intensified as the US has expanded its surveillance apparatus, detaining and deporting a greater number of immigrants, mostly Black men with green cards and undocumented Latino/a/x men (Golash-Boza 2011; Golash-Boza and Hondagneu-Sotelo 2013). And it's not only immigration officers tasked with enforcing immigration laws, but local and state police officers, guidance counselors, employers, and everyday citizens (Coutin 1993; De Genova 2002; Menjívar and Abrego 2012). Under this surveillance and deportation regime, some undocumented immigrants experience intense and pervasive fears of deportation, leading them, at times, to eschew making claims on the state (even when they or their family members are entitled to certain goods or services) and to avoid any interactions with the police, even when they might be victims of crimes (Abrego 2011; Asad 2023; Calavita 2007; De Genova 2002; Gleeson 2010; Hacker et al. 2011; Jimenez 2021). These fears of deportation are not unfounded, as undocumented immigrants from Latin America, especially men, are disproportionately detained, arrested, and deported during routine traffic stops and other everyday interactions (Golash-Boza 2011; Golash-Boza and Hondagneu-Sotelo 2013).

But Ricardo, a tall, athletic, 1.5-generation Brazilian of Portuguese descent, was not arrested or detained when his car was stopped by Border Patrol on a northeastern highway.[2] And Ricardo knew, without a doubt, that his ability to pass as white had helped him avoid the negative impacts of illegality. As described in the Introduction, "looking Latino/a/x" is conflated with illegality and has become the legal and de facto interpersonal basis for discrimination (Chavez 2013; Romero 2006). Ricardo, however, with his light skin that tanned easily in the sun and his straight, dark brown hair, blended in with his white teammates. While law enforcement officers and personnel, including Border Patrol officers, Immigration and Customs Enforcement (ICE) personnel, and the police, stop Black and brown immigrants and American citizens for mundane activities or minor offenses—jaywalking, broken taillights, and cracked windshields (Epp, Maynard-Moody, and Haider-Markel 2014; García 2019)—Ricardo and his white American rugby friends were not even asked for their driver's licenses.[3] They were presumed innocent of immigration violations.[4]

I first met Ricardo in 2007 when he was just nineteen years old. He was "fully" undocumented at the time, ineligible for a Social Security number and work permit. He had managed, however, to overcome enormous legal and financial barriers to college, receiving a full private scholarship to attend a highly selective liberal arts school. There he joined the rugby team. His white teammates did not know his legal status. Indeed, he was confident that he had been able to conceal it from them, just as he had been able to conceal it from the Border Patrol.

But while Ricardo could pass as white, his whiteness in the US was not always so clear-cut.[5] In Brazil, Ricardo was unambiguously white, meaning he did not question whether others saw him as white. But as described in the Introduction, differing racial projects in the US have led to more exclusive boundaries of whiteness.[6] Ricardo reported that he was sometimes racialized as Latino (but only "15% of the time") and sometimes asked "where are you from?," a question levied by inquisitors against someone who appears racially ambiguous or "foreign-looking" (Bashi Treitler 2013, 12). Most of the time, however, he told me that Americans most often perceived him as Southern European. His whiteness not a given in the US, Ricardo and other 1.5-generation Brazilians sometimes consciously constructed and performed whiteness. These strategic racial performances, or what sociologist Wendy Roth (2012) calls "racial strategies," involves using cultural knowledge about "styles, routines, and action to signal who they are and, sometimes, who they want to be seen to be" and can "collectively constitute broader racial strategies for positioning oneself within a racial hierarchy" (151). In Ricardo's case, these strategies often involved wearing preppy men's fashion that ruled the 2000s: black pea coats, polo shirts, khaki cargo shorts, and black crewnecks with baggy jeans.

To be sure, these strategic efforts to "pass" as white in this era of neoliberal racial capitalism can protect against the negative stereotypes and consequences associated with racialized illegality. Indeed, I argue that "passing as white" is a form of what sociologist Angela García (2019) refers to as "legal passing." According to García (2019), under the disciplining power of capitalism, undocumented Mexican immigrants in California, especially those living in more hostile local contexts, engage in strategic self-presentations to mask illegality by adopting behaviors, wearing clothes, and consuming products associated with mainstream US-born groups.

Erving Goffman (1959) first conceptualized the idea of "passing" to describe situations in which people attempt to cross group boundaries between stigmatized and dominant groups by managing how others perceive them, thereby avoiding uncomfortable and/or dangerous situations. In capitalist societies structured on white supremacy, Harris (1993) argues that "passing as white" for Blacks has an economic logic that helps to ensure both short-term economic gains and long-term political, economic, and social security. Meanwhile, other scholars have shown that undocumented immigrants engage in efforts to conceal illegality by showcasing expensive clothes and cars (Rouse 1992) or covering up skin color with hats and clothing (Willen 2007).

This chapter examines how power without papers shapes 1.5-generation Brazilians' experiences with deportability under neoliberal racial capitalism by focusing on their everyday interactions in public life, including with police and other law enforcement officers. On the one hand, I argue that passing as white, as it did for Ricardo, is a specific "legal passing" strategy and serves as a protective mechanism against the negative consequences of illegality.[7] In so doing, I draw not only on the work of sociologist Angela García, but sociologists Laura Enriquez and Daniel Millán (2019), who argue that there are protective social and spatial and locations for some 1.5-generation immigrants—such as being a college student on a college campus—that can limit exposure to immigration enforcement mechanisms. I argue that for most 1.5-generation Brazilians that I met, these protective locations are connected to whiteness.

Importantly, passing as white functions as a protective mechanism both because of the existing ethno-racial hierarchy in US society—including the social meanings of whiteness and white racial solidarity from other whites—*and* because of 1.5-generation Brazilians' own strategic efforts at constructing whiteness, which often involves boundary-making from other racialized groups, especially Latino/a/xs. In this way, 1.5-generation Brazilians' attempts to navigate the ethno-racial hierarchy are not so different from other ethno-racial groups throughout American history. And while these strategic efforts offer important protections and benefits to individuals, they also reify rather than challenge the ethno-racial hierarchy (Bashi Treitler 2013), undermining the potential for them to form a collective identity with marginalized others that might propel them to join a movement for revolutionary changes (Yazdiha 2021).

To be sure, while passing as white serves as a protective mechanism from negative consequences of racialized illegality, there are *limits* to its power for individuals. First, working to conceal illegality can come with some emotional costs. Many Brazilians feel like they must lie (which causes frustration and/or stress) or adopt other stigmatizing characteristics to conceal illegality. For example, Álvaro, who was light-skinned with medium brown, wavy hair and whose ancestors had migrated from Portugal to Brazil, reported that he told his white American friends in high school that he was "lazy" and "carefree" rather than tell them the truth about why he had not gotten his driver's license. But keeping up the lie of "laziness" was "annoying" for Álvaro and took effort because it was "obviously" not true. In his words, "I'm obviously not lazy 'cause I walk to the gym, you know what I mean? Like I run around the treadmill!" Like most men (and unlike most women), Álvaro did not cry as he spoke of living a lie. But he was clearly exasperated and bothered by it, rolling his eyes and growing more animated as he spoke. Women, however, often did cry. For example, Leila, who strategically passed as white by straightening her hair and changing her tone of voice to sound high-pitched and calm, cried as she detailed hiding illegality from others, exclaiming "It's not a good way to live!" between tears.

Second, as undocumented immigrants, 1.5-generation Brazilians still experience the legal violence of immigration laws, including the threat of (and actual) deportation for themselves *and* their loved ones. In other words, as undocumented immigrants, they are still legally subject to removal from the US. At least five respondents reported experiencing the deportation of a loved one and one woman was deported herself. Others were conscious of the threat of deportation, at least in certain situations. As explored throughout this chapter, however, the threat of (as well as experience of) deportation is experienced alongside the protective mechanisms of whiteness, which mitigates their vulnerability as disposable, undocumented workers. For example, 1.5-generation white-passing Brazilians rarely experience their own deportability as a pervasive fear, but instead as a "situational trigger," which Enriquez and Millán (2019) define as "specific situations that prompt real or perceived risks of interacting with immigration enforcement" (9). This was true in Ricardo's case—as he rarely feared deportation for himself. Rather, it was only during the interactions with Border Patrol that his anxiety was "triggered" and he was reminded of his legal vulnerability.

This chapter, then, demonstrates that power without papers shapes 1.5-generation Brazilians' lives in nuanced ways as they navigate public life, demonstrating how privilege and marginalization work together under racial capitalism in this historical conjuncture. Passing as white serves as a protective mechanism for 1.5-generation Brazilians against being stopped, questioned, arrested, detained, and/or deported, even as they remain legally vulnerable to the threat of deportation, which nation-states use to "control workers" (Golash-Boza 2015). Yet, because nation-states largely control those who are racialized as nonwhite, successful constructions of whiteness matter in important ways. Specifically, successfully passing as white allows 1.5-generation Brazilians to largely avoid the deleterious impacts of deportability *and* experience what Du Bois calls "the public and psychological wages of whiteness." As detailed in the Introduction, W. E. B. Du Bois (1935) demonstrated that while poor white men who earned low wages during Jim Crow segregation could still access white public spaces, like parks and schools (public wages), and experience a sense of confidence that they would be treated with respect (psychological wages). In the contemporary era of neoliberal racial capitalism, undocumented immigrants face low wages in the labor market *and* the threat of deportation. Yet, despite their precarious legal status, I find that undocumented, white-passing 1.5-generation immigrants, like poor whites of the Jim Crow era, also benefit from the public and psychological wages of whiteness.

In the next sections I explore the mechanisms that enable 1.5-generation white-passing Brazilians to accrue the public and psychological wages of whiteness. First I examine how they benefit from the preexisting racial structures and racial meanings in society. Then I turn to their own strategic work to construct whiteness and draw boundaries away from nonwhites, especially Latinoa/x/s, as they work for racial and economic uplift.

PREEXISTING RACIAL DYNAMICS THAT ENABLE THE ACCRUAL OF THE WAGES OF WHITENESS

Social Meanings of Whiteness in Enforcement Encounters

Race is not a biological reality but instead a social and political formation that produces racial meanings and divergent experiences for US ethno-racial groups (Omi and Winant 2014). Humans use physical features—light skin, narrow noses, blue eyes (and other physical facial features associated with northern and western Europeans)—to put people into an artificial racial category we call "white" (Omi and Winant 2014). Who is considered white changes across time and space, including international geographic space (Nobles 2000). Nevertheless, whiteness brings power not just in the US, but around the world, as colonialism and racism are structuring elements of global historical capitalism (Du Bois 1965; Itzigsohn and Brown 2020; Quisumbing King 2019).[8]

Whiteness is also gendered and brings assumptions of innocence, especially for women (Christie 1986; Collins 1990; Hamad 2019; Wanzo 2008). Furthermore, it brings assumptions of being a "real American"—that is, someone who truly "belongs" in American society and is deserving of citizenship (Hing 2004). These social meanings of whiteness—as being a "real

American" who is innocent of any wrongdoing, including the violation of criminal and/or immigration laws—help undocumented 1.5-generation Brazilians accrue the public and psychological wages of whiteness. Meanwhile, those racialized as Arab are treated as "forever suspect," especially at airports (Selod 2018), while Black and brown immigrants and citizens are seen as criminal lawbreakers and are often treated harshly—sometimes fatally—while engaging in everyday activities, including shopping, walking home while wearing hoodies, driving, and bird-watching in parks (Armenta 2017; Feagin and Sikes 1994; Golash-Boza 2011; Ray 2020).

Like Ricardo, Sabine could pass as white in the United States. Sabine was petite, with light skin, dark brown eyes, and long, soft, wavy brown hair that she often pulled back in a ponytail, her sideswept bangs tucked behind her ear. During our second interview, Sabine described an unintentional interaction with Border Patrol. In her early twenties, Sabine and her friends were driving in upstate New York, took a wrong turn, and ended up in Canada. While she had a Massachusetts driver's license—as she had been in liminal legality for years due to her pending application for an adjustment in status—she did not have her Brazilian passport with her. Even if she did, the passport would have shown that she had overstayed her visa.

> We miss some exit, end up going to Canada, okay? So we're in Canada, and had no problem going in. But then we're like, we just need to turn around because we . . . took the wrong exit. . . . So [we] have to go into this little room, and I'm like, shaking inside, like, "This could be the end for me. Like, they could just hold me into a little room here and then send me on a plane back to Brazil." And this girl, like, has no clue about [my status]. I was kind of—I freaked out. So we go into this little room. The guy asks us questions: "Where are you from?" I'm like, "Boston." And, "Oh, we all went to college together." And they like, let us back in. You know, they kind of gave them a talking-to. So they let us back in, but just said, "You can't come in without bringing your passport next time." None of them—like, none of us had it. We just took a wrong turn. So they let me in. You know, I was in the back seat, so I wasn't very visible. But still, I was like right there in front of them. So I think that says something about, not just race—race and also racial judgments, but about education. Like I talked about where I went to school. I had a driver's license. You know, I didn't have an accent—I didn't speak with an accent.

In Sabine's eyes, the joining together of her racial appearance, education, and non-accented English-speaking protected her that day in the mid-2000s. She was not seen as a foreign "threat" and was assumed to be innocent of any violation of immigration laws, even though she did not even have a passport to produce.

She was, however, extremely anxious ("I freaked out") during the encounter. She was fearful not only of deportation, but of the stigma of illegality—after all, none of her friends she was with that day knew she was undocumented. Thus, while whiteness protected her from being detained and deported, it did not completely protect her from the anxiety associated with situational triggers, reminding her of her vulnerability (Enriquez and Millán 2019).

It was not just Border Patrol who assumed that undocumented white-passing Brazilians were "real Americans" innocent of any violation of immigration laws, but police officers too. Thais, who was light-skinned and had highlighted, straight blond hair, told me that the police officers never treated her as if she might be undocumented.

> We know all of [the cops]. They all play jokes with us. "Oh, Brazilians! We love Brazilians! They're the most beautiful women in the world!" You know, [the police officers are] really funny and nice. They're like "every time you have a problem." But it's this kind of thing—they're nice to us, but I'm pretty sure they don't know our status.

Thais's experiences with the police as an undocumented woman stand in stark contrast to the stories of Black and brown immigrants and citizens who are stopped by police for minor offenses, leading to arrests, detention, deportation, and, "justified" police killings (Armenta 2017; Epp, Maynard-Mooney, and Haider-Markel 2014; Gilbert and Ray 2016; Golash-Boza 2011, 2015; Ray 2020). To be sure, some Americans living in Greater Boston began conflating Brazilians with illegality in the mid-2000s (Sanchez 2008). But other stereotypes also existed, and Thais's experiences with the police in the early 2000s were shaped by gendered stereotypes of "beautiful" and "sexual" Brazilian women—stereotypes that were connected in part to light-skinned Brazilian supermodels of the 2000s—Adriana Lima, Alessandra Ambrosio, and Gisele Bundchen, the now-ex-wife of NFL hero Tom Brady of the New England Patriots.[9]

Importantly, these interactions with the police, which led Thais to seeing the police as "funny" and "nice," demonstrate the public wages of whiteness she experienced. But these interactions also resulted in psychological wages—most notably, in providing her the confidence to ask these police officers to forgive her mom's speeding ticket. While many undocumented immigrants (and their adult children) who are racialized as nonwhite avoid interactions with government officials or representatives of other bureaucratic institutions, even if it means losing out on services or benefits to which they and/or their families are entitled (Asad 2020; Dreby 2015; García 2018; Sommers et al. 2012; Yoshikawa 2011), Thais felt enough confidence to ask for a favor from the police.

In contrast to the stories of Thais, Ricardo, and Sabine is the story of Gabriel, who was one of the few Brazilians I met who was unable to pass as white in the US. In the US, Gabriel, who was tall, had dark brown skin, and usually wore his jet-black hair long and slicked-back straight, reported during our interviews that he had been racialized as Muslim (when traveling in airports), as Hispanic ("if I have facial hair and my hair is slick back and I wear a wife-beater") and as Black ("if I'm wearing my shorts, my football jersey, and I got my hair all puffed"). Because Gabriel was undocumented when he graduated from high school, he was unable to attend his dream school. He settled for a nearby public university, where everyone in his major was expected to participate in a cruise to Puerto Rico and Mexico. Despite his hesitancy to travel due to his precarious legal status, Gabriel was convinced that due to the special circumstance of the trip, they wouldn't check his passport. But unlike the white-passing Brazilians I met, Gabriel was put in jail in Puerto Rico and then detained on the ship for two months.

> All I have is my Brazilian passport, and this receipt that's eight or nine years old. So, like, you know, I went there. And they had dogs and everything. And they were checking everyone's passport one by one, and they're like, "Do you have a green card?" I'm like, "No." Like, "What do you have?" I'm like, "This is it." You know, and I was like, "Uh-oh." . . . So they take me to jail—in Puerto Rico. And I'm trying to get in touch with my family and lawyers. . . . And based on the information that I knew, I was honest with them. I was like, "Hey, you know, this is what I have." And to my knowledge, we had applied for our green card. . . . But, so I was put under custody, by the captain of the ship, during inspection. So I couldn't leave

the ship. So I was on the ship for two months. . . . But I was thankful, because I wasn't deported. 'Cause that was the other option. So I was brought back to Boston.

Gabriel was fortunate he was not deported to Brazil. This was the early 2000s. And while enforcement practices were ramping up in the wake of 9/11, they were not quite what they are in the present day (Selod 2018). Back in Boston, Gabriel's family was able to connect with a new (and better) lawyer who effectively argued for humanitarian parole for Gabriel. Nevertheless, Gabriel's story of jail and detention differs significantly from white-passing respondents who interacted with immigration enforcement officers during the same time period.

White Racial Solidarity
Another mechanism that allowed 1.5-generation Brazilians to accrue the wages of whiteness was white racial solidarity from other white Americans. Feagin (2020) argues that a "shared white identity" with other whites can facilitate "positive interactions" (16). One of the starkest examples of this white racial solidarity was told to me by Ana Maria. Ana Maria, whose ancestors had migrated from Germany to Brazil, had pale skin and straight brown hair. In the months after the 9/11 attacks, Ana Maria was flying home to Boston from Oklahoma. She described standing in a security line behind a man that she perceived as "Arabian or something" who passed through without any questions from Transportation Security Administration (TSA) agents. Meanwhile, Ana Maria, who showed the agents her Brazilian passport, was asked for her green card. She was nervous and implied to the TSA agent that she had a green card but had forgotten it at home. This, of course, was a lie, as Ana Maria was undocumented. Just then a white American man standing behind her in line emphatically interjected, angry that TSA was stopping Ana Maria and not the brown-skinned man. "And the guy behind me, he's like, 'What are you talking about, man? She's white. What are you talking about? Go talk to that guy!' (pointing to the brown-skinned man in front of her)."

Ana Maria was allowed to pass through without further questioning following the interjection of this white American man, who assumed that she was innocent of breaking any immigration (or other) laws. Indeed, he redirected TSA away from Ana Maria to question a man he racialized as an "other." Ana Maria recognized the injustice that was happening, but her illegality prevented her from standing up for the other man, fearing the consequences of what might happen if she redirected attention to herself.

White racial solidarity from other whites facilitated not only access to the public wages of whiteness, but the psychological and material wages of whiteness too. For example, in the case of Elisabete, whom we met in the Introduction's opening vignette, race articulated with gender, education, and (il)legality to shape her willingness to reach out to a woman she did not know in order to network for a corporate job. Elisabete described this networking attempt as a "ballsy as fuck" action; she not only did not know this woman, but she had no corporate work experience to talk about with her. Still, underscoring the articulation of gender, race, and education, Elisabete calculated that this white woman would relate to her, especially since they had graduated from the same public college (and it worked, the woman did network for her). In part, Elisabete had been motivated to reach out at this particular moment because she finally had a work permit (via DACA). Yet, from Elisabete's perspective, it was whiteness that gave her the extra confidence to actually advocate for herself. Indeed, later in our conversations, Elisabete reiterated how whiteness gave her the confidence to make demands on her bosses, including pay raises, telling me that white people in corporate America "can relate to who you are."

Sometimes, assumed racial solidarity from other whites did not facilitate entirely "positive" interactions—as 1.5-generation, white-passing Brazilians reported that some white Americans felt free to talk pejoratively about undocumented immigrants in front of them. For example, one night I was out to dinner with Cristine and Gabriela at a neighborhood joint popular with local, white college students. At one point a few white undergraduate men approached our table and began flirting with Cristine and Gabriela. The men told us they overheard the three of us speaking in another language and asked what it was. After we explained that I was American and Gabriela and Cristine were Brazilian, one man remarked that Gabriela and Cristine were the "good kind" of immigrants, not the "illegal ones." Both Cristine and Gabriela conformed to European standards of beauty. They were thin, light-skinned, and had long, straight hair. After the men left, Gabriela rolled her eyes and said, "If they only knew . . ."

Andréa, who was petite, pale-skinned, and had a heart-shaped face, told me that she had overheard so many racist comments about undocumented immigrants because most Americans usually perceive her as white and not as an immigrant. "You know, and I've heard so many people say racist things (about immigrants) on the bus or, you know, at a supermarket, not realizing that I'm an immigrant. And it's kind of ridiculous." But while Andréa knew she was "treated better" in everyday interactions by other whites given her physical appearance, she still faced discrimination on the basis of illegality.

> Depending on the situation, I'm either treated just like any other immigrant, or I'm treated like a white person. If I'm being treated just based on perception of my physical looks and the way I speak . . . I definitely get treated better. But if I'm in a situation where I have to put down, you know, my identification—and it has to be my green card—or my citizenship, then I definitely, depending on the person, get treated with a little less respect.

Thus, Andréa describes how racial privilege and legal marginalization hang together in nuanced ways. That is, she experiences discrimination on the basis of illegality while also experiencing the public wages of whiteness in many of her everyday interactions with strangers.

STRATEGIC WORK TOWARD WHITENESS

Importantly, 1.5-generation Brazilians not only benefited from preexisting racial dynamics in society; they actively worked to accrue the wages of whiteness. In other words, they did not just passively benefit from the social meanings of whiteness and white racial solidarity; 1.5-generation Brazilians often strategically navigated the overlapping power systems in their lives in order to pass as white and accrue its wages. Next, I examine how they strategically worked to construct whiteness and conceal illegality.

Legal Passing: Constructing Whiteness, Concealing Illegality

While some 1.5-generation Brazilians reported almost always being seen as white in their everyday interactions, most 1.5-generation Brazilians told me that they were sometimes racialized as nonwhite in the US, especially in their early years in the US when their English was not as strong. These experiences with racialization for white-passing 1.5-generation Brazilians underscores how race is determined by more than one's physical features, as class indicators (such as occupations), language (and accents), names, and other social cues impact racial judgments (Bertrand and Mullainathan 2004; Roth 2012; Saperstein and Penner 2012). Nevertheless, with some efforts, all but six of the 1.5-generation Brazilians I met could construct whiteness and conceal illegality, successfully passing as white.[10]

Álvaro, who was of Portuguese descent, called himself a "chameleon" who was able to blend in racially with whatever group he was with, including white peers. "If I'm with all white kids, they'll just assume I'm like one of them." However, he knew that being seen as white did not just "happen" to him—he also consciously presented himself as white. "The way I dress and, like, the way I speak and present myself, it's much more of, I guess, white." In part, dressing as white meant avoiding tight T-shirts and hip-riding denim with designs, clothing associated with Latino men in the early aughts.

Leila detailed the physical, cultural, and social cues she used to simultaneously conceal illegality and accrue the wages of whiteness. For example, one social cue Leila used was to strategically mark "white" on forms when her "(legal) status is a consideration" in order to present as white and conceal illegality. "If I'm going to the RMV (Registry of Motor Vehicles), I mark white. If I'm doing anything where my status is a consideration, I mark white." Underscoring her strategic decision-making in these situations, she contrasted these moments with how she filled out forms in others. "If I'm responding (to) any kind of census-like question—or any type of question where I can see that there's an intent to get a real understanding of the demographics—then I put in 'Other' and I put in Latin American, non-Hispanic."

Leila's strategic constructions of whiteness was not limited to how she marked forms; she also discussed how she consciously presented herself as white by straightening her hair, wearing glasses, and talking in a particular tone.

> When I walk into the RMV, I am going to straighten my hair, I'm going to wear my glasses, I'm going to talk as white as I can. You know? And I'm just going to walk in there and I'm going to say that I need to renew my driver's license or whatever. . . . And sound as white as possible. . . . I'm not going to lie, when I get into—when I go into the RMV, I'm like, "I need to renew my driver's license" [in a superpolite, high-pitched, soft, and earnest voice]. Like, that's how I talk. [She continues in a high-pitched, soft, and polite voice.] "So, what else do you need

from me?" You know what I mean? As ridiculous as it sounds, like, it just makes me feel more comfortable about what I'm doing. You know? Like I had to go in and get a replacement license because I lost mine and it was about to expire soon anyway. And I was like "You know what? Why don't I just." And I was sweating profusely because I had to renew my driver's license. And it is always that fear, you know what I mean? It's like—you always have that fear—any time you have to do something where you have to check that box that says you are a citizen. Any time you have to—I have to do something like that, like, my stomach freezes and it's just an awful experience.

While Leila detailed how she strategically used physical and social cues to present as white at places like the RMV, Leila did not always consciously present as white. Indeed, right after describing (for a second time) how she wore glasses and straightened her hair to "try to be a white girl," she told me she presented herself differently when going clubbing with her Latina/o/x friends. On those nights, Leila consciously presented herself as "Latina" by wearing large gold hoop earrings and embracing clothes that show off her "curves." In this way, Leila engaged in code-switching, strategically using different cultural codes when it was advantageous to her (Carter 2007; Molinsky 2007; Roth 2012).

Notably, Leila's efforts to construct herself as white allowed her to accrue the public and psychological wages of whiteness—as she was treated with respect by the staff at the RMV *and* felt "more comfortable" about what she was doing. And in this case, she gained access to a Massachusetts driver's license, despite the fact that in that historical moment, she was technically ineligible for one as an undocumented immigrant (Massachusetts did not pass driver's licenses for undocumented immigrants until June 2022). Importantly, Leila had been able to get a driver's license issued in another US state (by establishing residency there). When that license was about to expire, she decided to transfer the license to Massachusetts, renewing it there. Doing so was fraught, given that she was undocumented. But by consciously presenting herself as white, she was able to calm her "stomach freezes" and successfully obtain a Massachusetts license.

Because race depends not only on physical cues but on social cues (Saperstein and Penner 2012), strategies to pass as white sometimes included conscious befriending and hanging around other white people. For example, Ricardo described how he had a "goal in mind" and "made an effort" to befriend white students at his predominantly white college. Ricardo was conscious that he had befriended his white peers in ways that most of his first-generation peers of color did not. To be clear, Ricardo's physical features—his height, light skin, and facial features associated with Europeans—assisted him in his ability to pass as white. But he was also *strategic* in making friends with white students. It was an explicit goal of his. And as we saw at the beginning of the chapter, he knew that hanging with his white rugby friends allowed him to "blend in" as white.

Choosing to Navigate White Space and Avoiding Black and Brown Spaces
Boston is one of the most racially segregated large cities in the country (Logan and Zhang 2010), a result of centuries of racism, decades of racist housing policies and white flight. Immigrants, like all Americans, must make decisions about where to live when they settle in the US, and when they do, they "sort into neighborhoods across cities in patterns strongly shaped by the racial and ethnic and socioeconomic characteristics of those neighborhoods" (Gelatt et al. 2015). As Gelatt et al. (2015) argue, where people live is important, as it impacts their life chances (and their children's life chances) since living in higher income—and whiter—spaces means a greater likelihood of avoiding environmental toxins while accessing better-resourced schools, grocery stores that offer more nutritious foods, and safer outdoor spaces in which to play and exercise.

Most of the young people and their families whom I met rarely settled in the poorest communities of color in the Greater Boston area. Instead, most had settled in racially and economically diverse but still majority-white spaces. For example, sometimes they settled in communities in and around Boston's many colleges and universities. Other times they chose Boston neighborhoods or suburbs where working- and middle-class whites lived, including those of Italian, Portuguese, Polish, or Russian heritage.[11]

Some 1.5-generation Brazilians knew that their parents had actively avoided settling in primarily Black and brown spaces in the US. For example, Fausto talks about how his family—and other Brazilian families—specifically avoid living in Hispanic spaces.

> Basically, East Solon was all Hispanics. In fact, my parents didn't want to live there because of that. The Brazilians didn't want to live there. We settled in Pepper Square. We got our house. This is where my aunt's salon was.... [But East Solon]—that whole neighborhood, Brazilians avoided it.

According to Fausto, Brazilians avoided Hispanic areas because they "think they are above" other Latin American immigrant groups.

Meanwhile, Álvaro, who grew up in a neighborhood of Boston that was more than 60 percent white and was close to at least two prominent universities, discussed how his family actively avoided sending him to school in Black and brown spaces, using color-blind language (Bonilla-Silva 2017) to describe the school communities his parents sought to avoid.

> I got into School X and School Y. And my parents were scared of sending me to School X because it was in Dorchester. And then School Y was in Roxbury and they didn't like the neighborhoods.

When Álvaro says his parents did not like "the neighborhoods" in "Dorchester and Roxbury," he is using color-blind language that allows him to avoid saying "Black spaces."[12] In 2010, the areas surrounding School X and School Y were more than 60 percent black (and in some census tracts, more than 70 percent Black). Instead of these schools, Álvaro's parents chose one that is disproportionately white (compared to Boston's diverse population). Thus Álvaro's parents chose not only to live in predominantly white spaces, but to send Álvaro to school in predominantly white spaces too.

The ways in which some 1.5-generation Brazilians had occupied predominantly white spaces was not always readily apparent to them until after they left Greater Boston. For example, Andréa only noticed when she went with her Brazilian friend to Chicago to scout out graduate schools.

> We went into a neighborhood, and like, we got on the bus. And we were the only light-skinned people on the bus. And that was very different for us. Because everywhere we've been to in Boston, you see everyone grew up everywhere. So we were . . . Like it took us a while to notice it. But finally I was looking around, and then I said to her in Portuguese, I was like, "Angelica, why are we the only light-skinned people? This is weird. This has never happened before."

To be sure, some 1.5-generation Brazilians, like Andréa, often did grow up in economically and culturally diverse spaces of Boston: neighborhoods with college and graduate students, highly educated professors from around the world, and more recently arrived immigrant groups from Europe, Latin America, and Asia. Yet these neighborhoods are still predominantly white (and, to a lesser extent, Asian), with few Blacks and Latino/a/xs. Notably, then, we see here how whiteness not only provided opportunities for geographic mobility *across* borders (see Introduction; Rosenberg 2022); whiteness also provided Brazilians the freedom to consciously—and unconsciously—move around geographic space *within* the US, including into and through wealthier, whiter spaces, without too much concern over how they might be policed in these areas.

As 1.5-generation Brazilians grew older and established their own households, they often chose neighborhoods that were even whiter than the ones in which they had grown up. For example, Alexia and her light-skinned, undocumented Brazilian husband moved from a town with a sizable Brazilian population to a more affluent and whiter town with lots of green space. Indeed, her new hometown was more than 80 percent white. Meanwhile, Ana Maria and her white American husband moved to an affluent town northwest of Boston, a town whose population is more than 80 percent white, less than 4 percent Hispanic, and approximately 0.5 percent Black.

Living in whiter, better-resourced areas was something Gabriela pointed to as evidence that she had defied racialized and classed stereotypes of illegality. For example, Gabriela proudly described her ability to buy a home in her current neighborhood. "I'm not a stupid person, and I'm not, I'm not a criminal. The stereotype doesn't fit with me. You know, (my partner and I) own this house. All the neighbors—this is a good place to live." The neighborhood that Gabriela and her light-skinned partner had chosen was a solidly middle-class and mostly white neighborhood. In this way, Gabriela underscores how race, illegality, and class articulate together, and how she, through homeownership in a white middle-class neighborhood, defies stereotypes associated with undocumented Latino/a/xs.

Emphasizing Whiteness and Boundary-Making from Stigmatized Groups
One-and-a-half-generation Brazilians I met made claims to whiteness in a number of ways. Sometimes they emphasized that strangers in public usually saw them as some sort of European, a source of pride for them. Other 1.5-generation Brazilians emphasized that official documents in Brazil classified them as "white." In some cases, however, they also drew boundaries between themselves and other racialized and stigmatized groups in the US.

Henrique, who had light skin and light brown hair, made claims toward whiteness by discussing how "happy" he was that Americans usually perceived him as Italian. "I'm happy to say I look Italian, and I've had a lot of people say, 'Oh, I didn't know you were Brazilian!'" Like most 1.5-generation Brazilians I met, Henrique did not always pass as white in the US, especially when he was with darker-skinned relatives and spoke Portuguese. For example, he recalled an incident when his cousin slightly bumped a car when parking. The driver of the other car, who was white, started yelling at them: "Go back to your fucking country!" In most situations, however, Henrique said that people most often assumed he was Italian.

Even 1.5-generation Brazilians who were more likely to be perceived as Latino/a/x on a consistent basis in the US made claims to whiteness during our conversations, sometimes invoking Brazilian understandings of whiteness. For example, when I first started talking to Heloísa, who had medium-brown skin and wavy dark brown hair, about race in the US, she immediately told me that her birth certificate in Brazil would demonstrate that she was white.

> In my [birth] certificate, I am white. People [in the US] wouldn't see me, but you know on the birth certificate . . . But yes, I am. . . . [People in the US] would look [at] me and they would say, probably, Hispanic, you know? But on my birth certificate, I am white.

Heloísa's claims toward whiteness in the US did not rely upon US racial logics, but official classifications of race in Brazil (her Brazilian birth certificate) based in Brazilian racial logics. Schwartzman (2007) finds that "money whitens" in Brazil, as highly educated nonwhite parents are more likely to classify their children as white. Thus it would not be surprising that Heloísa, whose parents were highly educated, had listed her race as "white" even though most Americans would perceive her as nonwhite ("they would say, probably—Hispanic"). In this case, we see clearly how notions of race travel across borders and come into tension with logics of race in a new racial context (Joseph 2015).

Oftentimes, emphasizing whiteness was explicitly accompanied by efforts to draw boundaries away from racialized others in the US, particularly other immigrant groups from Latin America. As Osuji (2019) argues, boundary-making has long been shown to be a way for "expanding or limiting the range of people that are included within a category" (99). Indeed, Bashi Treitler (2013) demonstrates how outsider groups throughout American history—the Irish, Italians, Mexicans, Chinese, and Afro-Caribbeans—have strived to achieve racial uplift in American society by drawing boundaries away from racialized groups (especially Blacks), while emphasizing similarities to Europeans. In the case of 1.5-generation undocumented Brazilians growing up in the 1990s and 2000s, they often worked to limit being racialized as Latino/a/x while striving for racial uplift. For example, Gabriela told me that she would not mark "Hispanic" or "Latino" on any form because she "didn't want to be compared to a Mexican." When I asked her to expand on this, she said she didn't "want to accept the stereotype" associated with Latino/a/x immigrants as being "lower-class." For Gabriela, this was a stereotype she believes is a "half-truth." As she told me, "(Latino/a/xs) fit into that stereotype. They will act the stereotype without knowing it. That's how they got the stereotype. You just don't make a stereotype without the person having a little bit of that characteristic in them."

But she does not see the stereotype as true for Brazilians *like* her, who she perceives as being from a higher social class.

> We're middle-class. Or now are middle-class. I am not a lower-class where like, the Hispanics that . . . There are Latinos that are—they're not living very good. You know, their status here is lower class. . . . When you say that [you're Latino/a/x], the stereotype wins. You just can't . . . When you put "Hispanic," you're accepting that stereotype. I don't want to because I'm not like that, you know?[13]

As discussed in the Introduction, the idea that class and race are interconnected is deeply embedded in Brazilian racial consciousness (Schwartzman 2007). And here we can see how Gabriela, who migrated when she was four years old, clearly perceives class and race as articulating together in the US racial economy too, such that she perceives Hispanics as "lower-class."

To be clear, while Gabriela believes Brazilians are of a higher class than most Hispanics, she simultaneously worried that everyday Americans might perceive Brazilians just as negatively as they do other immigrants from Latin America, especially because so many Brazilians in the Greater Boston area were undocumented ("we're all illegals (to them)." Indeed, during my fieldwork from 2006 to 2008, Brazilian community leaders I met—and journalists—documented rising anti-Brazilian sentiment (Sanchez 2008), a phenomenon that dovetailed with not only increased numbers of Brazilians living there, but an increase in darker-skinned and poorer Brazilians who entered via the US-Mexico border post-9/11 (Braga and Jouët-Pastré 2008).

This macro context is important, as 1.5-generation Brazilians like Gabriela became acutely aware that Brazilians might be (or are) stigmatized the way that other Latin American immigrant groups are. And this ever-changing macro context impacts their boundary-making away from other Latin American groups as well as their assertions that white Americans perceived Brazilians as "better than" other Latin American immigrants. For example, during our conversations, Kátia emphasized that Brazilians, unlike Mexicans, came legally. For this reason, she claimed that (white) Americans perceive Brazilians more favorably.

> When Americans—well, at least, how I feel, when they think of immigrants, they don't really put Brazilians into that [negative] part. Like when they think about undocumented workers, they think more, like, Mexicans jumping the fence. . . . [Brazilians] came here by plane. Like, when we came here—in our terms—legal. We had our visa. We came here, but we overstayed our visas. So it was different in that sense. Like, we weren't really—we didn't, you know, go through Mexico to come into the country. Or go through Canada.

While Kátia told me that Americans perceive Brazilians more favorably than Mexicans, she was also clear that Brazilians *assert* themselves as better than Mexicans—and specifically points to mode of entry. In this way Kátia draws boundaries away from other undocumented immigrants, especially Mexicans, elevating Brazilians (like her) who enter legally and overstay visas from those who enter without inspection. Of course, what Kátia leaves out of this story is the historical and contemporary ways in which racism and classism are embedded in US foreign and immigration policies that have allowed Brazilians like her to enter legally on visas, while entering without inspection via Mexico is the only option for others, including more recently arrived Brazilians (Chomsky 2018; Rosenberg 2022; Watson 2018).

Marta, who had light skin and straight, dark silky hair and was in liminal legality when I first met her, also told me that Americans perceive Brazilians better than Spanish-speaking Latin American immigrant groups. She explained what she meant by "better": "These American are like 'these Spanish [speaking] guys are so lazy, I got to get Brazilians to work because they're all hard workers.'" Like Henrique, whom we met previously, Marta told me that most people see her as Italian. And yet, when she was working at the garage and wearing a name tag, revealing her Portuguese name, some Americans assumed she was "Spanish" (a word she uses interchangeably with *Hispanic* and *Latino/a/x*), which made her upset.

> When I worked at the garage, they always asked me if I'm Italian. But I think they see my name—[then] they ask me if I was Spanish too. But I think it's because they see my name. . . . But I had people who came up to me and asked me—they thought I was American by the looks. . . . I don't know why, but I don't like when they mistake me as Spanish. I don't know . . . like . . . I don't like the way that [Hispanics] dress and that they talk. They are always so loud. You know? I go, "No, I'm not Spanish! I'm Brazilian!"

Marta perceives Hispanics very negatively, explaining in the interview that she not only thinks Hispanics dress and talk differently—she thinks they have a different skin color.[14] "It's the color. I think that [Hispanics] are more dark. I don't know. The Hispanic—well, even the way they dress. I can see. I can tell a person who is Hispanic or not. The way they talk. The way they dress." Thus Marta pointed to darker phenotypical differences and pejorative stereotypes as she drew boundaries between Brazilians and other immigrant groups from Latin America.

Lúcia, whom I interviewed in 2007, was very direct that she perceives Brazilians in Boston as lighter-skinned than most Hispanic groups, and that this is the reason why white Americans see Brazilians as better than other immigrant groups from Latin America.

> I feel like, maybe there's . . . I need to like make a statement here. But I feel that people might view Brazilians, or at least some Brazilians, as like, more light-skinned than Hispanics. You know what I mean? Because . . . shit, I really don't wanna . . . [long pause] I don't know. Nobody says anything like, "Dirty Brazilians," they would just say that [about] Mexicans, you know?

Thus Lúcia directly described how race matters for immigrants' incorporation in the US—including how Americans treat newcomers. Of course, as the migration stream from Brazil changed, it is quite possible that Lúcia, who was not one of the Brazilians I reinterviewed (because she had secured legal status by age eighteen), would have feared—as Gabriela did—that Americans were starting to perceive Brazilians more negatively.

Indeed, throughout the interviews, some Brazilians not only drew boundaries between themselves and other Latin American groups; they also drew boundaries between themselves and more recently arrived Brazilians. For example, Fausto, who was tall, with dark brown hair and light olive skin, told me his parents wanted him to avoid interactions with newer immigrants from Brazil who migrated via Mexico because they "lacked character."

> If [Brazilians] did get a visa, it meant they had jobs in Brazil, had a house, had a career of some kind. . . . I mean, they were just looking for something better. Somehow, after midnineties, I don't know what happened, but Mexico became huge—I mean, through Mexico—became huge. A lot of people with fake documents. My parents, like, that was a big thing for them. Because they felt that these new Brazilians that were coming to the US. [My parents] didn't really want us to interact with them. Because a lot of them had come here illegally. And they had falsified all these documents. So my parents felt that that reflected on their character. You know what I mean? . . . I think after '95, '96, '97, was when [these newer Brazilians] really started to ruin it for those of us who were here honestly. My parents said this all the time, that the Brazilians who came here twenty years ago, they were here for an honest, sincere purpose. To really build their life.

Fausto, who had grown up undocumented before getting his green card as a teenager, used color-blind language of "character" to talk about why his family avoided more recently arrived Brazilians (Bonilla-Silva 2017). Yet he clearly describes class differences, indicating that earlier waves of Brazilians came from a higher social class ("had a house, had a career of some kind"). Fausto did not mention that these more recent arrivals were also darker-skinned. And like Kátia, he also did not mention the ways in which racism and classism embedded in US migration policy has made it more difficult for some immigrants—including later waves of Brazilian migrants who are poorer and darker-skinned—to enter lawfully on tourist visas (see Chomsky 2014; Rosenberg 2022).[15]

Danilo, who migrated at age eleven, echoed Fausto's assessment that there was a divide in the Brazilian community between older and newer arrivals, one that was readily apparent in middle and high school. Danilo came from an upper-middle-class family (his dad had a master's degree from one of the top universities in Brazil) but was one of the 1.5-generation Brazilians consistently racialized as nonwhite due to his dark brown skin, wide nose, and curly black hair. During our conversations, Danilo described how there were white-passing Brazilians in his middle and high schools who came at young ages and sat with the white American "cool kids" at lunch. These Brazilians, he said, looked down on the recently arrived Brazilians who migrated as teenagers as "invaders." Meanwhile, recently arrived Brazilians stereotyped the white-passing Brazilians who migrated before 9/11 as "white wannabes."[16]

Notably, Vitória, the one respondent whose family did migrate via Mexico, did express a sense of solidarity with undocumented immigrants from Latin America and had joined the DREAMer movement (Nicholls 2013). But Vitória was largely the exception in her activism. Many of the Brazilians I met, even when they saw similar struggles to other racialized groups, engaged in boundary-work from Latino/a/x immigrants *and* more recently arrived Brazilians. Scholars of Brazilian immigrants have long noted that many first-generation Brazilians struggle with being racialized as Latino/a/x (Beserra 2005; Joseph 2015; Margolis 1994; McDonnell and Lourenço 2009). Moreover, they also find that first-generation Brazilians have a strong individual identity as Brazilian, but not a strong collective identity as Brazilian (Margolis 1994). Here we see evidence that most 1.5-generation Brazilians have not formed a collective identity as Latino/a/x nor a collective identity as Brazilian. And without the formation of this collective identity, it is unlikely that most will become actively engaged in a solidarity movement for more systematic racial changes (Yazdiha 2021).[17]

THE LIMITS OF WHITENESS

Throughout this chapter, we have seen how 1.5-generation Brazilians can sometimes accrue the public and psychological wages of whiteness, which provide very real protections from stigma, detention, and deportation. In some cases, they also accrue real material benefits, including access to licenses or to networks for jobs, the latter of which is explored in more detail in Chapter 2. And yet the benefits of whiteness are circumscribed by illegality. In other words, as we will see, there are costs that come with concealing illegality and performing whiteness. Furthermore, passing as white may limit, but it does not altogether protect, 1.5-generation Brazilians from the deleterious impacts of illegality in this era of increased immigration enforcement.

Emotional and Other Costs of Concealing Illegality

First, there are emotional and material costs that come with performing whiteness and concealing illegality. For example, Leila, whom we previously met when she vividly described constructing whiteness at the RMV, cried throughout our interviews when describing the stress and anxiety of having "to live a lie" by keeping illegality a secret from friends, teachers, counselors, coworkers, and others in their lives. Meanwhile, for Thais, concealing illegality limited her access to college. Thais, whom we met earlier when she described asking police for favors, reported that she concealed her illegality from a school counselor who was encouraging her to apply for college. Rather than telling the school counselor the truth about her status, she told him that her papers were in "in process." As Gonzales (2010) argues, school counselors are important gatekeepers of information for undocumented students. But they can only be helpful if students confide in them. Thais did not reveal her actual legal status, limiting the school counselor's ability to help her navigate the college application process.

Like Leila, Gabriela said that concealing illegality from her peers and school mentors was stressful and that it felt "horrible" to lie. Moreover, the lies took effort on her part, as she attempted to explain decisions that seemed out of character for her. For example, Gabriela, like Thais, felt compelled to lie about the reason she was not applying to college. Rather than reveal she was undocumented, she told her high school mentors and friends that she was going to take a "year off." But Gabriela had been a self-described "teacher's pet" and loved learning. And she desperately wanted to go to college. Thus this lie did not make sense to people, given how much she loved school. Furthermore, her lie about wanting to take a year off also brought on new forms of stigma. Indeed, she said that she knew her teachers and school counselors thought she was "choosing a life downhill" by not pursuing education immediately after high school. Yet the stigma of letting them believe she was letting her life go "downhill" was easier for her to bear than telling them she was undocumented. She worried that her friends might "pity her," see her as "a step below" them, and not want to be friends with her. She explained it like this:

> If I had known you for ten years, and then you say you're illegal, I wouldn't look at you differently, but I would know you can't travel. And you're probably—you can't work here. You're already, just by saying that, you are

a step below me. You've been through school with me and whatever, but you now are not my equal. . . . How are you going to be like . . . [deep exhale] If you have a group of friends, and then everybody's going off to college, and everybody's going to be able to go to school, and everybody's going to be able to travel together. [But] you have now a friend who you know is not going to be able to do any of that with you—how are you going to one hundred percent be their friend? You can't include them in everything that you want to do. . . . You're now going to go off to college. You're going to get a better education. You're going to learn all these things in college. And this person is not. What will you have in common with this person now?

Ultimately, then, Gabriela said it was better to let her peers—and her school counselors—believe she was potentially risking her life by not going to college than to let them know she was undocumented. The stigma of "letting her life go downhill" still left "hope" in their minds that she would turn things around. "I think by saying, 'Oh, I'm going to take a year off,' there's still a little bit of hope that after that year, you're going to do something with your life. It's better than saying, 'Okay, I'm illegal.' Now you're—you have no hope. You're not going to do anything with your life." To Gabriela's knowledge, she had concealed her illegality successfully from her peers and school mentors. But concealing the truth about her legal status was still difficult.

Situational Triggers of Deportation
While being able to pass as white reduces situational triggers of the fear of deportation, it does not entirely erase them, especially for those 1.5-generation Brazilians whose whiteness in the US is not a given. And these situational triggers were anxiety-provoking and sometimes led to material loss. To be sure, very few respondents were overwhelmingly fearful on a daily basis of actual deportation for themselves. Yet the "situational triggers" they did experience were very anxiety-producing. For example, Alexia did not worry about deportation on a daily basis ("I'm not [stressed] about deportation. 'Cause I don't think they [will] ever come to my house and say 'you're deported'") but illegality was still a source of stress in her life as she thought about Trump ending DACA ("Is it going to get bad enough . . . that I'm gonna have to self-deport?") and she still got nervous if she was stopped by the police. She described

recently getting pulled over for a traffic violation—making a left turn where it was no longer permitted.

> [The turn] changed six months ago. And I had no idea. I've always been turning on that street to go to the hospital and get my medication all the time. But this time there was a cop. And the cop stopped me and I'm there, like my hands are sweating, like "Oh my god, he's gonna know I have DACA—he's gonna know my sit . . ." And [then], "Why the hell am I worrying about that when I have a license?" That's what I was thinking about. And then he was supernice. He gave me a warning. He was like "Oh ma'am, have a good day." I'm like, "He doesn't know anything!"

Like other white-passing respondents, Alexia's experience with the police was shaped not only by her illegality, but by her gender and race. She was anxious, but the police officer was "supernice" to her. Sometimes, however, these situational triggers that reminded them of their own deportability led to material loss. For example, Rodrigo, who was often racialized as Latino when out at Latin American clubs with his Latino friends, described how he avoided an argument over a jacket when leaving a club one night because he did not want to deal with the police. Thus while whiteness can empower immigrants to make claims to the police (as in the case of Thais, who asked the police to forgive her mother's speeding ticket), those who know they will be racialized as Latino/a/x in a particular situation often seek to evade encounters with the police, demonstrating how undocumented immigrants both engage and evade the police (Asad 2023).

Most often, 1.5-generation Brazilians discussed "situational triggers" of anxiety related to deportability when they knew they might have potential encounters with the police (like Rodrigo), state bureaucrats (like Leila at the RMV), and/or when interacting with immigration officers at US borders (like Ricardo and Sabine). Importantly, for white-passing Brazilians, these situational triggers were dramatically reduced once they had citizenship, underscoring how power *with* papers operates. Indeed, as lawful residents/citizens, they rarely feared police encounters. For example, Álvaro discussed how, once he had citizenship, getting a flat tire on the highway was no longer a reason for concern. He felt no trepidation calling the police. In contrast, he explained that when he was undocumented, he would have been anxious.

> I was driving on the tunnel, and my tire actually fell out in the tunnel. So like I was driving with like three tires—until I stopped. And like a cop came. Obviously, because I called 911 to get help. And it's something that like, say you are not, you know like, you're illegal—that's a huge problem already. You know what I mean? Because it's like, now you're afraid to call the police, which is like what you have to do, because you're afraid to get deported or whatever. When [the police officer] got there, I had my license and registration out. He was like, "I don't even need to see that."

Álvaro told this story to detail how much legal membership reduced situational triggers of fear. But his story also reveals how much whiteness impacted his life. In this instance, the police officer not only treated him with respect, but released him from normal protocol during a traffic encounter (providing a license and registration). Encounters with the police for citizens of color, especially Blacks, are often quite different, and sometimes fatal (Headley and Wright II 2020; Ray 2020).

The Experience of Deportation
While whiteness decreases the odds one will be deported, passing as white does not remove the fact that some of them—or their family members—will be deported. Indeed, at least five respondents had experienced deportation of a sibling or parent/stepparent. For Alexia, the deportation of her mother in an ICE sting had been particularly traumatic. Alexia was still a teenager—not yet eighteen—and was left parentless in the US. In the days and weeks following the sting, she was fearful that her mother had been forced to hand over information about Alexia's whereabouts. Worried that ICE would come after her, Alexia and her mom's boyfriend vacated the place they were living and Alexia was forced to find housing elsewhere.

In my nearly fifteen years of fieldwork and longitudinal in-depth interviews, only one 1.5-generation Brazilian—Bianca—experienced being deported. Bianca's deportation was emotional for everyone in her family, especially her twin sister, Roberta, who cried throughout our follow-up interviews. Bianca's deportation was also emotionally painful for her. She very much considered Massachusetts home, and once back in Brazil, still rooted for her beloved Patriots each week during the NFL season. When Bianca and I reconnected after her deportation, she told me it was "emotional" for her to talk with me once again, as it brought her back to a time in her life when she had so much hope for a future in the US. But now she was a world apart from her twin sister, having missed out on Roberta's wedding and the birth of Roberta's daughter. For the first few months in Brazil, Bianca admitted she was "pretty devastated."

> Knowing that I wouldn't step a foot in the US or see my sister, friends, and everything I left behind again was really difficult. I was pretty devastated the first few months. I didn't know where to begin. I felt like the US immigration system was completely unfair. They took a huge part of my identity. I was completely lost.... There were days that I would cry and just want to go anywhere else.

She wanted to come back to the United States. But like others who are deported, she faced a ten-year bar to reentry, as she had accrued "unlawful presence" in the US after turning eighteen.

The story of Bianca's deportation also demonstrates how race and class join together to shape the experience of—and life after—deportation. Unlike most stories of undocumented immigrants who get deported, Bianca's deportation was not set into motion because she was stopped by the police for a routine traffic violation—nor because she was charged with a crime and turned over to Immigration and Customs Enforcement. Rather, Bianca's story of deportation began years before she was actually deported, and demonstrates both the far-reaching impacts of a loved one's deportation (in Bianca's case, the deportation of her brother) *and* how the psychological wages of whiteness may have given her too much confidence to try to travel to Brazil after living illegally in the United States.

Three years prior to her own deportation, Bianca had actually traveled to Brazil once before. Soon after she graduated from high school, back in the mid-2000s, Bianca and her sister Roberta, feeling that they had "nothing to lose," decided to take a vacation and visit family members in Brazil. Their passports demonstrated that they had overstayed their visas and had accrued unlawful presence. Yet Roberta and Bianca benefited from the public wages of whiteness and were able to travel for a few months in Brazil and then reenter the United States without any issue. Both girls have light skin and straight hair and conform to white standards of feminine beauty.

This uneventful experience traveling internationally would likely be impossible under today's more hostile immigration enforcement. But it is remarkable that even back in the mid-2000s—years after 9/11—Bianca and Roberta were able to reenter the country without incident. And this experience gave Bianca the confidence to try traveling to Brazil and reentering the US again years later. This time, however, she went to Brazil because she wanted her own mother's help raising her son after becoming a young, single mother herself. Her mother was back in Brazil because of another deportation in the family. Bianca's younger brother, who had been racialized as Hispanic more than Bianca because of his darker skin and involvement with drugs, was deported when he turned eighteen. Bianca's mother had made the difficult decision to return to Brazil with her son, because she was worried about his ability to navigate life there since he had been so young when they had left for the US.

Thus Bianca's decision to return to Brazil for a second time before trying to reenter the US can only be understood by considering how illegality and whiteness join together. On the one hand, there were the impacts of immigration policy, and in particular the far-reaching impact of her brother's deportation on the family, all of whom were undocumented. It was his deportation that had led to Bianca's mother's "voluntary"' deportation. On the other hand, Bianca's decision to return to Brazil was also framed by the psychological wages of whiteness that she had accrued over time, including from her previous noneventful encounter with immigration enforcement officers. When Bianca left the US for a second time to see her mother, she had every intention of returning to the US in a few months and expected she would be able to. After all, she had been able to do so a few years earlier.

This time, however, in the late 2000s, Bianca did not have the same fortune. As she went through the US airport's customs, she was detained, held for questioning, and deported back to Brazil. But while deportation was very painful for Bianca, her experience in Brazil was far different from most 1.5-generation Mexican deportees who report facing stigma and blocks to education and work opportunities (Caldwell 2019; Silver 2018a). As she told me, after a few months she "put her big girl pants on" and was able to draw on her Brazilian middle-class networks to find opportunities for work and school. Her English came in handy too. Soon she found herself settling into a new middle-class lifestyle in Brazil. Within a few years, she described things as "great."

> My first job was as an English instructor . . . which paid pretty well. I got my first teaching experience there and that's when I decided I wanted to

become a teacher. I started working as a teacher assistant at a [renowned school]. I begun studying pedagogy, which is the teaching credentials you need here in Brazil and I am now finishing my second year. . . . Now, things are great. As with any change, I think we all need time to adapt. For me it took about three years to fully adapt and accept what I couldn't change. I love my job, I work with great people, and the best thing about Brazil is that you still manage to have a social life. It's a different culture, but it seemed that in the US, everyone is spending their time chasing after money, and not having enough time to enjoy life. I work Monday through Friday, I get out while the sun is still out. I am able to travel on the weekends. I have time to be with my son and partner.

In addition to earning her degree in teaching, Bianca carved out a well-balanced social life. She joined a gym, traveled on the weekends, and started dating a light-skinned Brazilian. Her partner, Jair, had grown up in Brazil but was an American citizen, as his own father was American. And Bianca's experience back in Brazil as a middle-class, light-skinned woman can only be understood through a power-without-papers lens that situates how her privilege and marginalization work together in a global racial economy. Tanya Golash-Boza (2015) argues that Brazilian deportees in the 2000s faced less stigma and fared better in comparison to deportees to other nation states because Brazil had implemented fewer neoliberal policies during this time. Indeed, this was likely true for Bianca too, given that she was deported in the late 2000s. But Bianca's experiences also suggest that her light skin, conformity to Eurocentric standards of beauty, and connections to the Brazilian middle class allowed her to live relatively comfortably back in Rio de Janeiro.

CONCLUSION

When undocumented immigrants raised in the US turn eighteen, they begin accruing "unlawful presence time." If deported, they face a three- or ten-year bar to reentry, depending on the amount of "unlawful presence time" they have accrued. Thus, turning eighteen increases the vulnerability to deportation for undocumented immigrants raised in the United States. This is particularly true in a historical moment in which the US is mass-deporting immigrants, especially Black and brown men from Latin America and the Caribbean (Golash-Boza and Hondagneu-Sotelo 2013). As sociologist Tanya

Golash-Boza (2015) argues, mass deportation is "part of the neoliberal cycle of global capitalism" and a "US policy response designed to relocate surplus labor to the periphery and to keep labor in the United States compliant" (5). But of course, not everyone who is undocumented will be deported—it would cost too much money and take too much time (Golash-Boza 2015). The goal is not to deport every immigrant. Rather, the goal is to keep a large group of racialized workers vulnerable and compliant (De Genova 2002; Golash-Boza 2015). This is the macro-level context that shapes white-passing 1.5-generation Brazilians' experiences with enforcement and their motivations to conceal illegality and perform whiteness.

Put another way, deportability is theorized as a key aspect of illegality (De Genova 2002; Golash-Boza 2015) and is one of the reasons that we might expect legal status to function as a master status. But as we see in this chapter, undocumented 1.5-generation Brazilians' experiences with deportability are circumscribed by whiteness. Often our statistics on deportation focus on national-level statistics, which are a proxy for race. Yet, given the racial diversity among immigrants from Latin America, this chapter suggests we should consider how deportation for each national-origin group might be stratified by race, and how white-passing immigrants from Latin America are relatively less vulnerable to deportation. That whiteness served as a protective mechanism from deportation is not surprising from a historical perspective. Indeed, in the 1920s, hundreds of thousands of Europeans who were living in the US illegally were allowed to remain in the US since deporting them was framed as "unjust" punishment (Ngai 2004).

Thus the master status lens is insufficient for understanding 1.5-generation white-passing Brazilians' experiences with deportability under neoliberal racial capitalism. Instead we need a power-without-paper lens to wrestle with their nuanced experiences navigating public life. On the one hand, undocumented 1.5-generation Brazilians are marginalized on the basis of illegality. They are legal "outsiders" and experience vulnerability to deportation, at least in certain situations. On the other hand, successful attempts to pass as white allow them to conceal illegality and be seen by other whites as "insiders" in American society. In other words, constructing whiteness is a form of "legal passing" (García 2019). But because their whiteness is often not a given in the US—especially when they are speaking Portuguese—1.5-generation Brazilians use physical and social cues to present themselves as white, choose to occupy white spaces, and draw boundaries between themselves and racialized others while emphasizing proximity to Europeans. While these self-constructions provide very real protections and often allow them to accrue the public and psychological wages of whiteness (Du Bois 1935; Roediger 1991), they also reify the ethno-racial hierarchy (Bashi Treitler 2013).

There are, however, limits to the power of whiteness for undocumented immigrants. Concealing illegality by constructing whiteness comes with emotional costs—and in some cases, material costs. Whiteness also does not remove the other stressors that come with illegality, including the fear of other anti-immigrant measures being implemented that would make their lives more difficult. Furthermore, passing as white does not eliminate the situational triggers that remind them of their vulnerability to deportation nor protect their loved ones from deportation.

Of course, the specific ways in which strategic efforts to pass as white and allow 1.5-generation Brazilians to avoid the deleterious impacts of illegality are bound to this particular historical conjuncture. For example, the ability to re-enter the US under today's surveillance apparatus without a valid passport—the way that Bianca, Roberta, and Sabine did—might be impossible, even for white-passing undocumented immigrants (as we saw with Bianca when she attempted it three years later). Yet it is notable that even in that time period, these young, white-passing Brazilian women slipped past enforcement officers in a way that Gabriel, who was never racialized as white, did not. Thus this chapter suggests that scholars will need to pay attention to the context-specific ways that race, class and illegality hang together to shape immigrants' public lives and experiences with deportability after age eighteen.

In the next chapter, we will see how power without papers shapes how 1.5-generation Brazilians navigate another key domain of 1.5-generation immigrants' lives: postsecondary transitions. On the one hand, we will see some support for the master status perspective as illegality does present a ceiling on socioeconomic mobility, even for those with racial and class privilege. And yet this is not the whole story as race, class, and (il)legality join together in nuanced ways to shape their prospects for socioeconomic mobility, including in the labor market.

TWO TRANSITIONS OUT OF HIGH SCHOOL

Navigating Higher Education and Work

Unlike most interviews I had done with other 1.5-generation Brazilians, which often took place inside homes, workplaces, or restaurants, Leila chose to meet in a beautiful state park in suburban Massachusetts, a place where her dog could splash in the small pond surrounded by lush green trees and where we both could take in peace and tranquility of nature in the warm, damp New England air. The drive to the state park took me through rolling hills to a town outside Boston that is predominantly white and upper-middle-class. Indeed, more than 80 percent of its population is white, while less than 5 percent identify as Latino/a/x or Hispanic and less than 3 percent as Black. Few families and households live in poverty here, the median income is well over $100,000, and the schools are consistently ranked as some of the best in Massachusetts. Leila didn't grow up there, but after breaking up with her boyfriend, she moved to this small affluent community. In truth, the community was not all that different from many others in her life, including her former educational and current professional communities.

At age twenty-nine, Leila was still undocumented, but she was far from ready to accept the typical life of an "undocumented immigrant" in menial-wage labor. The daughter of college-educated parents who worked as an accountant and a public school teacher back in Brazil, Leila had migrated at age twelve. They left during the Brazilian economic crisis in the 1980s, after her father lost his job for more than a year and her family struggled to maintain their upper-middle-class lifestyle, including her private schooling. Like most of the Brazilians I met, they came to the US on tourist visas and overstayed. While her parents experienced downward mobility in the US, working as undocumented house cleaners, they hoped Leila and her siblings would have better opportunities.

Leila worked hard in school and, against the odds, overcame the barriers to attending a four-year college. This was particularly striking for a few reasons. First, unlike some states across the country at the time, Massachusetts did not have a policy or law offering in-state tuition to undocumented immigrants. Second, she graduated from high school during a historical moment— the early 2000s—in which there were few prominent national, statewide, or local "DREAMer" networks helping undocumented youth navigate the college application process (see Gonzales 2011). Thus Leila did not have access to well-informed school mentors nor student immigrant organizations to help her figure out the college landscape as an undocumented student. Instead, she largely had to rely on her own Brazilian networks and ingenuity to navigate the college application process. But she did figure it out, attending a four-year college in the fall after she had graduated from high school. She was lucky. Coming from a Brazilian upper-middle-class background, Leila's family did not expect her to make substantial financial contributions to the household and was able to pay her tuition without the help of federal student loans or grants.

While many undocumented immigrants report that it is during high school that their undocumented status becomes more salient (Gonzales 2011; Silver 2012), for Leila it was during college. As Leila told me during our first interview, she did not feel that different from her high school peers because "everyone has a crap job in high school." She had always been confident she would go to college since her entire family was college-educated, including her older sister, who went to college in the states. But once in college, at a predominantly white institution, she felt unable to truly take advantage of the college experience. For Leila this meant doing things like going to the Bahamas over spring break with her college friends. Furthermore, she constantly worried about her work opportunities postcollege. While she had dreamed of being a journalist, she had decided against pursuing journalism as a major, uncertain of her career prospects without the right "papers" permitting her to legally work in the United States.

Roberto Gonzales (2016) heartbreakingly demonstrates how most college-educated undocumented 1.5-generation Mexican immigrants in California are forced to confront their "illegality" following their college graduations as they ultimately face the same fates as their non-college-going peers. That is, both college-goers and "early-exiters" are ultimately forced to take physically taxing and poorly paid jobs in landscaping, on assembly lines, or in back kitchens as dishwashers. But Leila's postcollege story is quite different than the stories of undocumented Mexicans that Gonzales encountered. At age twenty-nine, even before the Obama administration enacted Deferred Action for Childhood Arrivals (DACA), Leila was working as a bookkeeper.[1] By the time of our second interview, when Leila was thirty and DACAmented, she had been able to save enough money to buy her own business from another Brazilian (who was returning to Brazil). For Leila, one of her most salient identities during our second interview was not an "illegal" identity but a professional one, as a small business owner.

And yet, while Leila prided herself on being a small-business owner, her business involved doing work she and her parents never envisioned for her: Leila *cleaned houses*, just like her parents and many other undocumented Brazilians in Massachusetts. But significantly, she did not feel exploited. She worked for herself, not a hotel chain or some other company. Moreover, she had aspirations of growing her business—hiring others to clean while she works on the website, marketing, and networking. Indeed, she had recently joined a network of other young entrepreneurs in Greater Boston, entrepreneurs who were mostly white and upper-middle-class. But Leila consciously hid her legal status from these young entrepreneurs. As detailed in Chapter 1, she was able to do so by constructing whiteness in gendered ways. For Leila, concealing illegality was important to her, even after DACA. "(I) want(ed) them looking at me and seeing a girl who's thirty years old . . . who owns a business, and that's it. That's the only image that I want them to have of me." And she was able to do so because she was a light-skinned, college-educated young woman with no discernible accent. She could straighten her hair, "talk white," and use other social and physical cues to present as white.

Leila's story necessitates a power-without-papers perspective. Race, class, illegality—and gender—articulate together to shape her postsecondary experience of navigating higher education and the labor market. On the one hand, Leila has faced barriers to college (relying on her own ingenuity without the help of school counselors) and restrictions in the labor market (doing bookkeeping work was not her first choice career) due to illegality. And when I last interviewed her, she was doing "stereotypical work" associated with undocumented Latinas—house cleaning. On the other hand, Leila has been able to leverage her middle-class roots to pay for college without the help of federal aid/loans *and* conceal illegality by constructing whiteness as she navigated work. As she told me, this was a conscious decision. "It's much easier, for most things, for your day-to-day, to be white. To be perceived as white."

In this chapter, I examine the post–high school transitions for 1.5-generation Brazilians and how race, class, and (il)legality articulate together to shape these experiences. In some ways, Leila's story is exceptional among her undocumented peers. For example, most do not attend a four-year college immediately after graduating from high school. But in other ways, her story is unexceptional. That is, racial and class privilege articulate with illegality to shape how 1.5-generation Brazilians navigate postsecondary schooling transitions and the barriers they face to higher education and work. Furthermore, we will see how gaining legal status before age eighteen for white-passing immigrants brings about power with papers as they navigate postsecondary transitions. In contrast to their undocumented 1.5-generation Brazilian peers, those with lawful permanent residency and/or citizenship by age eighteen face few involuntary delays to college, can travel abroad and reconnect with family and friends in Brazil, and can pursue work options that are satisfying to them. But importantly, it is not just legalization that matters. Rather, whiteness articulates with legality to shape these experiences, including facilitating more favorable work transitions and environments.

To make sense of these postsecondary transitions, we must situate 1.5-generation Brazilians' stories in the larger global racial economy, which has undergone significant neoliberal transformations over the past few decades, transforming life in both Brazil and the US. As described in the Introduction, the families of most undocumented 1.5-generation Brazilians I met left Brazil during a time of economic crisis when their families could not sustain their lifestyles. According to Dalto (2019), Brazil's recession and financial instability were created by the financial interests of international creditors, especially in the Global North, who imposed neoliberal policy measures. Middle-class Brazilians—like Leila's parents—who were part of the large first wave of migrants in the 1980s and '90s became unemployed or underemployed during this crisis. They migrated to the US with the hopes of returning to Brazil more financially secure (Margolis 1994).

The labor market they encountered in the US, however, was also undergoing neoliberal structural changes, as the US moved from being a global power based on an economy of production to an economy based on investment (Harvey 2003). Neoliberal policies, born out of an ideology of laissez-faire capitalism, cut public welfare spending and decimated blue-collar industries, as many factories were automated or moved overseas under new free-trade agreements. Thus the US lost many jobs that had provided middle-class wages and did not require a college degree. In this transformed and bifurcated labor market, there are well-paid, good-benefit jobs that require a college degree and precarious low-wage work that does not. Undocumented immigrants from the Global South may not be desired by the nation-state and its citizens as "people like us" deserving of rights and benefits, but in this political economy there is a demand for their labor. Indeed, there are plenty of jobs in the low-wage service sector and the increasingly dangerous production plants that rely upon a vulnerable and racialized labor force (Golash-Boza 2015; Muñoz 2011).

Yet, importantly, even among jobs in this bifurcated economy that do not require a college degree there is a racialized, classed, and gendered hierarchy (Jayaraman 2011; Muñoz 2011; Wilson 2020). For example, in the food and restaurant industry, white men are given the highest-paid and least stigmatized jobs in the "front of the house" at fine-dining restaurants while Black and brown workers are concentrated in the "back of the house" in poorly paid roles as dishwashers and line cooks, especially in fast-service restaurants (Jayaraman 2011; Restaurant Opportunities Center United 2015; Wilson 2020). As we will see, most 1.5-generation Brazilians, even those who were undocumented and did not have a college degree, were advantageously hired in "front of house positions," often in fine-dining establishments, or quickly promoted within the restaurant industry.

In the next sections, I examine 1.5-generation Brazilians' experiences in accessing higher education, before turning more specific attention to their experiences in the labor market. In truth, there was no orderly movement from higher education to the labor market for most undocumented 1.5-generation Brazilians. Instead the majority pieced together work and higher education at the same time, and/or cycled through higher education and work over many years, largely a function of their (il)legality. Thus, like other scholars, I find that legal status is an important form of stratification impacting opportunities to access higher education (Abrego 2006; Gonzales 2011; 2016; Greenman and Hall 2013; Silver 2012). Those without permanent lawful status at the time they graduated from high school were more likely to face *involuntary* delays or interruptions to their college dreams. This exclusion was very painful for them, even years later.

Like Leila, however, their transitions to adulthood were also shaped by other interlocking structures of power. For some, their families' middle-class roots provided safety nets as they navigated postsecondary schooling options. Indeed, some families, like Leila's, could afford to help pay tuition without the aid of federal or state grants and loans, underscoring the financial assets their families had built over time. Gender and race also shaped the kinds of work 1.5-generation Brazilians found in the racialized and gendered labor market. Indeed, most drew on Brazilian and/or white American networks to find work, which led to relatively "better" jobs in the labor market than we might anticipate given illegality. This work was gendered, with undocumented women often working as administrative assistants or hostesses and undocumented men working as electricians, drivers (if they had a work permit), and bartenders. Yet, despite some racial and class privilege, illegality cut off occupational opportunities and led to workplace exploitation. Furthermore, labor market options became more limited over time as the US implemented increasingly hostile anti-immigrant policies.

STRATIFIED EDUCATIONAL TRANSITIONS AFTER HIGH SCHOOL: THE SALIENCE OF (IL)LEGALITY

Navigating Legal and Financial Barriers

With the aforementioned neoliberal economic changes, postsecondary education has become increasingly necessary for good jobs in the US labor market. But the reality is that getting to—and staying in—college remains much more challenging for economically and racially marginalized youth (Ray 2017). The United States has the most unequal education system in the

Global North (Smedley et al. 2001), with low-income youth of color disproportionately attending racially segregated, overpoliced, and poorly resourced public high schools, problems that have been exacerbated by neoliberal budget cuts to education and overinvestments in policing (Paulle 2013; Ray 2017). Far from public education being "the great equalizer," the education system serves as a school-to-prison pipeline and contributes to low-income youth of color's lower odds of graduating from high school and going to college (Francis and Darity 2021; Orfield et al. 2004; Wald and Losen 2003). For economically and racially marginalized youth who do go to college, they often struggle to balance classes and work, as the part-time jobs available to them in the neoliberal economy have unpredictable hours that interfere with their ability to attend class and do homework (Ray 2017).

Meanwhile, undocumented youth face barriers to going and staying in college that their peers who are citizens and lawful permanent residents do not (Abrego 2006; Gonzales 2010; 2011; Patler 2018). The Supreme Court's *Plyler v. Doe* decision in 1982 granted unauthorized immigrants access to K–12 education in public schools. The ruling, however, did not extend to postsecondary education. While no federal law prohibits access to college, no federal law *guarantees* access to higher education either. Instead, each state sets its own tuition and enrollment policies for its public schools. While Texas, California, and other states passed in-state-tuition laws for undocumented immigrants in the early 2000s, Massachusetts denied access to in-state tuition for undocumented youth until August 2023, making the cost of state schools, including community colleges, nearly three times more expensive. In 2007, during the first full year that I was conducting my fieldwork, the Massachusetts Board of Higher Education allowed immigrant students with work permits—that is, those in liminal legality—to access in-state tuition. But my own fieldwork suggests that this policy was not well publicized and that many in the Brazilian community did not know about it. Moreover, the 2007 policy was implemented *after* many of my respondents had graduated from high school.

Undocumented and liminally legal youth across the United States are also ineligible for federal grants and loans. Thus they must pay the full cost of tuition—whatever the institution decides to charge—out of pocket unless they can secure private scholarships.[2] The enormous cost of higher education means that many undocumented and liminally legal 1.5-generation Brazilians simply could not afford to go to a four-year college immediately after high school. Indeed, of the 32 respondents who were still undocumented or in liminal legality by the time they graduated high school, only Leila and three others transitioned *immediately* to a four-year college and never experienced interruptions to their postsecondary educational dreams. How were they able to do this?

Both Ricardo and Rodrigo attended Boston's elite entrance exam high schools (two different schools) and were able to secure *private* scholarships for college—Ricardo to an elite liberal arts school and Rodrigo to a state school. In both cases, they had supportive high school mentors who helped them navigate the uncertain legal and financial landscape. Meanwhile, as previously described, both Leila and Elisabete, who attended the same public suburban high school years apart from one another, downgraded their college dreams to attend state schools rather than more elite and financially costly private institutions. In both cases, their families' Brazilian middle-class roots provided a financial safety net that helped them to afford a college education without taking out loans or securing private scholarship money.

These 4 respondents were the exceptions, however. The other 28 respondents who were still undocumented when they graduated from high school—even those who had been tracked high in school and/or attended one of Boston's elite entrance exam schools—found themselves unable to overcome the barriers to college and to transition, without interruptions, to a four-year college experience. In other words, in the face of legal and financial hurdles to college due to illegality, *most* undocumented and liminally legal Brazilians significantly downgraded their schooling choices, often begrudgingly settling for community colleges and extension programs.

Marta, who had migrated at age eleven and was in liminal legality when we first met, wanted to go to a four-year college. Instead, though, she took a semester off before enrolling at a local community college. She lamented that her past two years at the community college have been unlike her peers' experiences at the University of Massachusetts Boston, a four-year college.

> I really wanted to go to UMass Boston. Because it's closer and the environment—the campus is beautiful. I feel like I'm in high school still [at the community college].... [As] the student, you just go to class. And leave. You don't really interact with people. And I have friends at UMass Boston too. And they say it's a great school.... They have way more friends than I'm having at [my community college].

Marta's story of going to community college, and wishing she could go somewhere else, was common among undocumented 1.5-generation Brazilians. Yet, while attending community college was the last resort for many of them, their ability to pay out-of-state tuition rates for community college still underscores having some financial privilege relative to their undocumented peers.

Sometimes, undocumented 1.5-generation Brazilians did not realize the extent of financial barriers they would face to attending a four-year school until they were already enrolled. For example, Andréa had originally enrolled in a Boston-area private liberal arts school. She went to orientation, met her roommate, and then sought help from the college's financial aid office. One person on staff, however, threatened to call "Immigration," saying it was the only way to help Andréa. Frustrated, embarrassed, and scared, she ran out of the office crying and enrolled in a community college later that day. Yet, despite how harrowing this experience was for Andréa, the ability to attend a community college was only made possible because of her family's ability to help her pay the nearly $10,000 out-of-pocket, out-of-state tuition and fees she was charged for one year there.

Underscoring their families' relative financial security, some 1.5-generation Brazilians, like Álvaro, did not perceive the thousands of dollars they were forced to pay for community college as expensive.

> I'm going as an out-of-state [to the community college]. So I'm paying three times as much.... Which is not bad. I mean, it's cheap. So, you know, it's—I think with the three times [for the] out-of-state [tuition], it comes out to as much as a regular UMass tuition. So it's not bad.

For many undocumented families, this would be an inordinate amount of money to pay. But for Álvaro, it wasn't just doable, it was perceived as "cheap." Álvaro's family owned property in Brazil that they rented, providing passive income for his family. Thus, even as stigmatized undocumented workers in the US (his parents' owned their own house-cleaning business), their Brazilian middle-class roots provided some financial stability.

At the same time, going to community college was something Álvaro had to make peace with. He had graduated from Boston's top public school, whose degree is "supposed to be worth, like, gold." For a while, he thought he was "too good for community college," especially given the fact that his friends from his elite public high school looked down on it. But he had learned "to be humble" and told himself "if you want to succeed, it doesn't matter where you go."

Rather than enrolling in community college as a last resort, some undocumented 1.5-generation Brazilians chose to keep their four-year college dreams alive by delaying any postsecondary educational decisions while they worked to save money and gathered information on their options, information their high school mentors lacked. For Kátia, the strategy worked—she got in touch with an undocumented Brazilian friend who had managed to enroll at a four-year public university and helped Kátia navigate the process. A year after her high school graduation, Kátia enrolled at a public four-year university. Importantly, however, this strategy was only possible due to her family's middle-class roots. While Kátia had saved money during her year of working, her family still helped her pay the tuition and other expenses out of pocket since she was ineligible for public grants and loans.

The Information Vacuum
As Kátia's story underscores, undocumented 1.5-generation students faced more than financial barriers to college. They also faced an information vacuum on how to navigate this hostile terrain, a vacuum that was particularly acute in Massachusetts in the early 2000s when many of my respondents were graduating from high school. In-state tuition legislation in California, Texas, and nine other states in the 2000s not only removed financial barriers to college; the laws also provided a legitimizing identity (that is, students could call themselves AB 540 students in California) and the movement that led to the legislation created a network of well-informed undocumented students and their allies (Abrego 2008; Nicholls 2013). In 2006, when I began my research in the Greater Boston area, however, no similar legislation had been passed and the state's undocumented youth network was not as well developed.[3] For example, the Student Immigrant Movement (SIM), based out of Boston, was in its early stages and was not well-known.[4] Indeed, most respondents I interviewed in 2006 and 2007 had never heard of SIM. Nor did they know about the Board of Higher Education's policy allowing those with work permits to attend college. Furthermore, because they came of age before 2010, the national DREAMer movement was not yet well publicized and social media was in its infancy (Nicholls 2013).

Mentors are extremely important in helping undocumented college students overcome barriers to higher education (Enriquez 2011; Gonzales 2010; 2012; Sánchez et al. 2022). But with a few notable exceptions (Rodrigo and Ricardo), most undocumented Brazilians I met did not have access to well-informed and/or culturally sensitive school mentors. This information vacuum had chilling effects on their higher education dreams. On the one hand, school gatekeepers—teachers, guidance counselors, and mentors—are important sources of information for navigating the college application process. But undocumented 1.5-generation Brazilians reported having very few (or no) school officials "signaling" to them that they might be potential allies, sympathetic to the immigration issues they faced. Instead, many Brazilians who were still undocumented and liminally legal during high school reported that stigma and fear prevented them from disclosing their status to school mentors, including guidance counselors and teachers.

For example, Bianca told me she did not tell her guidance counselor about her status because she did not want the counselor to "judge her." Meanwhile, Ana Maria was more fearful about who else might get access to the stigmatizing information once she disclosed her status: "Who know(s) who (the guidance counselor" might tell?" Without information, neither Bianca nor Ana Maria knew how to overcome the hurdles to attend college in the US after high school. Both started working, forgoing their college dreams.

These stories of unhelpful mentors stand in stark contrast to the experiences of 1.5-generation Brazilians who had been able to adjust their immigration status to lawful permanent resident (and in some cases, had become citizens) by the time they were juniors in high school. Indeed, in their cases, we see how power with papers shapes their experiences. For example, both Camila and Amara had been undocumented as children, but had lawful permanent residency by the time they needed to apply for college. Both young women were white-passing, had been tracked high in school, and had developed strong relationships with teachers and other mentors who helped them through the college application process. With the help of these mentors, both young women enrolled in a four-year college immediately after high school. As Amara said, all "(My AP teachers) all offered me help. You know, like proofreading my essays and stuff like that." Meanwhile, Camila, who got her green card when she was in ninth grade, had mentors who set her up on a college pathway soon after she started high school, nominating her for prestigious summer programs and encouraging her to enroll in Advance Placement (AP) courses. Neither Amara nor Kamila discussed the ways in which light-skin privilege may have shaped the responses they got from their teachers. But in a comprehensive review of colorism's effects in education, Crutchfield et al. (2022) find the persistent privileging of lighter skin and more Eurocentric features in academic outcomes. Racialized tracking within schools is part of that persistent privileging, and it leads to racial segregation and disparate outcomes (Francis and Darity 2021). Thus we cannot ignore that their experiences in school likely were shaped by the joining together of their adjustments in legal status and racial privilege.

(In)voluntary Delays and Interruptions to Higher Education
The importance of legal status as a source of stratification was also underscored when talking to respondents about *why* they experienced delays and/or interruptions in accessing higher education. As the stories of Andréa, Álvaro, Kátia, Bianca, and Ana Maria highlighted, most undocumented 1.5-generation Brazilians described their reasons for delaying or forgoing their educational dreams as *involuntary* decisions. In stark contrast, green card holders and citizens often perceived their choices as *voluntary* decisions to not go—or to delay going—to college. For example, João, who was eighteen and a lawful permanent resident when we first met, told me he had never really wanted to go to college and instead was excited to be working as a car salesman. Meanwhile, other 1.5-generation Brazilians who were lawful permanent residents or citizens took advantage of their ability to travel to Brazil (and *legally* reenter the US) after graduating from high school. For example, Fausto went to Brazil for a year in order to get more "in touch" with his Brazilian identity. After taking this gap year, he came back to the US, enrolled in a four-year college, and was getting his MBA at the time I met him. Meanwhile, Karla went back to Brazil with her younger siblings and enrolled in classes to buff up her Portuguese skills. She eventually returned to the US, put herself in photography classes, and had a thriving photography business the last time we spoke.

Not one of the Brazilians who had lawful permanent residency or citizenship when they graduated from high school recalled their post–high school educational decisions with pain. In contrast, for those who had been undocumented or in liminal legality when they graduated from high school, the pain of not being able to go to a four-year college immediately after graduation was still palpable many years later. Some women cried during interviews remembering their blocked paths to mobility, even as they described being content in their current lives. For example, during our second interview in 2013, Fabiana (who was in liminal legality when I first met her) was a US citizen, happily married with two children, and enjoying her job as a lead administrator for a company in downtown Boston. The job provided good benefits and placed her in a supervisory role. But when we started talking about DACA, which had recently been implemented, she started crying as she described DACA's impacts on her younger sister. When I asked her why she was so emotional talking about DACA and her sister, she told me, between tears.

> I wish I had [DACA] ten years ago. . . . It all brings back, because [not having legal status] was one of the reasons why I didn't go to college. Because of my status. And I'm happy for [my sister and her friends]. Yeah [crying harder now]. Over-the-moon happy for her.

Despite being happy for her sister, Fabiana still lamented that those opportunities had not been available to her, as contented as she was when we spoke.

Roberta also cried when thinking about her struggles accessing higher education and the ways in which her career ambitions to be a doctor had been derailed. When I first met Roberta, she was two years removed from high school, working at a local grocery store, and still considering how—and where—she might go to college. Eventually she got into a four-year state school but decided to attend a community college instead, drawn to its nursing program. Once DACA was announced, she was finally able to work as a nurse, underscoring the importance of obtaining a work permit to find more meaningful work. But Roberta was twenty-five when DACA was implemented. And it was impossible for her to not wonder what could have been had DACA been available to her at age eighteen. She choked back tears as talked about the involuntary educational delays she experienced and the career shifts she had made.

> I think things would have been easier. I think that I would have probably gone to college right out of high school and done my four-year degree, you know? [Sniffling] . . . So, because I think, it. Even like right now, I think that [sniffling] I was held back [voice quivering] because of the [legal status] situation. I think academically speaking, I . . . Because I've always wanted—I probably would have gone to medical school. Because that's

what I wanted to do. But I feel like, it's too late now [voice quivering]. Like, I can't—I'm not going to go to, you know? I want to get my bachelor's in nursing [sniffling]. But I think if I had gone to . . . school right out of high school, I would have been like, so much further along now, you know?

At the time of this interview, Roberta was twenty-five and married to another undocumented immigrant. She felt like it was too late in her life to pursue medicine.

Thus legal status is an important form of stratification for 1.5-generation Brazilians, not only affecting *opportunities* for higher education, but *the specific pain* they experience with blocks to higher education and upward mobility. In Massachusetts during the 1990s and early 2000s, the legal, financial, and institutional hurdles were particularly great. Yet many undocumented and liminally legal youth did access some form of higher education—a testament to their resilience *and* their relative privilege.

For many undocumented 1.5-generation Brazilians, accessing higher education took much longer than they had hoped, even with relative privilege. For example, while Andréa's familial safety net had been able to help her pay the $10,000 for one year of community college classes, she was unable to complete her bachelor's degree until she was in her late twenties and had her green card, making her eligible for financial aid and underscoring how adjustments in status *do* matter. At the same time, unlike many of her undocumented peers around the country (Gonzales 2016), Andréa had largely avoided lengthy stints in jobs that required long hours doing menial wage labor during her twenties and early thirties. This was true for many of her undocumented 1.5-generation peers.

POWER WITHOUT PAPERS AND LABOR MARKET EXPERIENCES

With neoliberal economic changes in the US economy, the road to adulthood has gotten harder and more complicated for all Americans (Furstenberg 2010; Osgood et al. 2007). Without a college degree, young adults, regardless of legal status, are more vulnerable to mobility stagnation and downward trajectories (Terriquez 2014). Importantly, however, most American young adults without a college degree can *legally* work in the United States. Undocumented youth who lack work permits—even those who have college degrees—are largely relegated to low-wage, physically exhausting, dead-end jobs (Gonzales 2016).

However, few of the respondents I met were in physically exhausting, dead-end jobs following their (temporary or permanent) exits from formal schooling. To be sure, they had not altogether avoided these jobs, as some had briefly joined their parents working in house-cleaning and janitorial jobs (like Elisabete) or found work in grocery stores or fast-service restaurants (like Roberta) after graduating high school. But rarely did they work in these jobs for long. Sometimes shifts toward partial or full legal inclusion, which provided a work permit, provided a pathway out of these low-wage, low-status jobs. But often, undocumented 1.5-generation Brazilians, even those without permits, were able to successfully draw on their Brazilian or white American networks to find more meaningful work than we might otherwise anticipate. For example, Leila, whom we met in the introduction of this chapter, worked as a bookkeeper (before buying her own house-cleaning business from another Brazilian), Gabriela found work as an administrative assistant at a small insurance company (for a white American owner), and Bianca worked at a technology store, quickly becoming promoted to manager. While these women had varied levels of education, none of them had work permits when they found these jobs.[5] Yet, as we will soon see, their stories were not exceptional among the 1.5-generation Brazilians I met.

How can we make sense of these labor market experiences? Well, first it's important to understand that despite not having a work permit, it is possible to work as an undocumented immigrant. Some undocumented immigrants find work "under the table" or off the official record books (and are usually paid in cash), some provide fake identity documents to employers, and some use an Individual Tax Identification Number (ITIN).[6] But as we will see, their postschooling work experiences are also shaped by the articulation of (il)legality, and race and class. That is, despite ceilings on mobility due to illegality, their relative class and racial privilege provides financial safety nets to explore more meaningful passions/work *and* positions them—and many in their social networks—advantageously in the Greater Boston labor market relative to other immigrant and minoritized groups.

Indeed, previous research finds that Brazilians in Greater Boston outearned all other immigrant groups from Latin America (Boston Planning & Development Agency Research Division 2017). Meanwhile, data from 2010 show that Brazilians had the highest rate of households earning a middle-class standard of living—and the lowest poverty rates—of any immigrant group from Latin America (Boston Planning & Development Agency Research Division 2017). These findings are particularly striking when we consider that 70 percent of Brazilians were undocumented in 2007, while only 8 percent of Dominicans were (Marcelli, Holmes, Estella, et al. 2008; Marcelli, Holmes, Troncoso, et al. 2008). Their relative privilege, despite illegality, in the Boston labor market is connected to their pre-migration characteristics—coming from relatively higher social classes and having a history of self-employment in Brazil (Boston Planning & Development Agency Research Division 2017; Mineo 2007). But it is also a function of the racial economy in the US that privileges those who are lighter-skinned, especially if they can pass as white.

The picture, however, is not all rosy. Over the past few decades, undocumented immigrants, including 1.5-generation Brazilians, have faced an increasingly hostile labor market as E-Verify and other tools of the state become more widely implemented. Furthermore, illegality does make 1.5-generation Brazilians vulnerable to workplace exploitation, even in "good jobs" and from owners/managers with whom they had long-term working relationships. Thus, power without papers is a nuanced story of how race, class, and illegality articulate together as 1.5-generation Brazilians come of age and navigate the labor market, trying to not give up on higher education dreams and career ambitions altogether. To be sure, gaining a work permit through DACA or other legal dispensations is significant, but it is not the *only* important structural aspect of their lives shaping their experiences.

Financial Safety Nets: Avoiding Menial Wage
Labor and Pursuing Passions
Despite their parents' undocumented status in the US, 1.5-generation Brazilians' families' middle-class roots afforded some respondents a financial safety net that allowed them to live at home, rent-free, while pursuing more creative pathways. For example, Marcus, whose Brazilian middle-class family had migrated to the United States from the state of Rio de Janeiro when he was ten years old and had settled in a nearly all-white community just north of Boston, did not face long hours working in menial wage labor in the years after he graduated from high school. Like other undocumented immigrants, he faced legal and financial barriers to a four-year college. After briefly

enrolling in some community college courses (and quickly deciding he "was just wasting money") he started taking other courses to nurture his creative passions: a ten-week writing course through a local nonprofit, broadcasting courses at an out-of-state institution, and screenwriting courses at one of Boston's universities.

At age twenty-four, when I met him for the second time, Marcus was still living at home rent-free and was reluctant to take on work that would require long hours. This way he could focus on his passion—writing. "I do want a job, but I don't know. I just—I'm just really scared that that will be—that that will mean sacrificing my writing."

Marcus *did* work, but he was not working long, grueling hours around the clock, which he acknowledged *he could* be doing in order to make more money. But at the time, Marcus had a safety net in his parents. He was living at home and was not required to make significant financial contributions. Thus he had more time to work on his creative passions. He wrote film scripts and music and eventually published his first book. He played music at local venues and directed a play, one that starred some of his white American friends. To be sure, Marcus provided important financial, emotional, and logistical support to his family, especially during family crises, including when his father suffered a serious injury and his family needed funds to pay for unanticipated legal fees. But until that specific crisis, he was not relied upon for steady, significant monthly financial contributions to the household.

Importantly, Marcus's family had been able to start the process for an adjustment of status when he was under age eighteen, providing Marcus with key documents for much of his young adulthood: a work permit, Social Security number, and driver's license. And these documents certainly expanded his labor market options. Indeed, while he worked on his creative passions during the day, he worked as a delivery driver at night. He enjoyed this job, as it gave him some solo time in the car to listen to his favorite political and writing podcasts while he earned money. However, the precariousness of his liminal legality was exacerbated when his father's adjustment in status (on which Marcus was listed as a dependent) was denied when Marcus was in his early twenties. Thus Marcus lost his work eligibility and became more vulnerable to deportation. Fortunately for Marcus, however, DACA had already been implemented when this crisis happened. His increased legal insecurity was only temporary.

Marcus certainly experienced obstacles to his dream career (in Hollywood) due to illegality. But his relative privilege (especially as compared to other undocumented immigrants), including his family's financial resources, his work permit, and his driver's license, made a real difference in being able to avoid long, grueling hours in menial-wage labor so that he could pursue his artistic passions. But what about Marcus's peers who did not have work permits? How did they fare? They fared better than we might anticipate, drawing on networks in both co-ethnic niches and outside them.

Co-Ethnic Niches: Finding Work in Brazilian For-Profit and Nonprofit Organizations

Esther Cho (2017) argues that while illegality is an important source of stratification in the labor market, *ethno-racial background* mediates the work experiences of undocumented 1.5-generation Mexicans and Koreans in California, with Koreans being able to find work in a greater diversity of occupations given the extensive web of Korean businesses in the area. Importantly, she argues that the ability for Koreans to find these jobs was a function of the location of Korean co-ethnic niches—which she defines as being both for-profit and nonprofit businesses—in the broader occupational hierarchy. This begs the question: What was the nature of Brazilian co-ethnic niches in the Greater Boston area? And how might they impact the work experiences of undocumented 1.5-generation Brazilians?

Studies over the past fifteen years consistently find that Brazilians in Massachusetts have a very high self-employment rate. In 2017, more than 24 percent of Brazilians in Massachusetts were self-employed. In contrast, only 4 percent of Hispanic workers and 9 percent of all Massachusetts workers were (Boston Planning & Development Agency Research Division 2017). In fact, there are more Brazilian-owned businesses in Massachusetts than anywhere in the country (Lima and Siqueira 2007). According to Álvaro Lima of the Boston Redevelopment Authority, the high rate of self-employment is due to a combination of factors, including Brazilians' high educational levels, higher social class, and a "culture of self-employment in their home cities" (Mineo 2007). In the Boston area, Brazilians opened up businesses in restaurants, grocery, travel, insurance, and other sectors. There are also a number of Brazilian nonprofit organizations, many of which are closely connected to organizations serving the region's Portuguese-speaking immigrant communities (including Portuguese and Cape Verdean communities).

Like Cho (2017), I find that these for-profit and nonprofit ethnic organizations are important for undocumented 1.5-generation Brazilians, as they provide a range of jobs. For example, Jéssica, a light-skinned Brazilian who was twenty-three when we first met, was working for a Brazilian for-profit company. Jéssica had been a good student in high school and had dreamed of becoming an obstetrician. But like so many of her undocumented peers, she had been unable overcome the legal and financial barriers to college due to illegality. During high school, Jéssica had worked alongside her Brazilian immigrant friends in low-wage jobs for corporate retailers and supermarkets. But after high school, she drew on her parents' American and Brazilian networks and found a number of jobs: as a dental assistant, in sales for a small American-owned apparel company, and finally, as an administrative assistant with a Brazilian-owned moving company. This is the place that Jéssica was still working when we met. Jéssica told me she not only liked working with other Brazilians; she also had gotten more in touch with her Brazilian identity and valued the work she was doing.

Meanwhile, Mayra, who was twenty-five when we first met, was working for one of the Brazilian nonprofit organizations in the Greater Boston area. Like Jéssica, she had gotten the job through family connections. Mayra also really enjoyed her work there and found it "rewarding." Specifically, Mayra appreciated that her work with this Brazilian nonprofit had increased her knowledge of political issues and reconnected her with the Brazilian community.

> It [is]a rewarding job—because I [am] helping my community. My people. You know, Brazilians, I consider them to be my people. . . . I have been in their feet . . . shoes . . . well, [we] say feet in Brazil. . . . I work with wonderful people. [I] can connect with them. . . . They are very strong. They send me strength. Now, I'm a little bit stronger.

Thus, both Jéssica and Mayra were working in jobs they enjoyed, that provided steady paychecks, and which allowed them to connect with their Brazilian identities in meaningful ways. To be sure, they were not doing their dream jobs. Illegality had derailed their educational dreams—neither had earned a bachelor's degree—and career aspirations. And indeed, as we will see, illegality also shaped their work journeys, filling them with countless curves and detours along the way.

Finding Work Outside Co-Ethnic Niches

A closer look at Mayra's winding journey from high school to the time I interviewed her at age twenty-five helps to reveal how power without papers operates as 1.5-generation Brazilians find work outside co-ethnic niches in a racialized, classed, and gendered labor market. When Mayra graduated from high school, she not only had to navigate the labor market without a college degree or work permit; she also had to navigate finding work as a single mother. Mayra had gotten pregnant at age fourteen. And soon after her daughter was born, her much older, twenty-four-year-old Brazilian boyfriend became "somewhat abusive." But her high school—a top-rated high school in the area—linked her up with a tutor and counselor. Meanwhile, her family, especially her "wonderful" mother, provided crucial economic, emotional, and logistical support that allowed her to leave the abusive relationship and to graduate from high school on time.

Yet, as a single mother without a college degree or work permit, Mayra's options in the labor market were extremely limited. She was the primary caretaker of her child, limiting the hours she could work. Thus, after she graduated from high school, she bounced around various part-time jobs for a few years. Indeed, it was not until her daughter entered public school that Mayra found steadier work. Mayra's dad was particularly helpful in helping her find work at this time, getting her a job as a hostess at the chain restaurant where he worked, right in the middle of one of the most desirable neighborhoods in Boston. At the time, Mayra did not have a work permit (or Social Security number for work purposes) when she started hostessing. Thus his networking was crucial for her.

Mayra discovered that she really enjoyed working at the restaurant. "I just liked the people and I liked the atmosphere. And I liked the fact that I had a job and I had independence. I can take care of myself and my daughter. I don't necessarily have to rely on my parents all the time." For Mayra, this was not just "a job" for money; it was a job that gave her a sense of independence and social connection. Over the next two years, she received several promotions, including to supervisory roles. Those positions were particularly rewarding for her, spurring her desire to enroll in business classes at a local community college.

As previously mentioned, the restaurant industry is a highly racialized, gendered, and classed industry, with higher-paying managerial, server, and bartender positions (the latter two of which are "front of the house" jobs) in full-service, formal restaurants dominated by white men (and to a lesser extent, white women), and poverty-level positions as line cooks, bussers and dishwashers in casual and quick-service restaurants dominated by Black and brown men and women (Jayaraman 2011; Restaurant Opportunities Center United 2015; Wilson 2020). Mayra, an undocumented light-skinned Brazilian of Southern European descent who did not have a college degree, not only entered the industry as a hostess (and thus in the "front of the house") at a full-service restaurant, but was also quickly promoted to supervisory positions. Thus, despite being undocumented, she had avoided the poorly paid and stigmatized work in the "back of the house."

Mayra's progress in the restaurant industry, however, was stymied by an increasingly hostile anti-immigration context during the late 2000s. In truth, the foundation for increasingly hostile workplace enforcement had been implemented decades earlier with the passage of the Immigration and Control Act in 1986. But in the wake of 9/11, the US government ramped up its commitment to "internal enforcement" mechanisms, including (but not limited to) workplace enforcement. In 2005, the work-site enforcement system—which came to be known as E-Verify—became entirely internet-based, with employers able to check I-9 forms (which verifies workers' eligibility to legally work in the US) against federal databases (such as Social Security Administration records).[7] In 2008, then-president George W. Bush signed an executive order requiring all federal contractors and subcontractors to use E-Verify.[8] While the program largely remained voluntary for businesses in Massachusetts, the number of businesses opting to use E-Verify consistently increased between 2006 and 2012.[9]

Still, by 2013, only 8 percent of all US employers used E-Verify (Zamora 2013). Mayra's restaurant, however, was one of them. Fearful of what might happen, Mayra decided to "voluntarily leave" before her employer asked her to fill out the I-9 form. She was sad to leave, but told me that her personality was such that she always remained optimistic and was certain that "something else better will come along." Her optimism was rewarded. Within a couple of months, her older sister successfully helped her network for the aforementioned job with the Brazilian nonprofit organization.

Mayra's ability to find meaningful work, despite illegality, at this chain restaurant and later with a Brazilian organization was not an outlier. Indeed, several 1.5-generation Brazilian women reported that they also worked as hostesses in fine-dining restaurants. For example, Ana Maria and Andréa, both of whom were white-passing, had worked as hostesses at fine-dining restaurants in some of Boston's trendiest areas. In Ana Maria's case, she was promoted to a managerial position.

I first met Ana Maria in 2007 when she was working in this capacity—as a manager—at a high-end restaurant in one of Greater Boston's upscale neighborhoods. As previously mentioned, she had started out as a hostess, getting the job through her aunt's connections to the American owners.

> So [my aunt and the owners have] known each other for a long, long, long, long time. And then they needed a hostess at the old restaurant. That's how I kind of got in. And then, eventually, one of our managers quit. And I've always been good at taking care of computers too, so that's how I got offered the [manager] position.

Ana Maria notes that her skills with computers led to her employer offering her a manager position. But importantly, employers are not race- or gender-neutral—and their hiring and promotion decisions reflect and maintain racialized and gendered system of privileges and disadvantages in the labor market (Branch 2011). Indeed, Ana Maria was one of several white-passing undocumented respondents I met who had been elevated to the position of "manager" at their place of employment.

Furthermore, even the entry-level positions that 1.5-generation Brazilians received must be understood within this macro context. For example, 1.5-generation Brazilian women I met were hired as hostesses, not as bussers or dishwashers. And while hostessing does not pay as much as male-dominated jobs like serving and bartending, hostessing is a customer-interfacing job, thereby allowing 1.5-generation women to not work in stigmatized "back of the house" jobs. For example, Andréa, who also worked as a hostess when she was undocumented, told me that being a busser or dishwasher was much less desirable than hostessing, as being a busser or dishwasher left workers with burns on their arms and spills on their clothes.

Meanwhile, Rodrigo, who was undocumented and white-passing, found work in a more male-dominated job in the industry—bartending—at a popular tourist spot in downtown Boston. This was not his ideal job, as he had earned his bachelor's degree from a state college and had hoped to work in corporate America. But he did enjoy bartending and was good at it, especially given how charismatic and outgoing he was. As much as he liked the job, however, he was frustrated that he could not pursue better opportunities that would allow him to take advantage of his bachelor's degree in business. Especially when his customers offered to help.

> I've met people at work, in the business world, and they like my personality. And they're like "Well, what do you do?" And I said, "I do this." You know? And they're like, "You have a business management degree. Why don't you want to get into business?" A couple of times I've been offered positions, small positions, or whatever. I just tell them, "I don't have [a work permit]." And they're like "Oh yeah, well, that's definitely a problem." I can't join any corporation or anything. And they're like "Okay, well," and like, they'll give me their cards and they'll be like this and that.... There's another situation—my mother works for a lady whose husband is into—big software company. And they really like my parents. So through my parents, they said, "How old is your son?" This and that. "He graduated, that's great. Tell him to give me a call, I'll give him a job." So they didn't even meet me yet and they were willing to give me a job because of my parents. So I spoke to him and he said, "The moment you get your papers, call me. You're in." Just like that. So I have that lined up if I get my papers. I'll definitely try it out. Software is not really my thing. But then again, *business* is a very vague word. So I could go there, and he's like "All you have to do is talk to people all day." And I'm like "Perfect!" Because that's what I do at bartending. All I do is talk to people.

Even with his college degree and affable personality, Rodrigo's legal status presented a ceiling on his mobility. Importantly, however, being male and passing as white shaped Rodrigo's current work as a bartender in the "front of the house."

Whiteness helped other undocumented 1.5-generation Brazilians gain access to other industries too. For example, Marcelo, a light-skinned Brazilian of Southern European descent, was someone scholars may have predicted would experience downward mobility (Portes and Rumbaut 2001; Zhou 1997).

He was not only undocumented for most of his life in the US, but was also a high school dropout. When I asked him why he dropped out, he explained that he always knew that going to college would be difficult for him because of his undocumented status. During our interview, he repeated a myth that other 1.5-generation Brazilians had told me: "If you're not legal, you don't get your diploma (from college)." This belief, combined with the fact that many of his male friends in his "new" school community (he moved in eighth grade) had also dropped out of high school, led Marcelo to make the same decision.

While there were external pressures that shaped Marcelo's decision to leave school (pressures connected to illegality and his gendered peer networks), the necessity for him to contribute financially to the household was *not* one of them. Indeed, he was able to live rent-free in his family's home. Thus his story of dropping out stands in contrast to undocumented Mexican immigrants in California who are forced to leave academic trajectories earlier than they desire in order to financially contribute to their households (Gonzales 2016).

Furthermore, Marcelo was also able to draw upon his family's connections in a racialized, gendered labor market to find meaningful work. Marcelo's white-passing Brazilian uncle was a contractor and had developed connections to blue-collar trade workers, including Irish electricians in the area. Marcelo used these connections to find additional training and eventually went to work for a white American.

> And then, after that, I went to another American guy. Out of Berthaville. He's my father's cousin's neighbor. So, the guy needed a person. . . . So my father's cousin called me, and invited me to go there. And the guy did, like, a quick interview with me. So that's—I started working with him. And I worked with him for three and a half years.

Higher-paid blue-collar trades have long been dominated by white men due to nepotism and racism toward nonwhites (Alexander, Entwisle, and Olson 2014). But as a light-skinned Brazilian who told me that everyone perceived him as white, Marcelo (and his white-passing family members) did not face this racism. Indeed, his family's networks included white electricians, facilitating an apprentice-like opportunity for Marcelo, even when did not have a Social Security number or work permit.

While Marcelo did not explicitly name how whiteness mattered for him as he navigated the labor market, there were some 1.5-generation Brazilians who were very conscious of how whiteness mattered. For those who experienced shifts toward legal inclusion, whiteness articulated with legal status to improve their labor market experiences, demonstrating once again how power with papers operates. For example, Amara, who was able to adjust her status before high school, was working at a bank when I met her and was conscious that she was treated more favorably by clients than her darker-skinned coworkers. "I think, I think I've had it easier, so to speak, my being fair-skinned, and not having an accent, you know?" Amara, who migrated at age six, had blond hair, light skin, and spoke without an accent. And her work story underscores how whiteness not only helps 1.5-generation Brazilians *access* jobs (as it did for Marcelo and others) but positively impacts *their everyday work experiences*. In this way, her experience dovetails with research that finds that lighter skin color is associated with fewer experiences with racial discrimination for immigrants from Latin America (Marrow et al. 2022).

Elisabete, whom we first met in the Introduction, was also very conscious of the ways in which whiteness impacted her ability to *access* jobs as well as her *experiences* on the job. Indeed, as discussed in the Introduction and Chapter 1, getting access to the corporate world was something that Elisabete directly attributed to her whiteness and to shifts in legal status. As we recall from Chapter 1, after DACA was passed, Elisabete cold-called a white alum from her college, assuming that the woman would be able to relate to her as another young, white, college-educated woman from the same state university. And it worked, as this woman networked on her behalf, leading to her corporate job, where she had been promoted numerous times. But importantly, Elisabete reiterated to me that her whiteness not only helped her get the job; it helped her *succeed* in her career. She identified three specific reasons. First, according to Elisabete, others in the company, who are primarily white, assume they can relate to her. Second, because others perceive her as white, she feels a sense of confidence and faith in herself. Thus she does not shy away from asking for and in some cases even demanding opportunities (including pay raises). Third, none of her coworkers suspect her of being undocumented, even though there are "red flags" about her life that should raise suspicion. For example, she told me that no one questioned why she had not seen her husband in four years. As explored in the next chapter, Elisabete, who was in liminal legality due to DACA when we last met up, could not travel to Great Britain to visit him, and he could not come to visit her, as he had been denied a visa by the US government in recent years. But no one suspected that immigration laws and her legal status were the reasons they were apart.

ILLEGALITY AND EXPLOITATION IN THE LABOR MARKET

Despite relative privilege that eases some of the burdens of illegality in the labor market, some 1.5-generation Brazilians recounted exploitation and discrimination in their workplaces because of their legal status. For example, Sandra told me that she was never paid for 190 hours she worked at a department store around the holidays. She feared that if she pressed payroll for payment, the company might contact immigration and/or other law enforcement, who would arrest her and send her to jail. So, as she told me, "I think I'll just not get the money. It's best."

Others, like Ana Maria and Gabriela, gradually realized that longtime employers they had trusted had been taking advantage of them. As previously mentioned, Ana Maria had worked, first as a hostess and later as a manager, at a fine-dining restaurant. By the time of our second interview, she had been manager of this restaurant for at least a decade. But as she took on more responsibilities in this managerial role, she realized that in comparison to her coworkers, she was being asked to do more double shifts and being given less priority when requesting time off. She also discovered she was making much less money than coworkers who had less experience.

> I was doing payroll. And I was doing—'cause whenever the payroll person left I would do their job plus my job on top of it. I was also helping the private events coordinator, getting events set up, and doing menus, and putting together menus. 'Cause she'd never had any private events-coordinating experience.... Why would you hire someone that has never put a party together in her life? I'm like, it sounds like it's easy, but it's not. There's all these other details you gotta know. And she just wasn't detail-oriented. And she wasn't organized, and there were so many issues when she was here. Like, every day we were correcting something—reprinting menus. Like, every day! We killed so many trees. So many trees because of this woman. Plus, like, they're all getting paid over $800 a week, I'm getting like $400/450. Maybe. Our accountants get paid like $1,500 a week, events coordinator was getting like $900 to $1,000 a week. And then [the owners]

> have the nerve to tell [me], like, *as [I'm] doing the payroll* . . . and they have the nerve to tell [me], "We don't have money to give you right now. It's just too slow."

Ana Maria was not only bothered by being paid less than her less experienced and less competent coworkers; she was also angered by her employer's justifications for not paying her more. She became further incensed after one particular incident when her boss scolded her in disparaging ways, an incident that led Ana Maria to finally take a risk and seek new employment.

> I'm up [before work] leisurely taking a shower. A leisure[ly] breakfast. All the sudden I get this phone call, it's like "Where are you? You are so irresponsible." And I'm like, "Excuse me? Where am I? I'm home. It's eight [a.m.]. Like, why would I be there?" Like [she says] "You need to get your ass in here right now!" And I've never been spoken to like that before in my life. Not by a boss. And never anyone else. I'm like "I'm sorry, what?" She's like "Who's gonna make [the coffee]. . . ." They can't make coffee! They don't know how to make fucking coffee! "Who's gonna set out the dishware? And who's gonna make coffee? And who's gonna put out cookies?" I'm like "Oh my God! Really?" That's why I'm going there? To put out coffee and cookies? . . . You can't literally brew a cup of hot coffee? How do you live at home? It's not that hard." And she had me so worried that I took a cab here. I thought I was gonna lose my job. I was crying, I was in hysterics. I get here—she doesn't even apologize. Sees that I'm upset—she's just like "You should just be grateful that Lilly was here"—the pastry person—"she made the coffee and she put the cookies out. You should really thank her."

Ana Maria worked the rest of the day but then immediately went home and started looking through Brazilian newspapers for new work. For years she had been scared to seek new work because her managerial job was a relatively "good" job for an undocumented immigrant. Thus she had dealt—begrudgingly—with poor treatment from her employers. But with this incident she reached her breaking point. As she pointed out to me during the interview, even if she had made a small mistake and had failed to come to work on time that day (which she didn't really think was the case—her boss had only asked her informally during casual conversation to come in early and had never put the early hours on the official work schedule), the mistake did not merit the hostile treatment she received.

Like Ana Maria, Gabriela felt taken advantage of by her longtime white American employer. But she was also fortunate, relative to other undocumented immigrants, to be in a position in which her employer had been able to sponsor her for an adjustment in status. Thus for a long time Gabriela felt she was unable to leave her job even though he was not paying her what she should have been paid.

Gabriela was an administrative assistant for an insurance agency, a small business she had been with since age sixteen. When I met her in 2006, she was undocumented but was holding out hope for a pathway to citizenship because her father had filed for an adjustment of status under Section 245i before the April 2001 deadline. While the process under her father did not advance, Gabriela's employer agreed to sponsor her. He was able to do so because she was "grandfathered" under Section 245(i). Her lawyer, who was helping her adjust her status, was the one who told her that her employer was taking advantage of her.

> The lawyer calculated the hours I had been working and calculated how much I made, and he was like "This guy's completely underpaying you. Like, you don't get benefits. . . . I used to get salary. Now I'm hourly again. [It's] convenient for (m–boss)—salary, hourly, salary, hourly. . . All I know is . . . after twelve years, it doesn't seem like what I should be making, you know what I mean?

Gabriela was upset she was being underpaid and that her boss had shifted her from salary to hourly wages when it suited his interests. But she was not in a position to find new work given that her employer was helping her adjust her status. By the time I met with Gabriela for a second time, nearly six years later, she had her green card. Yet she continued working for the insurance company. She told me she believed her employer was a good man. ("He's not a bad person. Because he did help me. And he is a good boss.") but she also explained that she felt trapped. In part she felt indebted to him, since he had employed her when she did not have work authorization and because he helped her "get her papers." But she was also scared that if she quit, her employer would no longer agree to sponsor her younger brother for an adjustment in status.

CONCLUSION

Leaving the institutional protection of school is a jarring experience for undocumented 1.5-generation Brazilian immigrants, just as it is for other undocumented immigrants, who grow up in the United States and are educated and socialized alongside their American-born peers. However, because of relative racial and social class privilege, the undocumented 1.5-generation Brazilians I met had a more varied and nuanced experience as they transitioned out of postsecondary education than did many of their undocumented peers from Latin America (see Gonzales 2016). Their ability to access some form of higher education, even when they downgraded their choices, was particularly striking given the financial and information barriers they faced to higher education in Massachusetts, which did not offer in-state tuition nor have an extensive, well-known organizing apparatus for undocumented youth at the time. Indeed, even 1.5-generation Brazilians who experienced events that could have put them on a downward spiral often found they had cushions—in the forms of networks and resources—that softened the landing for them. These cushions were shaped by their Brazilian middle-class roots and/or their abilities to pass as white in the US. Thus, while 1.5-generation Brazilians experienced illegality as salient in their lives when they left the institutional protection of high school (Gonzales 2011; 2016), their other social locations profoundly shaped their postsecondary schooling experiences.

Specifically, Brazilian middle-class roots allowed some families to help pay expenses for college without the help of federal or state aid and/or to allow their kids to live at home, rent-free, as some 1.5-generation Brazilians pursued creative interests. Several white-passing 1.5-generation Brazilians were also tracked high in school, which can only be understood in a longer history of racial tracking (Francis and Darity 2021). Meanwhile, race, gender, and (il)legality worked together to shape the work they found in a racialized and gendered labor market. To be sure, illegality rendered most top-tier jobs in the neoliberal racial economy unavailable to them, even for those with college degrees. Furthermore, gaining a work permit was significant in opening up job opportunities. But even when 1.5-generation Brazilians did *not* have work permits, they rarely worked in the lowest-tiered jobs of the low-wage service-sector economy. Some found work in the extensive web of Brazilian co-ethnic businesses and nonprofit organizations while others drew on white American networks to find work in blue-collar industries, the corporate sector, and small businesses.

Yet, to be clear, an undocumented status does limit their opportunities in the labor market in significant ways. This was particularly true over time as workplaces implemented E-Verify and other anti-immigrant measures. Furthermore, illegality does lead to workplace exploitation, even in relatively "good jobs," including by owners whom 1.5-generation Brazilians had trusted. Given the ways that illegality did limit their educational and career dreams in the neoliberal racial economy, we might anticipate that undocumented 1.5-generation Brazilians would do anything within their power to pursue the very limited pathways to citizenship available to them. As we will see in the next chapter, the most viable pathway to citizenship for most who are still undocumented when they turn eighteen is not through an employer sponsorship as it was for Gabriela, but through marriage to a US citizen or lawful permanent resident. But few 1.5-generation Brazilians wanted to instrumentally marry for papers, despite the socioeconomic opportunities that legalization through marriage would bring. Instead they wanted to marry for love. And often what was more important to them in a love match was not citizenship, but the race and nationality of their partner.

THREE   LOVE LIVES
Romance and Marriage

Ana Maria, a self-proclaimed "bookworm," loved reading, libraries, and romance. From an early age, she devoured stories about romantic love. First, fairy tales. Later, Jane Austen novels. After one particularly bad breakup in her early twenties, she dreamed of writing the next great American romance novel. ("Didn't happen!" she told me.) Nevertheless, when I met her at age twenty-five, she was still a hopeless romantic who dreamed of meeting her soulmate.

    Being a hopeless romantic in American society isn't unique. But Ana Maria's search for her soulmate was, like everything else during young adulthood, complicated by illegality. According to her lawyer, her only potential pathway to citizenship was marriage. Ana Maria had sought the lawyer's legal advice about pathways to citizenship she may have overlooked after she was thwarted by impediments to higher education and better jobs. But even after the lawyer told her that marriage to a US citizen was her *only* option for a pathway to citizenship, she was emphatic that she was *not* willing to marry a US citizen *just* to get her "papers."

> I was just like "Oh, I am so lost right now. I really need to take a different course again." And I was just like "Oh my God, what am I going to do?

There's got to be some loophole, there's got to be something." [The lawyer] I, "The only way you can do anything right now is to marry someone. That's American." And I was like "I am not going to marry anyone for a—a paper." I'm sorry, I'm not. Because if I do end up—if I marry someone, that means I am going to have to deal with them and what if I don't like them? Or I mean, what if I do like them? But still, I want to go to Europe by myself. I want to backpack Europe by myself. I want to have a good time by myself. Because I'll meet interesting people and I don't want to have to—to meet interesting people and not be able to, you know, hang out with them or something because I'm married. You know, what if I meet the true love of my life in Europe or somewhere? Or Africa.

Ana Maria's refusal to marry for papers underscores a number of dynamics. First, the prospect of marrying for papers looms large in the minds of undocumented immigrants—and they often receive messages, including from lawyers, that it is their best prospect for legalization. Second, Ana Maria did not want to get married at that point in her life, because she saw her twenties as a time for self-exploration rather than settling down ("I want to go to Europe *by myself*"). Third, her refusal to strategically marry for papers underscores how important romantic love-based relationships were to her. She wanted the chance to travel the world and "meet interesting people," including the potential "love of (her) life." Meeting your soulmate while traveling abroad was a storybook romance; strategically marrying for papers was *not*.

But who did she imagine the love of her life to be? Not a Brazilian man. Indeed, as a teenager, she had been engaged to a much older Brazilian. But according to Ana Maria, she had sworn off dating Brazilians after breaking off that engagement. She saw her Brazilian ex as too patriarchal and that experience had soured her on dating other Brazilian men.

> He wanted me to quit school. Not go to college. Have six kids and be barefoot and walk around the house all day. And that really wasn't going to go well with me. I wanted to do something. I wanted to make something out of myself, you know? Progress. I really have never dated Brazilians ever again after that one. And I don't. And I never intend to.

Instead, Ana Maria—who was of German and Italian heritage with light skin, silky dark brown hair, and dark almond eyes—envisioned the "love of her life" as a white American man with blond hair and blue eyes. "My thing was, I would always marry a blond, blue-eyed guy. Like, that was like, my dream guy." This physical description of Ana Maria's "dream guy" embodies a Northern European appearance that is the epitome of "white racial purity" in many places in the world (Pande 2021), including Brazil, where blond hair and blue eyes are highly idealized (Osuji 2019; Twine 1998).

By the time I reconnected with Ana Maria for a second interview, years later, she had met her "dream guy" on an online dating site. Luka is a white American and has blond hair, blue eyes, and pale skin. But dating someone who is a white American and unfamiliar with the nation's harsh immigration laws complicated Ana Maria's relationship, especially in the early stages. Specifically, she feared she would no longer be desirable to him if he found out the truth about her immigration status. In order to conceal her illegality from him, she found herself telling little lies. "I just haven't had time to go down, to go back to Brazil . . . I'm planning a trip very soon," she lied when trying to explain why she had not seen her siblings or parents for more than a decade. Ana Maria lived with her grandmother in the US but her nuclear family members were all in Brazil, unable to "get papers" to come to the US. And without a green card, Ana Maria was unwilling to visit Brazil, knowing that when she left US soil, she would trigger the ten-year bar to reentry.[1] But rather than explain this to Luka, she told little lies in order to conceal the stigma of illegality.

A month into their relationship, however, Ana Maria began to feel "guilty" that she had not shared her "(immigration) situation." The relationship was getting serious. Luka had shared his medical struggles and Ana Maria had shared other painful details of her life, including her history of sexual abuse. But disclosing her legal status felt scarier to her. She worried that if he knew the truth about her legal status "this perfect little relationship that I'm building in my head is all going to disappear. In a blink of an eye."

Finally, Ana Maria decided it was time to tell him, but it was incredibly emotional for her. "I started bawling. Like—just bawling." Much to her relief, however, the relationship did not end. And by the time of our second interview, Luka and Ana Maria were engaged. Still, there was no rush to the altar in order for Ana Maria to get her papers. Rather, Ana Maria was content to have a long engagement and to plan the ideal wedding. It was important to her that people knew she was not marrying Luka for papers; she was marrying him for love.

Ana Maria's story of finding and navigating romantic love necessitates a lens that not only accounts for how illegality matters, but how race, class, illegality, and gender articulate together. On the one hand, a power-without-papers perspective underscores the powerful role immigration laws play in penetrating the most intimate aspects of undocumented young adults' lives. As Laura Enriquez has also argued, (il)legality shapes all aspects of romantic experiences—feelings of desirability, ways of relating to partners, and decisions about if and when to advance a relationship. And the potential of "marrying for papers" looms large in Ana Maria and other 1.5-generation Brazilians' minds. Given the nation's restrictive immigration laws, it is often the only viable pathway to citizenship and thus their hopes for reuniting with family members in Brazil, exploring the world *and* seeking better opportunities in the US labor market. Yet (il)legality leads them away from wanting to strategically marry for papers, despite their desires for US citizenship and the political, civil, and social rights that brings.

On the other hand, a power-without-papers lens also brings to the forefront the ways that family formation, including romantic partnerships, remain a powerful site for the reproduction of race and class inequalities. Indeed, for many 1.5-generation Brazilians, it is not a partner's citizenship status but rather nationality and race that play a profound role in shaping *who* they desire as a partner. For example, like Ana Maria, some 1.5-generation Brazilian women cite a desire to be with American men, whom they perceive as less patriarchal, while some 1.5-generation Brazilian men told me that they do not want to date American women, who they perceive to be feminists. Furthermore, most 1.5-generation Brazilians stated they wanted to date or marry partners with European physical features—whether they were American or Brazilian—with some expressing clear anti-Blackness. One 1.5-generation Brazilian woman, Pamela, explicitly articulated that marrying someone who is white would elevate her own racial status. In this way, Brazilian notions of race (that whiteness is expansive and fluid and that marriage is one way to "become white") travel across borders (Joseph 2015) and are passed down over generations.

In the next sections, I begin with a discussion of the larger historical and structural contexts in the US and Brazil that shape the romantic lives of 1.5-generation Brazilians, including historical laws regulating marriage and citizenship and contemporary laws governing family reunification via marriage. Then I analyze how power without papers shapes all stages of romantic relationships before I take a closer look at romantic partner choices. Illegality penetrates all aspects of romantic lives and leads them away from wanting to strategically marry for papers, while cultural gendered norms and race shape who they desire as a partner.

LOVE, MARRIAGE, FAMILY, AND THE STATE

The American Context

Romantic love is dominant in Western societies. That is, most people living in Western societies want to marry for love. Indeed, under current US immigration law, romantic love is necessary for demonstrating to the US federal government that the marital relationship is "legitimate" for legalization purposes. But the idea of marrying for love is a relatively new historical phenomenon. For most of history, marriage has been an explicit economic arrangement, evolving over time to fulfill the economic needs of societies and kin (Coontz 2006). Today, despite the emphasis on romantic love, young people often have other requirements they hope to meet before getting married. Indeed, with neoliberal economic changes that make the transition to adulthood longer and less orderly, Americans are delaying the age at which they marry as they focus on achieving other adulthood milestones, including going to college (and/or graduate school), becoming "financially set," and/or exploring their own identities (Arnett 2004; Edin and Kefalas 2011; Furstenberg 2010; Kefalas et al. 2011). In other words, like Ana Maria, many young Brazilians do not want to marry in their early twenties since they see this life course period as a time to explore themselves, their education, their careers, and the world (Cebulko 2016).

Importantly, marriage and the family have historically been key institutions for state-building, governing which spouses and children can gain access to migration, citizenship, and the full social, civil, and political benefits of citizenship. As such, laws and policies governing marriage and family formation have not only been shaped by patriarchy, heteronormativity, white supremacy, and capitalism; they have worked (and continue to work) to uphold these interlocking systems of power. For example, from 1907 to 1922, the Expatriation Act stripped women of their US citizenship if they married noncitizen men (Batlan 2020). Meanwhile, until the Supreme Court repealed the Defense of Marriage Act in 2013, US laws prevented gay and lesbian couples from providing citizenship to their spouses (López 2021). And of course, the US at both the federal and state level has a long history of regulating marriage and family formation between whites and nonwhites, especially Blacks, in order to protect "white racial purity" (Pascoe 2009).

Antimiscegenation laws were on the books as early as 1691 when the Maryland General Assembly criminalized interracial marriage. In some US states, antimiscegenation laws would not end until 1967, when the Supreme Court, in *Loving v. Virginia*, finally guaranteed the federal right to interracial marriage (Osuji 2019). But importantly, even as state laws forbade interracial marriages, other laws rewarded white male sexual violence against women of color. For example, during slavery, laws in some US states legally classified the children of white slave owners and Black slaves as Black and thus as slaves. This ensured that white male violence against Black women was lucrative in the slave economy (Osuji 2019). Meanwhile, sexual relations—real or imagined—between Black men and white women often led to the lynching of Black men, stoking fear in Black communities, maintaining white patriarchy over white women, and exacerbating the stigma of interracial relationships (Osuji 2019).

It was not just state laws that served as legal bulwarks against interracial marriages in order to protect white racial purity. Legal scholar Rose Cuison-Villazor (2011) details how interracial relationships between white men and Japanese women were forbidden on US soil using an entire system of federal race-based marriage restrictions. These immigration, citizenship, and military laws and regulations sought to uphold white racial purity by preventing men who had served or were serving in the US military from marrying any woman from a racial group who was ineligible for citizenship at the time (Villazor 2011, 13).

This long legal and social history governing marriage and family formation continues to impact the present in several ways. For example, most Americans marry someone of the same race, with whites being the least likely to marry someone of another race (Wang 2012).[2] Couples in interracial relationships report social sanctions, including opposition from families (Childs 2005; Harris and Kalbfleisch 2000), especially from families of white women who are dating Black men (Osuji 2019). Historically, as bell hooks (1981) argues, interracial unions between white women and Black men threatened white male power over white women, whom they saw as their "property."

Importantly, contemporary immigration laws and social norms governing family reunification via marriage also continue to reflect—and maintain—these interlocking systems of power. For example, laws and norms governing US citizens sponsoring a spouse for an adjustment of status prioritize better-educated, wealthier, white men who seek to sponsor better-educated, wealthier, non-Latino women (López 2021). Furthermore, couples who can project idealized marriages and families rooted in white, heterosexual upper-middle-class norms tend to be more successful in their applications (Gomberg-Muñoz 2016; López 2021).

There are at least three immigration laws that are important for understanding the contemporary legal landscape shaping if and how a US citizen can sponsor an undocumented immigrant for lawful permanent residency. All of these laws are discriminatory (López 2021). First, in 1952, the Immigration and Nationality Act (INA) limited family sponsorships to "nuclear family" relationships (spouse, siblings, parents/children) and codified the requirement that couples must be *legally* married. In so doing, the INA centered the post–World War II, suburban, upper-middle-class, white, nuclear family model (López 2021). These codifications discriminated against alternative household family models, more common in the Global South and among non-white families in the US, in which grandparents and other extended relatives act as important caregivers (Cohn et al. 2022).[3] Indeed, this exclusionary law is why Ana Maria's grandmother, the woman who had been her primary caretaker since age five, could not sponsor Ana Maria for a pathway to citizenship even once her grandmother became a US citizen.

Second, the Immigration Marriage Fraud Amendment (IMFA) of 1986 forced mixed-status couples to prove their marriage was a "legitimate" love relationship. Worried about marriage fraud, the US government requires couples to *submit evidence* demonstrating the quality of their love and commitment to one another. As López (2021) details, the IMFA standards for demonstrating the legitimacy of a love marriage are rooted in white, upper-middle-class, patriarchal norms. As we will see later in this chapter, couples who do not perfectly conform to these standards often experience anxiety that the US government will not perceive the relationship as legitimate.

Third, the Illegal Immigration Reform and Immigrant Responsibility Act (IIRIRA) of 1996 implemented a number of anti-immigrant measures, two of which were specific to mixed-status couples and were discriminatory in nature. First, IIRIRA introduced a new requirement that US citizens who seek to sponsor a spouse *prove* that their individual income is at 125 percent of the poverty level. In so doing, this "minimum income requirement" both prioritizes US citizens who are better educated, wealthier, white, and male (as they earn higher wages in the labor market) to sponsor a spouse *and* negatively impacts US citizens who are structurally disadvantaged by capitalism (including nonwhites, women, and disabled Americans). Second, as described in the Introduction of this book, IIRIRA implemented the three- and ten-year bars to reentry. Under family reunification laws governing marriage, these bars negatively impact undocumented immigrants who entered without inspection (EWI), but not visa overstayers. This is because EWIs, but not visa overstayers, are required *to leave* the US and to complete the process for an adjustment in status via marriage at a consulate in their native country. Visa overstayers can complete the process in the US and avoid triggering the three- and ten-year bars to reentry. Thus these laws disproportionately negatively impact poorer, darker-skinned immigrants who come from Mexico and Central America, since they are more likely to have entered without inspection.[4]

Together, then, what does this legal context mean for 1.5-generation unauthorized Brazilians I interviewed? First, in the restrictive immigration context, marriage is often the *only* potential pathway to citizenship—just as Ana Maria's lawyer told her. Unlike other familial relationships under US immigration law, petitions for spouses are not subjected to quotas. Second, because 1.5-generation Brazilians largely overstayed their visas (a function of their relative racial and social class privilege in Brazil), getting papers via marriage is more realistic for them than for many of their unauthorized peers who entered without inspection. Third, if they choose (and are chosen by) romantic partners who are advantageously positioned under capitalism (white, middle-class, able-bodied), they are more likely to have success adjusting their status.

As Enriquez (2020) details, these legalization realities can create pressure on unauthorized immigrants to date and marry a US citizen. Furthermore, the anti-immigrant legal context can shape all stages of romantic relationships, affecting men's and women's feelings of desirability (often in gendered ways), their emotions navigating early courtship, and their long term partnerships (Enriquez 2020). But importantly, for 1.5-generation Brazilians, it's not just the American legal context that matters in shaping their romantic lives.

Indeed, as much as they may receive messages about the desirability of US citizens as romantic partners (Enriquez 2020), they also receive messages about the racial desirability of romantic partners, messages informed not only by US racial logics, but by racial logics particular to Brazil.

The Brazilian Context

In contrast to the US, where racial mixing, especially between whites and Blacks, has been heavily policed and antimiscegenation laws prohibited interracial marriages in order to protect white racial purity, racial intermixing between Blacks, whites, and indigenous peoples has been common in Brazil since Portuguese colonization. The Brazilian nation-state's legitimation of miscegenation was rooted in white supremacy and was endorsed alongside the ideology and practice of *embranquecimento*, or whitening. As discussed in the Introduction, Brazilian elites argued that miscegenation would lighten rather than darken the population, since they believed that white genes were stronger and that Brazilian people would choose partners lighter than themselves (Skidmore 1992).

Embranquecimento, however, is not just a Brazilian *elite* ideology. Indeed, nonwhite Brazilians have purposefully sought social status and movement up the racial hierarchy through marriage to whites (see Osuji 2019). According to Degler (1986), there has long been a "mulatto escape hatch" that allows individuals of mixed ancestry in Brazil to enjoy freedom from the stigma of Blackness and engage in upward mobility through marriage and having children. More recently, Osuji (2019) finds that some Black Brazilian women deliberately set out to marry white Brazilian men, and situates this racial preference in Brazil's long history of women of color increasing the possibility for upward mobility through marriage to European men, especially because their offspring would not automatically be considered Black or indigenous. While scholars disagree on the extent to which there is actually evidence for a mulatto escape hatch in Brazil (Loveman, Muniz, and Bailey 2012; Sheriff 2001; Telles 2004), many Brazilians *believe* that intermarriage with whites can increase someone's social status and prefer that their children marry partners with physical features associated with Europeans. For example, Twine (1998) finds that working-class Brazilian families, including Afro-Brazilian families, valorize whiteness, sanction children who date Black partners, and erase their own family histories of Black ancestors.

In the next sections, I examine how these American and Brazilian structural contexts come together to shape the romantic lives of 1.5-generation Brazilians. I find that immigration law penetrates their *experiences* in romantic relationships at every stage: early courtship, long-term partnerships, and in marriage and family formation. But importantly, (i)legality hangs together with other structural positions—race, class, and gender—to shape these experiences in dating and long-term romantic partnerships. Yet it is race, even more than legality, that shapes *who* they desire as a partner. I argue that we cannot understand these racial preferences for whites without understanding how Brazilian racial logics transfer across borders and are passed down intergenerationally in families.

US IMMIGRATION LAW, ROMANTIC LIVES, AND ARTICULATION WITH OTHER INEQUALITIES

Illegality and Early Courtship

> Like, honestly, when [I] ask a girl on a date, I can't pick her up. That's what sucks the most . . . [Imitating a hypothetical conversation with a girl] "You want to take a train out to East Boston?" [Girl:] "Uhhh, not so much."—Rodrigo

Rodrigo was an athlete—a *futebol* (soccer) star who oozed charisma, flashing a bright white grin throughout our conversations. In many ways, Rodrigo embodied the hegemonic masculinity that is often associated with male athletes, projecting confidence and downplaying sadness—even while talking about his experiences navigating illegality (Pleck 1995). Unlike 1.5-generation Brazilian women I met, he never cried when talking about blocked opportunities due to illegality. Instead he used taciturn language like "it sucks." And for Rodrigo, what "sucked" the most at age eighteen when I first met him was that he was unable to engage in traditional gendered dating norms. He wanted to pick a girl up and take her on a date. Underscoring just how important this dating ritual was to him, Rodrigo reached out to me when his DACA application was finally approved in his midtwenties, telling me, "I finally experienced the long-awaited date where I pick a girl up at her house and not at a train station! Life's good!"

Traditional dating norms place the responsibility of date planning on men. But illegality constrains undocumented men's abilities to adhere to this traditional form of masculinity (Enriquez 2020; Pila 2016). Rodrigo did not worry that girls did not find him attractive, but he did worry how he appeared to women when he could not court them in traditionally gendered ways. In this way, illegality negatively impacted his *feelings of desirability*.

Marcus also told me—more directly than Rodrigo—that he felt undesirable in dating relationships. He used words and phrases like *outsider, awkward*, and *not normal* to describe himself and told me directly that he had a "lack of confidence" in dating relationships.

> I've only dated women who pursued me. The idea of "trying" gives me a lot of anxiety. I wouldn't want me coming up to you! . . . It's a lack of confidence. One hundred percent. I've been going to the gym so that helps a little bit. But I feel like [girls not wanting to date me] is based on evidence. So I don't feel crazy.

Importantly, in Marcus's case, the "lack of confidence" in dating was not only a function of illegality but also the result of his experiences growing up as an undocumented, white-passing Brazilian in a mostly white suburb (more than 90 percent white) and his nonconformity to the "alpha male" stereotype that he believed women were attracted to. He wasn't athletic (although he was trying to go the gym more); he was artistic and creative. He was not confident and assertive; he was sensitive. "I'm too sensitive though. Not really in a healthy way. Like I feel things too much." Writing—and specifically, writing horror—had become his creative outlet for processing his feelings of being an outsider in society. "(Horror can be) a metaphor for anything. Like if you feel like an outsider . . . you just take whatever you feel and you make it physical." His current horror screenplay explored the idea of being "the immigrant other" who is "not welcomed" in a small "cult town." The cult? "Basically white people," he told me while laughing. But the screenplay did not completely reflect his reality as the immigrant "other" protagonist in his horror movie was dating a white American girl. Marcus at the time was single. But he acknowledged that if he did date, it would mostly like be a white American. After all, he told me, most of his peer group was white.

For undocumented women, feelings of undesirability mostly emerged when they recalled the early stages of their relationship with a non-Brazilian romantic partner. For example, like Ana Maria, Mayra worried that Jacob, a white Canadian whom she met at a camp in the US, would not date her if he found out the truth about her legal status. When Jacob first came to Boston to visit Mayra once they started dating, Mayra could not bring herself to tell him she was undocumented. She was worried for two reasons. First, Mayra was fearful that Jacob would not want to deal with the logistical stress that would come with dating her ("He would be the one coming (to Boston) all the time"). Second, she was nervous to disclose her status due to the stigma of illegality.

> And I was also afraid, you know? Because some people—they think that "illegals" are criminals. And they shouldn't be here. And obviously I didn't think that Jacob would think that. But I was afraid that he might have thought that is was very wrong . . . for me to be here. Or [think] why didn't I ever do anything about it? Even though we did, you know?

Like Ana Maria, Mayra found it easier to tell Jacob other stigmatic aspects of her past than to disclose illegality. In Mayra's case, she shared that she had gotten pregnant at age fourteen and was a single mother to a little girl. It was not until Jacob's second trip to Boston that she finally told him that she was undocumented. "And then we talked. And it was at Bread and Bagels Co. And until today—I hate Bread and Bagels Co. Hate it! Bad memories . . ."[5] The memories of that day, despite the fact that they stayed together, are so painful she cannot bring herself to go to the restaurant anymore.

Long-Term Romantic Partnerships with Non–US Citizens

Illegality continues to impact romantic relationships after the initial courtship stages. The impact differs, however, depending on their romantic partner's nationality and immigration status in the United States. For those who are in a relationship with an undocumented immigrant, the most realistic pathway to citizenship via marriage is closed and the legal precarity for both partners can create stress in relationships. Meanwhile, for those in long-term partnerships with non–US citizens who called Canada and/or Great Britain home, the couples were forced to live separately across borders, which also creates stress in relationships.

Roberta's story helps underscore how immigration law creates stress in romantic partnerships between unauthorized immigrants. Roberta, who had

DACA by the second time I met her, married her light-skinned, unauthorized Brazilian husband when she was in her early twenties. But while she had DACA, he was ineligible since he arrived to the US when he was sixteen. During our second interview, she told me that their legal precarity in this country made her uneasy about planning their future. Specifically, she wasn't sure she wanted to have children or buy a home.

> Without a legal status, you can't really truly settle down. Like, I would never buy a house without having a documentation, you know what I mean? And maybe even have kids because you don't know, you know, what tomorrow is going to bring. If we're going to have to pack up and leave.

In this way, the far-reaching impacts of immigration law are clearly seen in Roberta's marriage and family formation processes. As Enriquez (2020) argues, making decisions about future plans in a relationship is complicated by legal uncertainties.

Meanwhile, Mayra's and Elisabete's relationship stories demonstrate how US immigration law separates couples across international borders, negatively impacting their relationships. As mentioned above, Mayra's partner, Jacob, was a Canadian citizen, not a US citizen, who had never lived illegally in the US. But Mayra's undocumented status prevented her from going to Canada—and meeting the people and seeing the places which had shaped Jacob's life. "I wanted to go there (to Canada), I wanted (to) meet, you know, his church. I wanted to meet his friends and everybody." Jacob was getting to know more about her family and life in Boston, but she could not reciprocate.

As their romantic relationship became more serious and neared a potential engagement, (il)legality also shaped decisions about *when* to move closer to one another and *where* to live and raise a family. Given that neither Jacob nor Mayra had a pathway to citizenship in the US, they made the decision that Mayra and her daughter would move to Canada after Jacob and Mayra married. Due to her undocumented status in the US (which prevented her from leaving the country), her own experiences with illegality (which made her reluctant to move anywhere without status), and the Canadian government's rules over granting a Canadian spouse residency, she remained in the US even after she and Jacob were married.

> It's—it's a long process. We had no idea it would be this complicated. The reason why I'm still here [in the US] is because [the Canadian government]

said that if I stay here then I can get my papers faster than if I go to Canada. If I stay [in the US], it's about six to eight months. And if I move to Canada it's about two years. And I don't want to go to another country and be illegal all over again. So I just want to wait here. Because I know the frustration. And I know what it is to not have a driver's license, and not be able to work. So I—we—made the decision to just wait here.

Thus, due to US immigration laws—*and* Canadian immigration laws—Mayra and her partner had to endure separation across international borders despite being married.

In Mayra's case, she was at least able to see Jacob during their long-distance, cross-national relationship (only, of course, when Jacob came to visit her). Elisabete was less fortunate—she found herself separated from her British husband for more than four years. Keith and Elisabete met as teenagers in the US and dated long-distance. During this time, Keith had never had an issue getting a visa to visit the US. But after they were married and Elisabete got DACA, things changed. According to Elisabete, Keith was denied a student visa to attend graduate school in the US—and was told it was because of his marriage to her.[6] Thus Keith and Elisabete became separated by an ocean after they married due to US immigration laws. He could no longer get a visa to the US and she could not visit him in Great Britain since she did not want to leave the US—and her ailing father—permanently behind.

Long-Term Relationships and Marriage with US Citizens
Several of my respondents, all of whom were women, fell in love with US citizen men, both naturalized US citizens from Brazil and US-born white Americans. Their marriages opened up realistic pathways to citizenship for the following reasons: the 1.5-generation Brazilian women were *visa overstayers without criminal records*, their romantic partners met *the minimum income requirement*, and they were in *heterosexual relationships*.[7] Yet, even in these relatively privileged cases, immigration law created stress in their romantic relationships.

For Sabine, a white-passing, 1.5-generation Brazilian who married Jonah, a white American citizen, immigration issues in her relationship became particularly salient *after* she got married. Jonah and Sabine met during college and had nearly a decade-long courtship. During that time, Sabine had a work permit and Social Security number since she had a pending immigration process (she had been listed as a dependent on her father's petition). Thus Sabine did not plan on applying for an adjustment in status via her marriage.

But seven months into her marriage, her father's application for an adjustment in status was denied, and thus so was hers. After speaking with a lawyer, Sabine quickly realized her only option to adjust her status was through her marriage. It was a very "scary" and "awful" time, she told me. But for Sabine, there was a silver lining: her family's case was denied *after* she married her husband. Thus her legal situation did not become a reason for marriage.

> I'm just so thankful to God that like, and I'm thankful that [her father's application was denied] now and not before I got married because then it would have been like, "Oh, let's get married so that I can have papers." And that—it's not what I want, you know? I didn't. I wouldn't have wanted to get married that way. So, as bad as [having the application denied] is, there's also like, the good side. Which, like, it could have been worse.

Sabine's silver lining underscores how strongly she felt about *not* having her marriage—one that was based on love—be used for instrumental reasons like papers.

While Sabine's application for an adjustment in status through her husband was ultimately successful, it was still a daunting, stressful, time-consuming, and expensive process. She worried the US government would be skeptical of the legitimacy of their relationship since she was four years older than her husband, bucking society's gendered expectations that women marry older men, not younger men. "The only thing in our way, I'm like, is our age difference, I think. Because they're going to be like, 'What? Are you sure?'" In this way, Sabine understands that couples who adhere to norms rooted in traditional heterosexual white middle-class relationships will be most successful. Indeed, she did not anticipate any other aspect about them—including their race and social class—standing in their way.

Moreover, the process was stressful on their marriage in other ways. Indeed, the bulk of the logistical labor navigating the paperwork fell on her, not her husband. "I did most of the work. He said 'we' can do it. . . . But meaning 'you' can do it. And it was mostly me." Sabine's white American husband also could not truly empathize with immigration struggles. During our interview, she realized that she had never truly confided in him about the stress of legal insecurity. In part, she had been able to avoid this conversation because she had a work permit, Social Security number, and pending legal process in place for an adjustment in status. But she also said that she was not confident that he, as a white American man, could relate. As she explained to me why she had not confided in him, she told me she really only talked with her friend, Annie, who had direct experience with immigration.

> I feel like nobody [besides Annie] understands or can relate. It's just, like, a deer in the headlights. Like, well-meaning . . . I don't know how to explain it. But it's like, this is something that I just have to keep to myself because unless you're in the same situation as me, you just don't get it. And you mean well. And you hope for the best for me. But you're not going to understand it.

Sabine was happily married and saw her husband as a supportive, kind man. But she did not believe he truly understood immigration issues. And this lack of understanding became particularly salient to her as she took on the emotional and logistical work of navigating the adjustment-of-status process via her marriage. As we completed the second interview, Sabine told me she wished her husband would listen to this conversation so that he would have a better understanding of how immigration issues had impacted her life.

Sabine's experience underscores how relative privilege does not mean that immigration laws do not create stress in intimate relationships. To be sure, US immigration laws privilege immigrants like Sabine (female, visa overstayer, highly educated) and her US citizen husband (white, highly educated male who made above the minimum income requirement) in *opportunities* for successful adjustments of status via marriage. At the same time, Sabine's story also demonstrates the ways in which the state, via immigration laws governing family reunification, negatively impacts *experiences* in marriages (and in adjusting one's status).

The Pressure of Marriage Myths and the Desire to Avoid Strategic Legalization Relationships
Despite the economic opportunities and security from deportation that US citizenship brings—nearly all 1.5-generation Brazilians I met did not want to strategically marry for papers. US cultural mythology, as exemplified in Hollywood movies like *The Proposal* and *Green Card*, suggests that marriage is an

easy and straightforward pathway to citizenship for all immigrants (Enriquez 2020). The reality of "getting papers," of course, is far from this Hollywood trope. As Sabine's story indicates, getting papers through marriage is expensive, time-consuming, and brings about complicated emotions and anxieties (Enriquez 2020; López 2021). Nevertheless, marriage myths persist, sending "pervasive" messages to undocumented young adults that they "should consider their immigration status and legalizations desires when choosing romantic partners" (Enriquez 2020, 25).

Alexia, a white-passing DACA beneficiary who was married to an undocumented, white-passing Brazilian, told me that prior to her marriage, she received pressure from friends and other community members to marry a US citizen in order to get papers. She described one situation in which her friend told her to "take advantage" of Jair, a Brazilian-American Iraq War veteran she was dating, and his "disturbed" mental state to get him to marry her. But Alexia did not feel the romantic chemistry she sought in a partner and broke up with him. Her friend responded by telling her she was "stupid." "She's like 'You're so stupid, you could have married him and had your papers in four months because he was in the army!'"

Nor was it only Alexia's friend who told her to date and marry US citizens. Her boss also encouraged her.

> My own boss—he's from Costa Rica—he was encouraging me [to date US citizens]. "Oh you have so many options here!" 'Cause it's a medical building with a lot of a young American men. And "You can have so many options here if you just go out!" But they were not my type! I can't do that. I can't go out with someone if I don't like them.

Ultimately, Alexia found love with her white-passing undocumented Brazilian husband, closing off any opportunity to adjust her status in the US unless federal laws changes.

For Leila, a white-passing DACA beneficiary, the pressure to marry for papers came from her parents. Her best friend, Devon, had offered to marry her. But Leila refused, despite parental pressure.

> [Devon] actually offered to marry me when were in college. He offered to marry me. We were already broken up and he was just my friend at the time. And he said, "I will marry you if you want." And I thought about it

a lot. And my mom really wanted me to do it. My parents were pushing hard for me to do it. And I was . . . at his house all the time, you know, and I knew his mom very well. I knew his dad very well. And I'll tell you why I didn't do it. I didn't do it because I thought his mom would hate me forever. And, um, and I also—it sounds stupid I guess. But I also thought, you know, Devon. This is a commitment. He might not know what he's in for. He would have to be married to me for three years. We would have to file taxes jointly. We would have to pretend we were a couple for three years, you know what I mean? What if [he met] somebody in that time? Is he going to—is that going to jeopardize his relationship because he's married—you know what I mean? . . . I just—I didn't, I didn't want it to screw up our friendship in any way. . . .

Like Ana Maria, whom we met at the beginning of this chapter, Leila did not want to marry strictly for strategic reasons. She understood that, despite marriage myths, legalizing one's status through marriage would be complicated, requiring a lot of paperwork. Leila also did not want to ruin her friendship with her best friend nor deny him opportunities to date and marry his romantic match. In this way, Leila underscores the importance of strong relationships that provide a sense of inclusion in the larger hostile context of legal exclusion (Cebulko 2016).

When I met up with Leila for a second interview, she was in her early thirties and still did not have lawful permanent residency. Yet she was still thankful that she had not married Devon for strategic reasons. Indeed, during the three years that they would have had to remain married, he met his wife. Leila had been in the bridal party and her friendship with Devon was strong. It was not weighed down by the emotional and financial burden of keeping up the façade of a sham marriage.

Ana Maria and Leila were not the only ones who refused to strategically marry for papers. In Marcus's case, he had four friends—including his "dream girl"—offer to marry him after he thought he might be getting deported. But having his dream girl offer to marry him because she took pity on him was not the storybook romance that Marcus had in mind. He wanted her to desire him because she loved him, not because she felt sorry for him.

Moreover, like Leila, Marcus also understood that getting papers through marriage was not as easy as marriage myths implied, and he did not want to put his friends through the stress of a fake relationship.

> The government isn't stupid. They know people do this. The first thing you have to do is prove that you didn't get married just for a green card. You have to show that you had a relationship and have the same address and such. Not to mention the interview you have to pass, which is a lot of pressure to put any of my friends under.

Marcus did desire an American citizen partner. Indeed, he told me the "best-case" scenario would be to fall in love—"for real"—with an American citizen. "The best case would be what happened with my sister who just got lucky and found a nice American guy and it was all real." But his desire to marry an American citizen, rooted in the structural reality of being undocumented, would not lead him to pursue a romantic relationship with an American citizen *solely* for papers.

Stories of refusing to marry strategically for papers demonstrate the value that 1.5-generation Brazilians placed on genuine friendships and romantic relationships. At the same time, their stories also underscore how immigration law—and the reality that marriage may be their only option for adjusting their status—looms large in their lives. Sometimes they must resist pressure from family members and turn down offers from well-intentioned friends.

For women, there were often gendered reasons for wanting to avoid strategic marriages. For example, Kátia told me she did not want to enter into a marriage for papers because it was so much like an "arranged marriage" and that the marriage "could be used against (her) if (she was) caught." Furthermore, Kátia was emphatic that she did not want to have to rely on a man.

> [Marrying for papers] always felt—it felt wrong in terms of having—relying on another man for that.... Like I didn't wanna have to. Like, well for me to get [papers], I have to marry somebody. And I have to marry this man to get whatever I want. Then it becomes, like, a negotiation. Like, okay, what am I giving him?

As a woman, Kátia is already more vulnerable in heterosexual romantic relationships. But being undocumented and relying on a US citizen would exacerbate her vulnerability, as she would be relying on him for papers. And she wondered what she would have to "give him" in return.

Another reason 1.5-generation Brazilians gave for not wanting to marry for strategic reasons was that they did not want to "live a "lie" by keeping a sham marriage a secret. Vitória, who was an undocumented youth activist, said that being forced to hide her illegality when growing up had made her reluctant to marry for papers.

> Like I didn't want to have to lie in order to get papers. And I know a lot of people have to do that. And it just sucks. I had to keep my undocumented status hidden—or lie—to my friends all the time. I didn't want to keep having to, like, live this lie for the rest of my life. Because that's essentially what you do when you get married for papers. You can't really tell a lot of people, "Yeah, I got married for papers and divorced because it wasn't a real marriage." If you get caught for that, it's serious. And I was like, I don't want to have to keep that lie going forever.

As an undocumented youth activist, Vitória is now "out" about her illegality. And after years of hiding, she wanted no more secrets. Thus illegality had led Vitória away from wanting to marry strategically for papers.

Vitória's fears about living a lie were not unfounded. Ricardo was the only 1.5-generation Brazilian I met who strategically married a friend for papers. After three years, they divorced. While he never had concerns that his ex-wife would betray him, he was careful telling his postdivorce girlfriends how he gained access to citizenship. As he told me, "you never know how (the) relationships end. And how that is a weapon that somebody can have against me at all times."

Thus, despite a legal context that creates structural pressures to marry a US citizen, 1.5-generation Brazilians did not want to strategically marry for papers. But did their structural positions with legal marginalization lead them to *preferring* a US citizen romantic partner?[7] Marcus clearly stated that it would the "best-case" scenario. But contrary to what we might anticipate, very few undocumented 1.5-generation Brazilians expressed such explicit romantic preferences for a US citizen. In part, stating such explicit preferences may have seemed too instrumental and at odds with their belief in romantic love (Enriquez 2020). Yet 1.5-generation Brazilians I met were often very explicit about their *cultural* and *racial* preferences in romantic partners. In the next section, I further examine these explicit cultural and racial romantic preferences, situating them in the larger structural contexts.

CHOOSING A ROMANTIC PARTNER

Power Without Papers and Marriage Markets

Given the dominant cultural norms around marrying for love in US society, it is not surprising that undocumented 1.5-generation Brazilians *wanted* to marry for love, not for instrumental reasons. Yet who we love, and who we desire, are shaped by our structural positions in intersecting power systems. Thus we need to consider how the larger structural context shapes who undocumented 1.5-generation Brazilians *want* to date and marry and who they *actually* marry. As we will see, most undocumented 1.5-generation Brazilians wanted to date and marry (or were dating/had married) someone who was a white American or a white-passing Brazilian.

Some scholars explain who we choose to date/marry as a function of opportunity in the marriage market, arguing that most people marry someone of a similar racial and class background due to extensive US racial and economic segregation, which limits people's opportunity to work and mingle—and thus meet a romantic partner—from a different racial and/or economic group (Blau, Beeker, and Fitzpatrick 1984; Harris and Ono 2005). These networks can change over time, however. For example, going to college can change the dating pools for some young people. Laura Enriquez (2020) finds that college-educated unauthorized 1.5-generation Latino/a/xs are more likely to date romantic partners who are *US citizens* than they were before they went to college, arguing that higher education expands their dating pools beyond their low-income, mixed-status Latino/as/xs neighborhoods.

Importantly, however, the dating pools for 1.5-generation Brazilians who are not college-educated are very different from the unauthorized 1.5-generation Mexicans and Central Americans respondents whom Laura Enriquez interviewed. This is because 1.5-generation Brazilians I met did not grow up in similarly racially and economically segregated neighborhoods. Instead, as described in Chapter 1, unauthorized Brazilians who migrated in the 1980s and '90s largely settled in ethno-racially and economically diverse neighborhoods and/or working class (or middle-class) white neighborhoods. Thus their peer networks—and dating pools—at school, church, work, and in their neighborhoods were primarily composed of white Americans, Brazilians, and other immigrant groups from Europe, the Middle East, Asia, and Latin America. When they described who they were interested in dating, they often mentioned that they preferred to date white Americans or Brazilians, and explained this as a function of who their peers were.

For example, Marcus, who did not go to college and who had grown up in a predominantly white town, told me that he would likely date a white American because that's who he mostly "hangs out" with. Similarly, Álvaro, who grew up in a multicultural neighborhood near some of Boston's most prestigious universities and went to a predominantly white public high school, told me that most of his friends were white and that he would likely marry an American woman because of his networks.

> There is a ninety-nine percent chance that I'm probably going to marry an American girl, you know what I mean? Just in a sense, just because of . . . Obviously I'm not going to be like, "No, you're Brazilian; I'm not going to marry you." But it's like, you know, just from the people I hang out with, the people I'm around—you know what I mean—I go to school with. It's like, odds are that, you know, that's going to be it.

Álvaro said he would marry an "American girl," but like other Brazilians, he used *white* and *American* interchangeably throughout the interview, conflating whiteness with being an American.

While Marcus, Álvaro, and others discussed their networks as predominantly white and thus shaping their likelihood of dating white Americans, other 1.5-generation Brazilians said they often dated Brazilians and explained it as a function of their networks. Emilio was dating a second-generation, white-passing Brazilian woman whom he had met through church. He explained that he had mostly (but not exclusively) dated Brazilians because "I'm involved in the Brazilian community, so, like, it ends up like that." Emilio was also not alone in meeting his romantic partner through Brazilian churches as several 1.5-generation Brazilians, including Roberta and Fabiana, met their boyfriends (and eventual husbands) there.

But marriage markets alone cannot explain why people date and marry the people they do. Indeed, a strict focus on *opportunities* to meet and mingle neglects the ways in which people make *meaning* of and *navigate* the interlocking structural positions in their lives. As Vasquez-Tokos (2017) argues, this is a "proverbial black box" that needs to be filled in when considering romantic desires. For example, previous research has demonstrated that young people in the United States report being the least attracted to Black men and women (Bany, Robnett, and Feliciano 2014), romantic desires that can only be understood in the context of the long history of white supremacy and anti-Blackness. Meanwhile, other scholars find that men and women pursue social acceptance (especially from family) and/or upward mobility through their romantic partnerships (Osuji 2019; Twine 1998; Vasquez-Tokos 2017). For some migrant women from the Global South, marriage to white European men can bring upward class mobility and status and help them fulfill gendered norms, such as taking care of their extended families back at home by remitting money (Fresnoza-Flot 2022; Fresnoza-Flot and Merla 2018; Groes and Fernandez 2018).

Among Latino/a/xs, studies find that some Latino/a/xs do not want to date Blacks, with some college-educated Latinas also preferring to not date Asian men (Feliciano et al 2011; Muro and Martinez 2018). Vasquez-Tokos (2017) finds that Latina women in the US—but not Latino men or white men and women—want to improve their class position through marriages to white men. She argues that Latina women's "triple oppression" creates a structural preference for marrying those with race, class, and gender privilege. In the next sections, I consider the cultural and racial romantic preferences of 1.5-generation Brazilians and situate these desires not just in marriage markets, but in larger cultural dynamics and structural forces.

Culture and Gendered Norms
Several 1.5-generation Brazilians told me they usually dated other Brazilians not just because of opportunity structures, but because of the cultural connections between them. For example, Cristine, a light-skinned woman with golden blond, sun-streaked hair, told me she had previously dated a (white) American but that she usually dates other Brazilians. She explained this in part as a function of who she hangs out with. ("I mostly—not always—but mostly hanging out with the Brazilian people. So that's the people that I get to know . . . that's why we mostly date Brazilian people.") But she also said that she hangs out with and dates Brazilians because of their shared connections, connections that differ from the American man she dated.

> I dated an American guy before. . . . He was the only American. It's not . . . something that I wouldn't do [again] just because he is not Brazilian. . . . It's just because it's a lot of differences, you know what I mean? Like, the way that we—the things we like to do, and all those kind of things.

Throughout the interview, Cristine elaborated on these connections, sharing that Brazilians like Brazilian food and sports, are "friendlier" than Americans, and spend more time with their families and friends, especially on Sundays. These cultural differences became stark for her in her previous relationship with an American man.

But while some Brazilians, like Cristine, were drawn to other Brazilians due to shared culture, other 1.5-generation Brazilian women were adamant that they did *not* want to date Brazilian-raised men. Like Ana Maria, who we met at the beginning of this chapter, these women told me that Brazilian-raised men are too macho, embracing traditional patriarchal gender norms that expect women to stay home and care for their husbands and children. Thus these women, who saw themselves as Americanized—especially in comparison to other Brazilian women—preferred to date American men *or* Brazilian men who grew up in the US.

For example, Camila was dating a white-passing Brazilian man when I met her. But she emphasized that he had migrated when he was young—and thus had largely been raised in the United States. Therefore, according to Camila, he was not "macho."

> Like, my boyfriend. He's not macho at all. . . . And he came here when he was little too. So, yeah, it's different . . . I see, like . . . my parents' friends. Like, how their relationship goes. And I'm like, "Oh my God!" . . . Yeah, [Brazilians] got that whole "macho" thing. Like, guys have to be better. . . . But here in America, [it] is different. Because women are getting themselves in the same level as men. It's not like that in Brazil.

As Camila discussed later in the interview, by women "getting themselves in the same level" as men, she was referring to women's potential to go to college and be *productive wage earners* in the labor market. Importantly, Camila's understanding of Brazilian gender norms is rooted in her observations of Brazilians living in the United States. She sees Brazilian women doing all the housework and caretaking for their husbands and children. In contrast, she told me that "American guys treat women better." Thus she sought out a partner who was raised in the United States and who would appreciate a woman being "on the same level" as him, getting an education and working outside the home.

The perception that Brazilians embrace more traditional gender norms than Americans was not limited to 1.5-generation Brazilian women. Indeed, some 1.5-generation Brazilian men told me they preferred to *not* date American-raised women because they had become too "independent." For example, Fausto told me he likes to date Brazilian or other women from Latin America, like his current Ecuadorian girlfriend, because they appreciate "macho" men like him.

> I'm dating someone that, you know, likes the whole macho thing. . . . She likes it. . . . Most American girls here in Boston, they're very—more independent. They have the more feminist type of mentality. Whereas if they are Brazilian, and just came from Brazil, you say, "Oh, I don't want you to do this," and they're like, "Okay."

Fausto also sees himself as more "jealous" and labeled that characteristic as being very "Brazilian" of him. "I think Brazilians are more—they are very jealous. Very jealous. They're very emotional. That type of stuff . . . They're very protective, you know. So, in ways, I can be like that." It was this gendered and cultural identity that shaped how he perceived not only himself, but who he desired as a romantic partner. He wanted to be the dominant one in the relationship and therefore did not want an "Americanized woman" who he perceived to be "feminist."

The belief that the US is less patriarchal than other places is a sentiment echoed by other 1.5-generation and second-generation young women from Latin America and Asia (Enriquez 2020; Pyke and Johnson 2003). As scholars remind us, however, the perception of gender equality in the US "obscures the day-to-day materiality of American patriarchy" (Pyke and Johnson 2003, 38). But while patriarchy is the reality in the US, most 1.5-generation Brazilians *perceive* the US as having more gender equality than Brazil, dovetailing with scholarship on first-generation Brazilian men and women who perceive the US similarly as they experience changes to gender roles after migration to the US (De Biaggi 2001). These perceptions shaped 1.5-generation Brazilians' romantic partner choices.

White Racial Preferences and Anti-Blackness
As Ana Maria's story at the beginning of this chapter revealed, it was not just perceived cultural gender norms that shaped romantic desires, but race. Indeed, nearly all 1.5-generation Brazilians I met were in relationships with white or white-passing Brazilians. And several respondents, like Ana Maria, were quite explicit about their racial preferences. For example, Camila, whom

we just met, not only wanted to date an American-raised man; she wanted to date white Americans or white American-raised Brazilians. When I asked her why, she responded: "I'm just attracted to them, I don't know. I just can't find myself attracted to an African American.... I don't know, I just can't." In stating her preferences for a white racial partner, Camila was quite explicit in her anti-Blackness. And like the young adults whom Erica Chito Childs (2005) interviewed in the US, she framed this anti-Blackness in terms of "attraction." But importantly, anti-Blackness in romantic relationships is pronounced in Brazil too (Osuji 2019; Twine 1998). Meanwhile, white partners are—and have been—generally seen as more desirable in both the US and Brazil (Chappetta and Barth 2022; Osuji 2019; Twine 1998) and this cannot be separated from white men's dominant racial and economic positions and Black men's disadvantaged economic and racial positions in society.

Camila was not alone in stating this anti-Blackness so explicitly to me. Rodrigo, whom we met earlier in this chapter, also told me he was not attracted to Black partners. Initially he told me he "dated everyone" before stating that he really prefers to date American women. But like other 1.5-generation Brazilians, by "American" he really meant "white American." "I think American women are beautiful. Maybe that's an American thing. I usually just date American girls." When I pushed him on whether he meant American women of all ethno-racial backgrounds, he responded with "No, no. Blond, blue-eyed. White Americans . . . I have dated Black Americans. Um, (one) individual. There was this one girl. Black girl. American girl. Beautiful and I liked her a lot. But definitely an exception on my personal taste."

Rodrigo's stated racial preference reflects a long history of valorizations of light-skinned women who have physical features associated with Northern Europeans and the devaluation of Black women in both the US and Brazil (Goldstein 1999; Osuji 2019; Twine 1998). In the US, Black women are the most likely racial and gender group to be excluded by heterosexual young adults as potential romantic partners (Bany, Robnett, and Feliciano 2014). Indeed, Bany, Robnett, and Feliciano (2014) find that even when white, Asian, and Latino men are open to dating outside their race, they often exclude Black women from consideration, citing a lack of physical attraction.

Pamela, the daughter of an Afro-Brazilian father and a white Brazilian mother, also stated strong preferences for dating—and marrying—a white American. Pamela had inherited many of her mother's European features: a long, narrow face, thin nose, high cheekbones, and light skin. In the winter months, when she stayed out of the sun and straightened her hair, she could pass as white. But other times, especially in the summer months when her skin darkened and her hair curled into ringlets in the New England humidity, Pamela was racialized as brown—especially as "Puerto Rican" or "Indian." But Pamela believed she could climb the ethno-racial hierarchy in the United States by having white children through a marriage to a white American man.

Pamela began the conversation about achieving racial uplift through marriage by telling me that she does not see herself ever marrying someone who is Brazilian or African American.

> I don't see myself marrying somebody that's not American. . . . I mean, I wouldn't marry a Brazilian or somebody that's an African American. Like, I won't date African Americans because of my dad. I don't know why. I'm just not attracted.

According to Pamela, her lack of attraction to Black men was connected to her bad relationship with her Afro-Brazilian father. But as we continued talking, it was clear that there were other racial dynamics at play. It wasn't just "an American" Pamela was interested in marrying—it was a white American. And this preference had been shaped by her own maternal family's racism toward her father. Indeed, Pamela told me that her mom's family had always "joked" that her Afro-Brazilian father had "dirtied" up the family. And when her mother divorced him, her grandfather "joked" that Pamela's mother had finally "cleaned the family up." These racist "jokes" are common in Brazil as white family members of mixed-race couples often use "openly racist humor" that is a "combination of friendliness with antagonism" (Osuji 2019, 164).

Pamela learned very clear messages through these racist jokes that whiteness was good, Blackness was bad, and marrying someone who was Black would further "dirty up" the family. Given her family's racism and their belief that one could "clean up" or "dirty up" through marriage, it's not terribly surprising that Pamela articulated to me that she could improve her own racial status through marriage to a white man.

> That's why I want to marry the whites. [laughing] Get in there good with them! [Laughter] . . . And eventually my fam—I'll be here [moving her

hand up high to indicate the top of the ethno-racial hierarchy]. Because I'll have a white kid! [laughing]

Osuji (2019) argues that mixed-race women in Brazil have long negotiated racial boundaries to their own advantage through marriage in order to achieve racial and social uplift. Meanwhile, Twine (1998) details how many working-class Brazilians with African ancestry have an explicit desire for a white romantic partner in order to have "more beautiful" children; that is, children with lighter skin, straighter hair, and other physical features associated with Europeans. Here we see Pamela express desire for white children to help elevate her own racial status. And while Pamela desired to marry someone who is a white *American*, it was the desire for whiteness, even more than American citizenship, that mattered to her.

Many Americans might be surprised at Pamela's belief that she could "whiten herself" through marriage to a white man and having "whiter kids." But these ideas about race and racial positioning reflect Brazilian racial logics and practices described in the beginning of this chapter. In Brazil, interracial marriages have been common and Brazilians have long perceived that mixed-race people can "whiten" and gain racial and economic status through their marriages. These ideas have traveled across borders (see Joseph 2015) and over generations, impacting Pamela, who had not been to Brazil for over twenty years when we sat down for this interview.

But of course, undocumented 1.5-generation Brazilians are not solely shaped by Brazilian racial ideologies; they also learn about race, racial logics, and racial constructions from their experiences living in the United States. Anti-Blackness is global, and Gabriel, the one respondent who had been racialized as Black in the United States, acutely felt this anti-Blackness. When I first met Gabriel, he had graduated from college and was dating a white American. He said that when he was flying on airplanes, he was often racialized as Muslim (see Garner and Selod 2015; Selod 2018). But during high school, when he was a football star in his mostly white suburb, he was most often racialized as Black and experienced racism, including when he went to the prom with a white American women.

> I was really—what do you call it—viewed as African American when I was growing up. More than Hispanic. I was called the N-word a bunch

of times. . . . In high school, I was a football player. So, I had a lot of fans for the work I did on the field, you know? But I remember one time, I was brought home [by a white girl] and the attitude completely changed. . . . It was like, "Whoa." Almost like a racehorse, you know? I thought of the racehorse called Seabiscuit. They bring the horse inside the living room. [laughing] "What's this horse doing here [laughing] in our home?!"

Gabriel clarified that it was the girl's father, in particular, who had this reaction when Gabriel showed up at her house, underscoring the threat white men feel when Black men date white women (Ferber 1999). Gabriel laughed when telling me story. But like other men I interviewed, he rarely showed sadness when discussing this or any other negative experiences. Laughter was one way of coping. But this experience with white racism from this white woman's family members stayed with him in profound ways. Indeed, it was the only specific example he named as racism during our interviews.

CONCLUSION

A power-without-papers lens demonstrates how immigration law penetrates the most intimate aspects of immigrants' lives, shaping all stages and aspects of their romantic relationships. Hostile immigration laws do negatively impact the romantic lives of 1.5-generation Brazilians, causing uncertainty around revealing a stigmatic identity to a non-Brazilian partner and raising questions about if—and when—to advance a relationship and/or plant roots in the US. Importantly, however, a power-without-papers lens also reveals how illegality articulates with gender, race, and class to shape feelings of desirability, experiences in romantic relationships, *and* choices of romantic partners.

US immigration laws, which offer very few pathways to citizenship, do create structural pressures to marry US citizens. But even with legalization pressures to marry for papers, including from friends and family members, illegality leads the overwhelming majority of 1.5-generation Brazilians *away* from wanting to strategically marry for papers, despite the economic and security benefits that "papers" would bring. That is, despite immigration law "push(ing) young adults to think in terms of papers" (Enriquez 2020, 24), very few 1.5-generation Brazilians explicitly stated that they wish to date and marry US citizens. In part, they did not want to conform to negative stereotypes about undocumented immigrants engaging in marriage fraud. But in the larger anti-immigrant context, they also valued spaces of inclusion and did not want to instrumentally use friends and romantic partners. Furthermore, after hiding illegality for much of their lives, they did not want to keep additional secrets.

Rather than a partner's American citizenship, it was a partner's adherence to traditional gender norms and race that determined who 1.5-generation Brazilians desired to date and marry. Both 1.5-generation Brazilian men and women perceived Brazilians as embracing more traditional gendered norms. Some 1.5-generation Brazilian women in particular had strong preferences to date American-raised men who they believed would support their educational and career ambitions to be productive wage earners, not just reproductive laborers.

Nearly all 1.5-generation Brazilians were in relationships with white or white-passing partners or expressed a desire to marry someone who was white. Some 1.5-generation Brazilians were also explicit about their desire to *not* date Black people. These racial preferences cannot be understood without situating them in the global system of racial capitalism and the histories of racial projects in the US and Brazil, where whiteness is valued and Blackness is devalued. Yet, while whiteness is valued and brings material, public and psychological wages in both contexts, racial logics and practices differ in each national context. And these Brazilian ideas about race—especially the perception that one can whiten themselves through marriage to white partners and have white children—is evidence of what Tiffany Joseph (2015) calls "the transnational racial optic," where ideas about race transfer across borders and take on new meanings in a new national context. In this case, Brazilian ideas about whitening through marriage are one way for 1.5-generation children in the US context—whose families experienced downward racial and class mobility when they migrated, working as racialized undocumented immigrants from Latin America—can try to regain lost status. Pamela was the most explicit about this process of status climbing. But the importance of dating or marrying a white partner was apparent as only a few 1.5-generation Brazilians I met were *not* in relationships with someone who was not white or white-passing.

Thus the articulation of race, class and illegality shapes romantic relationships. And as we will see in the next chapter, power without papers also matters for their sense of belonging in the US. Indeed, despite accruing some of the wages of whiteness, their experiences with illegality, a racialized and stigmatized status in the US, keeps most 1.5-generation Brazilians from identifying as "white." Furthermore, most 1.5-generation Brazilians are ambivalent about identifying as American or eschew identifying as such altogether. Power without papers, then, undermines their sense of belonging in the US.

FOUR   **SENSE OF BELONGING**

American and Ethno-Racial Identities

[My] thought process and everything is American.... [But] I'm Brazilian. One hundred percent ... Especially now that I know—that I've been to Brazil. The culture. The way I am. And where—what I want to be a part of. Not because I want to by choice. But because of how things worked out. How people accept me. Like, how I was accepted in Brazil. And how I was ... I *am* accepted here. You have to pick the place that will accept you better and will give you more opportunities.... Even if I become a US citizen, like, it's been such a struggle. There was so much, "No." You know? "No, we don't want you. No, you can't go to school. No, you're going to have to wait. No—another seven years." Why would you say, "Oh, now I'm American"? And wave the flag? Are you kidding? Like, you know what I mean? After somebody, like you—somebody's basically spit in your face, and now you're going to go, "Now I'm American"? That's not going to happen.

—Gabriela, 29

When I met with Gabriela for the second time at her home in suburban Massachusetts, she was no longer undocumented. After migrating to the US at age four and living in the US illegally for the next two decades, she finally got her green card in her early twenties (see Chapter 2). But even though she was (finally) a lawful permanent resident and felt culturally American in some ways ("my thought process and everything"), she did *not* identify as an American. Nor did she anticipate identifying as American in the future, even if she became a US citizen. She emphasizes legal exclusion from American institutions, especially education, and the lack of acceptance she felt. This exclusion felt particularly stark when contrasted with the feelings of acceptance she had when she was finally able to travel to Brazil for the first time in twenty years after getting her green card.

Some scholars might define Gabriela's refusal to identify as American—and to embrace being Brazilian instead—as a *reactive ethnicity*, one that arises due to rejection and exclusion from American society (Massey and Sánchez 2010; Rumbaut 2008). In this chapter, I build upon this work emphasizing the negative impact of exclusion on American identification to argue that Gabriela's identity as Brazilian—and not as American—is a story about the complex articulation of race, ethnicity, class, *and* legal status in the US. That is, Gabriela and most other 1.5-generation Brazilians who grew up undocumented largely do not identify as (fully) American as they receive messages—through policy, discourse, everyday interactions, and opportunity structures—that "real Americans" are white citizens whose ancestors *only* hail from Europe (*not* Latin America too) and who are economically advantaged in American society. In contrast, they perceive white Americans and white institutions racializing undocumented immigrants as nonwhite (Asad and Clair 2018; Menjívar 2021) and stigmatizing them as poor, as criminals, and as "takers" in American society (Chavez 2013).

In Gabriela's case, she can pass as white in the US. Yet, as we will see, she does not *feel* white in the US—largely due to her experiences with illegality. In Brazil, Gabriela, who has a Portuguese last name and light olive skin, almond-colored eyes, a heart-shaped face, and long, silky, straight, light brown hair, *does* consider herself white. In the US, however, her ethno-racial identity is more complicated, just as it is for other Latin American immigrants (Dowling 2014; Golash-Boza 2006; Joseph 2015; Negrón-Gonzales 2011; Roth 2012; Valdez 2011). She told me she will sometimes mark "white" on official forms, especially if there is no option to write in "Brazilian." She has also sought and successfully benefited from the wages of whiteness (as seen in Chapters 1 and 2). But marking "white" on forms and sometimes passing as white does not mean she *identifies* as white in the US. "White in America," she told me, is:

> All the American kids who don't care about school. Mommy and Daddy are paying. I'm not one of those....White in the US is one hundred percent white. American. That kind of life... Born in America. Went to school. Is probably in college. Will move on. Parents own a home somewhere. That's white.

Importantly, for Gabriela, being white in the US is not just about European ancestry or one's skin color and physical features; it is also about *citizenship* and *social class*. In other words, in Gabriela's mind, whiteness in the US is so inextricably linked to citizenship and class that for her to racially identify as white would mean she had citizenship since birth ("born in America"), come from a family who enjoys a certain economic standard of living in American society ("parents own a home somewhere"), and have access to opportunities to increase one's economic standing (that is, "is probably in college, will move on"). Meanwhile, her life as an undocumented immigrant has been in stark contrast to white Americans. For much of her life, she could not access in-state tuition, federal loans, and federal grants in order to pay for college, legally work, travel internationally, or vote. Thus, because she was not a legally recognized member of the US political community, she was formally denied what T. H. Marshall (1950) refers to as *political rights*—those rights associated with legal citizenship that involve exercising political power (for example, voting in members of Congress). Furthermore, she had also been denied what Marshall refers to as *social rights*—rights associated with being able to achieve a certain economic living standard in society, including access to welfare programs like Pell Grants and loans for college), and *civil rights* (rights necessary for individual freedom).

How did she racially identify then? As explored in Chapter 1, Gabriela does not identify as Latino/a/x. To be clear, she believes that the racist xenophobia of white Americans and its institutions targets her, just as it targets all undocumented immigrants from Latin America. ("We're all the same. We're all illegals. And we're all from South America. People don't even know where Brazil is.")[1] But as explored in Chapter 1, in this racist context, Gabriela draws boundaries between herself and other Latin American immigrants, claiming that Brazilians come from higher social classes, work harder to assimilate, and are of a higher status in the US. Instead of embracing a white or Latino/a/x ethno-racial identity, Gabriela told me her race in the US is "Brazilian," echoing an ethno-racial identity claim of many first-generation Brazilians (Margolis 2007).

Gabriela's complicated sense of belonging—feeling Americanized, but not identifying as American (or even, as a hyphenated Brazilian-American), marking white on forms and working to accrue the wages of whiteness, but not identifying racially as white in the US—points to the need for a power-without-papers perspective, one that captures how power and marginalization articulate together to shape the identities of 1.5-generation Brazilians. By focusing on whether (and why) 1.5-generation Brazilians identify as American (or not)—and their ethno-racial identities—we can see how interlocking inequalities come together to configure internalized meanings of belonging. Specifically, in Gabriela's case, a power-without-papers perspective brings to the forefront how illegality as a racialized—and classed—status that denies her political, social, and civil rights leads her away from identifying as American *and* as white, despite passing as white at times.

The power-without-papers lens in this chapter also builds on the work of scholars who call for more attention to the intersection of race, ethnicity, *and* legal status in shaping the sense of belonging for children of immigrants (Joseph and Golash-Boza 2021; Negrón-Gonzales 2011). While race and ethnicity are often assumed to be—and are treated as—analytically distinct concepts, other scholars argue that there is overlap, which creates complicated dynamics for immigrants who do not fit neatly into preestablished US racial categories (Cornell and Hartman 2006; Telles 2018). Since the 1990s, assimilation scholarship has largely emphasized how some 1.5- and second-generation immigrants use ethnicity, which is often conceptualized as shared cultural heritage, to distance themselves from a stigmatized African American underclass and achieve upward mobility (Alba and Nee 2005; Portes and Rumbaut 2001; Portes and Zhou 1993; Waters 2001; Zhou 1997). But recently scholars have critiqued these assimilation perspectives for 1) failing to center race in the analysis, 2) ignoring how structural racism has created and perpetuated the US racial and economic hierarchy, and 3) disregarding the cultural and class heterogeneity that exists in Black America (Clergé 2019; 2014; Joseph and Golash-Boza 2021) .

Increasingly, scholars of the 1.5-generation have turned to the work of W. E. B. Du Bois, arguing that his insights are important for understanding the identities of children of immigrants, including 1.5-generation undocumented immigrants (Aranda, Vaquera, and Sousa-Rodriguez 2015; Joseph and Golash-Boza 2021). For the purposes of this chapter, there are several important Du Boisian insights. First, as detailed in the Introduction of this book, in *Black Reconstruction* Du Bois (1935) demonstrates how the lived experiences and identities of the working class are intersectional. For example, he details how *white workers*, despite being economically exploited by the capitalist class, identified as white because the capitalist class provided them with psychological, public, *and* material wages *relative* to Black workers. This included but was not limited to bringing them into the ranks of the police. Thus Du Bois underscores how race and class articulate together, detailing how working-class white men's racial position *within* the working-class structure led the white worker to identify more with his *whiteness* than his common economic interests with Black slaves. In so doing, Du Bois makes clear that we can't make sense of identity without understanding how race and class (and gender) articulate together in a particular historical conjuncture.

Meanwhile, Du Bois's work on "double consciousness," which Itzigsohn and Brown (2020) call "the pillar of Du Bois's analysis on subjectivity," is important for understanding how racialized people understand themselves in this modern era of neoliberal racial capitalism (27). In *The Souls of Black Folk*, Du Bois (1965) argues that the problem of the twentieth century was the "color line" separating the white world from the Black world. He argues that on one side of the color line, which he conceptualizes as a "veil" that operates as a one-way mirror, white people have the power to define themselves and other racial groups *and* can only see their own definitions and reflections. But on the other side of the veil, Blacks can see both worlds. Thus Black people know how the white world perceives and dehumanizes them.

According to Du Bois, these structural dynamics give rise to double consciousness, or a sense of twoness, for Black Americans. That is, Black Americans' sense of self is shaped both by how they appear to themselves *and* how they are dehumanized by white society. In this way, Du Bois's work on double consciousness captures the psychological impact of stratified citizenship for Black Americans. On the one hand, Black Americans have been granted *legal (political) citizenship*, which formally makes them members of the American political community and entitles them to certain rights denied to noncitizens. On the other hand, even with formal legal citizenship Black Americans do not receive *social citizenship* as they are labeled "problems" by white society and denied being treated as socially and economically valued members.

Joseph and Golash-Boza (2021) contend that in the twenty-first century, racialized legal status "represents a new variation of Du Bois' 'color line,' because of how these statuses generate cumulative disadvantages and exclusion for citizens and immigrants of color, particularly the undocumented." They remind us that Du Bois's conception of the color line is global—where race, color, nationality, and legal status shape the extent to which people are excluded or included by a nation-state. Furthermore, they argue that the lens of double consciousness resonates in the contemporary era for immigrants or citizens of color *and* undocumented immigrants, including *white* undocumented immigrants, as all these groups are treated as "problems" by white American society and its institutions. We see this in the case of Gabriela, who knows that she is culturally American, but that white society classifies all undocumented immigrants from Latin America as "illegals". Thus her sense of self is not only shaped by her own understandings of who she is in the world, but how white Americans and white institutions racialize, stigmatize, and exclude undocumented immigrants from Latin America.

Meanwhile, Aranda, Vaquera, and Sousa-Rodriguez (2015) also argue that 1.5-generation undocumented immigrants develop a sense of twoness because of the tension between feeling culturally like an American (having been raised in the US) and the trauma of being legally excluded. They argue that illegality is a source of personal trauma (because of laws that exclude them from opportunities and securities) *and* collective trauma (from laws and practices that target their families and communities) that ultimately leads to *ambivalently American identities* for undocumented immigrants. In Gabriela's case, however, she does not feel ambivalently American: she rejects an American identity altogether.

Ultimately, then, this chapter examines the articulation of race, ethnicity, class, and legal status—and the role of double consciousness—in shaping feelings of belonging. Specifically, I consider how privilege and legal marginalization hang together to configure internalized meanings of belonging. Do most 1.5-generation Brazilians, like Gabriela, develop a sense of twoness, leading them to eschew identifying as American? And how is this connected to their ethno-racial identities? Do those who pass as white, but who have been legally excluded from citizenship, identify as white in the US? And what about the few respondents who could not pass as white? What do their identities teach us about the articulation of race, ethnicity, class, and legal status in this particular conjuncture?

In the next sections, I examine 1.5-generation Brazilian's identities as American before turning my attention to ethno-racial identities.[2] Importantly, as the case of Gabriela demonstrates, their (non)American identities and ethno-racial identities are interconnected. I find that three-fourths of 1.5-generation Brazilians who were undocumented during the transition to adulthood report a sense of twoness—that is, they feel culturally American, but do not fully identify as American. While some 1.5-generation respondents who report a sense of twoness ambivalently identify as a hyphenated

Brazilian-American, others, like Gabriela, eschew an American identity altogether. Gender also matters. For example, women's sense of twoness is connected to feeling culturally like an *American woman*, not a Brazilian woman, as they reject patriarchal gendered norms they see as common in Brazil (see Chapter 3).

The vast majority of white-passing 1.5-generation Brazilians also do not racially identify as white in the US. They point to their legal exclusion from citizenship (and the rights and opportunities it confers) *and* racialized anti-immigrant discourses, policies, and treatment. Their perspectives underscore that being an undocumented immigrant from Latin America is a racialized immigration status (Asad and Clair 2018; García 2017; Menjívar 2021; Patler 2014) as the media, politicians, and everyday Americans conflate illegality with being poor, nonwhite, and coming from Latin America (Chavez 2013). In contrast, they see a white racial identity in the US as inextricably connected to citizenship, protection from deportation, access to welfare programs, and other civil and political rights.[3] Ultimately, like Gabriela, most have a hard time racially classifying themselves in the US and struggle to choose any ethno-racial categorization.

AMERICAN (AND NON-AMERICAN) IDENTITIES

As shown in Table 4.1, the American identities of the 43 respondents who experienced illegality fell into three groups: 1) ambivalent Brazilian-American identities, 2) non-American identities, and 3) secure Brazilian-American identities.[4] Importantly, both the respondents who expressed ambivalent Brazilian-American identities *and the* respondents who rejected an American identity reported a sense of twoness. That is, both of these groups felt culturally American, often much more so than Brazilian. But the first group *hesitated to* embrace an American identity—while the second group *outright rejected* an American identity—due to their experiences as undocumented Latin American immigrants. In contrast, those with a secure Brazilian-American identity did not report a sense of twoness. Rather, their secure Brazilian-American identities were an *affirmation* of their ties to two cultures and not a response to exclusion in the US.

Of those who were still undocumented during the transition to adulthood and thus experienced the increased salience of illegality in their lives

TABLE 4.1. (Non)American Identities of 1.5-Generation Brazilians

	AMBIVALENTLY BRAZILIAN-AMERICAN (SENSE OF TWONESS)	DEFINITELY NON-AMERICAN (SENSE OF TWONESS)	SECURELY BRAZILIAN-AMERICAN (NO SENSE OF TWONESS)
LPR by age 18 [11]	0 (0.0%)	2 (18.2%)	9 (81.8%)
Undocumented after age 18 [32]	10 (31.3%)	14 (43.7%)	8 (25.0%)

(Gonzales 2011; Silver 2012), 31.3 percent ambivalently identified as American while 43.7 percent eschewed an American identity altogether. In contrast, only 18.2 percent of respondents who had their green cards by age eighteen reported similar struggles in embracing an American identity.[5] In this way, we see some evidence that illegality operates as a master status in shaping internalized meanings of belonging, since those who were undocumented at age eighteen were much more likely than their peers to reject and/or ambivalently identify as American. Yet at the same time, and as the next sections reveal, it is clear that race, class, nationality, and (il)legality articulate together in nuanced ways to shape the specific meanings of the identities they assert.

Ambivalently Brazilian-American Identities
In 1992, Toni Morrison, American writer and 1993 Nobel Peace Prize winner, told the *Guardian*, "In this country, American means white. Everybody else has to hyphenate" (Shah and Adolphe 2019). For Morrison, hyphenated American identities capture the reality for nonwhites of never being seen as fully American. Scholarship backs this up. Indeed, Golash-Boza (2006) finds that Latino/a/xs who perceive discrimination are more likely to identify as hyphenated Americans. Meanwhile, Flores-González (2017) finds that Latino/a/x/ millennial citizens are often uncomfortable identifying as American given their experiences with race and racism.

For 31.3 percent of the 1.5-generation Brazilians who were still undocumented at age eighteen, a hyphenated Brazilian-American identity also captures a sense of not feeling fully American. This group identified as *Brazilian-American* but they were ambivalent about whether they could truly claim the "American" part of their identity. They reported a sense of twoness, telling me that on the one hand they see themselves as culturally American and often feel little connection to Brazil. But on the other hand, they do not believe that white Americans or white institutions see or treat them similarly. Sometimes they emphasized that political citizenship—that is, being legally considered a member of the political community—would be enough for them to consider themselves American. But other times they were not so sure, given the lasting impacts of illegality.

Marcus, who was DACAmented and in his midthirties by the third time we met, described identifying as ambivalently Brazilian-American. At first he told me he most identified as Brazilian-American. In truth, however, he said he felt culturally American, not Brazilian. But he could not bring himself to just call himself "American" because he felt like "the other," underscoring his sense of twoness in the US. For Marcus, this feeling of being an other was not *only* about his legal status. Rather, it was a feeling connected to the articulation of all of his identities: he was an undocumented immigrant from Latin America who did not conform to hegemonic white masculinity. Indeed, Marcus perceived himself as sensitive and artistic and in contrast to "alpha males." And while he was proud of his creativity, he also felt like it made him less attractive to women.

He channeled his feelings of being "the other" through creative outlets, especially in writing horror stories. "Horror," he told me, can be "a metaphor for anything. . . . Like if you feel like an outsider . . . you can just take whatever you feel and you make it physical and that's (a) horror movie." One of the horrors Marcus had dealt with was the concrete possibility of being deported. During our second interview, Marcus and his family members had just had their adjustment in status applications denied, putting them in danger of removal. While Marcus was never deported—and eventually applied successfully for DACA—the insecurity of being an unwanted, immigrant "other" had stayed with him. And he used his life experiences, as well as stories of immigration raids in towns across America, to inform his latest screenplay, in which the main immigrant character moves to a small "cult town" of "white people." In this way, his horror story captures white society's racism toward immigrant "others" like him. Importantly, like most 1.5-generation Brazilians I met, Marcus was white-passing (especially when hanging out with his white American friends, who were the majority of his friends) but had also been racialized as nonwhite. For example, he told me that white people "who are in charge" racialize him as Hispanic when they find out he is Brazilian. "They (white people in charge) always assume if you're Brazilian, you probably speak Spanish . . . you are Hispanic." Thus, while he could pass as white, had a social circle of primarily white Americans, and felt more culturally American than Brazilian, his experiences with being a racialized, undocumented immigrant "other" in certain situations in his life led him away from confidently asserting an unhyphenated American identity.

Like Marcus, Rodrigo, who was twenty-four and still undocumented the second time we met, also told me he identified as Brazilian-American. Yet, as soon as he asserted this identity, he quickly wavered on whether it was accurate because he was not certain that he nor anyone else in any precarious legal situation could truly embrace the "American" part of this hyphenated identity. He briefly thought about calling himself an "Americanized Brazilian" before backtracking, telling me "Americanized Brazilian" sounded like "pasteurized milk"—as if he had altered some piece of himself rather than recognizing he is *both* culturally Brazilian and American.[6] Yet, as culturally Brazilian *and* American as he felt, he was still ambivalent about claiming the "American" part of this identity given his precarious legal status. He explained this by telling me how even those in liminal legality are not really "American" since they are excluded from political citizenship.

> They're not citizens. So they're not Americans. . . . So they're slightly documented. To be honest, I mean, they're really not [Americans]. If they were to get arrested, they would get deported. These papers don't keep you here. These papers are actually—they're negated the moment you get a criminal record. So, I mean, how much freedom do you have? You know, you are a traffic violation away from . . . they're not American. At all. Like, I use the word *American* because it initiates a process where they're being accepted. You know what I mean? But they're not. They're really not. . . .

Here Rodrigo underscores the vulnerability of those in liminal legality, or gray areas of legal membership (Cebulko 2014; Menjívar 2006). At the time of this interview, he was not in liminal legality. His initial application for DACA had been denied and he was waiting for a decision on an appeal he filed. But he knew that even with DACA, he would be vulnerable to deportation and have limited freedom, undermining his ability to identify as American.

Rodrigo, like Marcus, was white-passing. But he also had experiences with being racialized as Hispanic, including by public transit authorities. And given his deportability as an undocumented immigrant, these instances of racialization made him feel particularly vulnerable, especially when he compared himself to Latino/a/xs who had citizenship. Indeed, according to Rodrigo, Latino/a/xs *with* lawful status, like Puerto Ricans, have way more "confidence" than him, especially in interactions with the cops because they are *legally* considered Americans. From Rodrigo's perspective, Puerto Ricans might be arrested and go to jail for fighting, but he, as a racialized *undocumented* immigrant, could be arrested, jailed, *and* deported. He knew this reality on a personal level—his older brother had been deported.

Yet, despite not being sure he could claim an American identity, Rodrigo, like Marcus, felt that he was very culturally "American" and pointed to his schooling experiences in the United States.

> The way I formulate my sentences. Very American. It's almost like, the way they teach you in school, to make your thesis statement. Three supporting statements. Summarize. It's how I speak, you know? That's very American of me. Because of my schooling.

Thus, given his socialization experiences in the US, Rodrigo often felt more culturally American than some Brazilians that he knew, even those who are naturalized US citizens.

> One of the girls I work with ... she has her papers now. She married somebody. Ended up getting her papers that way. And she uses that word. She like, jokes around. She's like "I'm American!" And she has a very thick Brazilian accent. And it's very funny. Like if you were to compare "who is American?" [Not by the] paperwork. Just lifestyles. And I guess by any sense of the American culture, I'm much more American than she is. But, she has her papers. And she's a citizen. So at this point, for me to say, she's American ... she actually is.

Despite feeling he was culturally *more* American than Brazilians who are naturalized US citizens, Rodrigo emphasizes that someone with citizenship "actually" is an American. In this way, Rodrigo suggests that formal political citizenship, more than a cultural feeling, is what is necessary for an American identity. And without formal political citizenship, he is ambivalent about claiming the "American" part of the hyphenated Brazilian-American identity. Yet he just couldn't think of a better term to capture his identity.

Andréa, who is also white-passing and was a lawful permanent resident by the time of our second interview, also told me that she most identifies as "Brazilian-American." But as soon as the words "Brazilian-American" left her mouth, she immediately expressed skepticism over choosing this identity. "I'm not even really sure what (that identity) means." Andréa, who had been undocumented until she was in her midtwenties, explained how it was her experiences with illegality as a young adult that led to her skepticism.

> I tend to feel more American. But at the same time, I'm always told by American people that I'm not American. . . .You know, representatives. Like, elected officials or people who have to look at my immigration status to let me do anything . . . So it's kind of like, by the people who have the power to decide things for me, [they] are always very happy to let me know that I'm not American and, therefore, can't do any of the things that I was trying to do. Like the intern[ship] . . . Even before then, like going to college and getting a job and getting a driver's license. Like you're always very aware of the fact that you're not American.

Notably, Andréa explicitly connects her previous experiences of (il)legality with economic vulnerability in a capitalist economy (her inability to *legally* earn wages through a paid internship or job) *and* the US government's denial of basic social and civil elements of citizenship that (most) other Americans enjoy, rights that T. H. Marshall and W. E. B Du Bois argue are important for full inclusion in a democratic society. Specifically, Andréa names her inability to go to college, to get a job, and to get a license. As described in Chapter 2, the US government denies her, as an undocumented immigrant, access to federal grants and loans, a social welfare policy to which (most) low- and middle-income Americans who are lawfully present are entitled. Meanwhile, a driver's license, which Andréa could not lawfully get when she was in her late teens and early twenties, has long been an important marker of adulthood (Urry 2007) and "essential for participation in economic and civic life" (Epp, Maynard-Moody, and Haider-Markel 2014, 17).

Andréa was no longer undocumented during this conversation. But the negative material and social impacts of illegality during the transition to adulthood have remained. Andréa was twenty-eight and *still* pursuing her bachelor's degree when we met up for a second interview. And while she was glad to finally live on campus and have "the college experience" at a liberal arts school, this experience did not happen at the age she had hoped it would. Indeed, she was at least six years older than her college-aged peers at her school. Moreover, she had lost at least six years in the labor market working *with* a college degree.

Like Marcus and Rodrigo, however, Andréa emphasized that she truly did *feel* culturally American. This was especially true in comparison to her Brazilian female peers.

> The [Brazilian] culture as a whole—they're focused on raising their daughters to be wives and mothers. . . . A lot of Brazilian girls are focused on getting married or always having a boyfriend. And I know so many girls who are fifteen, they already have their weddings planned out. They just need the groom. Like literally. They just need the groom. Because they have it all planned out. And so they're always thinking about getting married and raising a family and so focused on their physical appearance. And I don't care about those things at all. They're like "Oh, you're Americanized. You grew up in America so those things aren't as important to you." . . . Let me go to college or get a job. Like having a baby and starting a family isn't a priority.

Andréa's sense of herself as culturally American is connected to her own aspirations to go to college and work in productive wage labor, aspirations she believes are a function of growing up in the US. In contrast, she sees Brazilian culture and Brazilian-raised girls to be focused on reproductive labor. In this way, Andréa's sense of self is shaped by transnational dynamics and rooted in the intersection of gender, class, and the nation-state. That is, she thinks about her gender, cultural identity, and labor market aspirations in relationship to women raised in Brazil, contrasting them with her experiences as the daughter of Brazilian immigrants who was raised in the US.

Leila, who was also white-passing and also identified as Brazilian-American, articulated a sense of twoness as well. She told me that she felt "more in touch with the American culture than the Brazilian culture" due to her "American upbringing." Her sense of being culturally American was reinforced by Brazilians who constantly reminded her that she is not *really* Brazilian. "Brazilians tell me left and right—'you are not Brazilian!'" Yet, given the way that

American society has excluded her as an undocumented immigrant, especially during the transition to adulthood, Leila could not bring herself to fully claim an American identity. In particular, Leila notes exclusion from accessing well-paying jobs in the labor market and from traveling freely around the world like other American students.

> I would feel silly saying that [I'm an American]. I would feel silly. Because my reality is that I'm an illegal immigrant. I always have been. Anytime that I'm by myself with the thought of, you know, where I live. And my life . . . I still feel very much like an illegal immigrant. Like when I was in school, when I was in college. I think that's where it made more sense. It sort of . . . was more real for me. Right? Because when I was in high school, everybody has a crap job anyway. Everybody works at Bob's store or everybody works at McDonald's. . . . But when you go off to college, you can study abroad. You are thinking about where you are going to work once you are [not at] school. . . . I remember my sister not returning for an interview at [a tech company] where they loved her because they were going to do a background check on her, you know? My sister was—she had a freakin' 3.9 in comp sci *at college*. Very smart girl. And she did excellent in her first two interviews or something and they were going to bring her back for a third round. But then she found out that she had to, you know, prove citizenship or something. So she didn't go back. So, you know, here I am in school and here are my friends that, you know, going to vacation in the Bahamas. They are doing fun stuff. Going other places that—I can't join them. And not only can I not join them, I have to lie about why I can't join them. You know? And when you're nineteen or twenty and your focus is on having fun, and just doing good school. That sucks. That's like the worst possible thing, you know? That's the worst possible reality.

As Leila described it, her legal status became more salient after she left high school (Cebulko 2014; Gonzales 2011; Silver 2012). But importantly, it is clear that illegality articulates with social class in shaping her sense of exclusion once she went to college. That is, she perceived everyone as having a low-status job in high school. Thus she did not feel too different from her peers. But expectations changed for her in college, as her new peer group pursued options that allowed them to reap their investments in a college education and travel internationally over spring break.[7] Importantly, Leila's Brazilian middle-class roots allowed her to overcome financial barriers to college (as described in

Chapter 2). But, once she was there, her undocumented status prevented her from engaging in the (upper) middle-class lifestyles of her American college peers (for example, traveling to the Bahamas) *and* she worried about her postgraduation workplace opportunities. Furthermore, due to the stigma of illegality, she did not feel like she could be honest about why she did not fully participate in their social worlds.

The negative impacts with legal exclusion were so profound for her that she was not sure she would ever consider herself an American, even if she became a US citizen.

> I feel like if I were to say "I'm American," it passes the impression that I was born and raised here. And I feel like my experiences are different. My experiences are very different. And because of my experiences, I am the person I am. And I have the beliefs I have. And I have the personality I have probably because of, you know, my experiences. So I don't know—I don't know that I would say I am an American.

Legal exclusion from formal citizenship during the transition to adulthood has led Leila away from saying "I am an American." Culturally, however, she feels much more American than Brazilian. Thus, this sense of twoness, of feeling culturally American but legally excluded, has led her to identify as "Brazilian-American" instead. Yet her adoption of a hyphenated Brazilian-American identity stands in contrast to some of her 1.5-generation Brazilian peers, like Gabriela, who eschewed an American identity altogether.

Not American: Eschewing an American Identity
Nearly 44 percent of 1.5-generation Brazilians who were still undocumented at age eighteen eschewed an American identity altogether. In contrast, only 18.2 percent of respondents (a dark-skinned man and a white-passing woman) who had their green cards by age eighteen did not identify as American.[8] Like those who asserted ambivalent Brazilian-American identities, respondents who rejected an American identity expressed a sense of twoness. That is, on one hand they did feel culturally American. But on the other, their experiences and perceptions of racialized legal exclusion by the American government, institutions, and white Americans in everyday interactions led them to reject an American identity, including a hyphenated American identity.

Like Gabriela, some 1.5-generation Brazilians who rejected an American identity asserted a Brazilian one instead. For example, Sandra, who was undocumented during our first interview but had DACA by the third time we met, only identifies as Brazilian, despite feeling culturally American:

> I mean, I have lived here [in the US] for such a long time. But I have had the struggles of anybody.... For example, if somebody just came here today, they would face the same kind of struggles, you know? So it's like, you can't really identify with the country that you're trying to fight every step of the way, you know?... They don't deserve—sorry, they don't deserve to have me as an American. No insult to you [nodding to me, the interviewer].

Sandra, who was white-passing, felt no ambivalence in rejecting an American identity. Given her experiences "fight[ing] every step of the way," she did not think the country "deserve[d her]."

Some 1.5-generation Brazilians who rejected an American identity refused to put themselves in any box. For example, Elisabete, whom we met in the opening vignette of this book, did not identify as American. But she also did not identify as Brazilian. "I don't fit in anywhere. I just feel like me," she told me. But underscoring her sense of twoness, Elisabete did *feel* very culturally American even as she rejected an American identity. When I asked her why she eschewed an American identity given how culturally American she felt, she emphatically replied: "Because they don't want me. So screw them."

By "them" Elisabete was referring to the white-controlled government. But importantly, while Elisabete was clearly frustrated by her formal legal exclusion from the political, social, and civil dimensions of citizenship by the US government, Elisabete also felt a disconnect from her American friends, many of whom were white. "My experiences are unique to me in my group of friends." She admitted that she sometimes grew frustrated with her American friends' complaints, given their privilege as US citizens who could pursue whatever opportunities they desired. "My friends complain and I just can't relate... [like] 'I can't believe you are complaining to me of all people!'"

Like Leila, Elisabete said that even if she became a US citizen, she wasn't sure she'd ever identify as American. While she wanted the legal rights that US citizenship confers (such as the right to vote), she told me she would have trouble "professing allegiance to the United States" because she is "very disappointed in the government." Ultimately, she said she could only imagine identifying as American *if* the American government treated all immigrants better. But in that moment, she told me, "I don't really feel accepted," not only because of how the US government treats her, but because of how it treats *all* undocumented immigrants, who she knows are racialized and stigmatized. Thus it was not just her direct experiences with illegality that mattered for her sense of belonging, but also the US government's treatment of all immigrants in her legal position.

Other 1.5-generation Brazilians who eschewed an American identity altogether asserted an "Americanized Brazilian" identity instead. This was the case for Sabine, who was also white-passing and knew she benefited from the articulation of her racial appearance, nonaccented English, and US education (see Chapter 1). Notably, Sabine said she felt very little connection to Brazil, Brazilian culture, or the Brazilian community. But due to legal exclusion in the US, she could not bring herself to identify as an American, even a hyphenated Brazilian-American, despite feeling culturally American:

> It's more like—not feeling like I am Brazilian. Like, I feel that, you know, it's part of who I am. But just no longer. I don't have a connection to that part as much. Except through my parents that keep that connection, you know? Except through like immigration. Which is a *huge* reality check. "You're not, you know, American. You're not—" It just reminds me that like, I'm not [American], you know? As much as I have all this life . . . that I feel like very similar to a lot of my friends who are US citizens who live here . . . I am constantly reminded that I'm not [American].

Sabine was married to a white American man and feels socially accepted in her everyday life. But the legal exclusion by white-controlled American institutions undermines her identity as American. Specifically, she points to "Immigration"—her term for US Citizenship and Immigration Services (USCIS), the Department of Homeland Security (DHS), and any branch of the US government that excludes her on the basis of her legal status.

Sabine was not the only one to choose an "Americanized Brazilian" identity. Alexia, who migrated as a young teen, also felt culturally American and disconnected from Brazilian culture. Yet she also felt unable to claim an American identity, even a hyphenated Brazilian-American identity, due to her experiences with a racialized immigration status. Underscoring the articulation of race and legal status and its dehumanizing impacts on her sense of self, Alexia explicitly talked about discrimination against her as an undocumented immigrant as racism. "It makes you feel like less of a person, especially if you have somebody that's racist against your immigration status. . . . I am not happy when people are racist against me."

Like most 1.5-generation Brazilians I met, Alexia is white-passing but has also faced anti-immigrant racism from white Americans, especially when she first arrived in the US and did not speak English. She also had experienced the pain of deportation, as her mother had been deported when she was a teenager (Golash-Boza 2015). These dehumanizing experiences with illegality—in addition to the blocks she faced to going to college and legally working—led to her sense of twoness, where she felt culturally American, but knew others, especially white Americans, did not see her this way because she was not a US citizen. She described her complicated sense of belonging and identity:

> I barely speak Portuguese at home anymore. I always criticize my husband when he says that certain Brazilian shows are good. Because my adolescence was here and this is not what I learned. . . . And all my friends are Americanized Brazilians. And we barely speak Portuguese. And we only do things the American way. And that's just how we are. [But] we're just not [American]. Because if I say that to someone, they're going to say, "Oh, when did you get your citizenship?" And like, "Oh, but I'm not [a US citizen]." I just feel [American] because I have been here for so long. . . . But "you are not an American!"

Throughout our conversations, though, it was clear that it was not just the government's treatment of Alexia that shaped her sense of belonging as non-American, telling me that to truly identify as "American" she would need more than formal citizenship from the US government. She would also need (white) Americans to see immigrants from Latin America as people.[9] "It doesn't matter how the government sees you, I guess. Everybody around you needs to see you as a person. 'Cause as long as you have discrimination, it doesn't matter how the government sees you." In this way Alexia underscores how important Du Bois's concept of the "veil" is to her sense of belonging and identity, as she is not only aware of her own humanity but is also hyperaware of (white) American institutions—and people's—dehumanization of immigrants from Latin America.

How Lawful Status Before Age Eighteen Matters: Affirming a Secure Brazilian-American Identity

While the majority of 1.5-generation Brazilians who were undocumented at age eighteen articulated a sense of twoness, 25 percent asserted a secure Brazilian-American identity. Like their peers who asserted an ambivalent Brazilian-American identity, this group chose a hyphenated Brazilian-American identity. *The meaning* of this hyphenated choice, however, was very different. That is, they did not choose "Brazilian-American" because they felt excluded from American society. Instead, choosing "Brazilian-American" was an affirmation of their connections to two worlds/cultures/and communities: Brazilian and American. Importantly, while 25 percent of those who were undocumented at age eighteen asserted a secure Brazilian-American identity, more than 80 percent of those who had a green card at age eighteen reported a secure Brazilian-American identity, underscoring the importance of being able to adjust one's status *before* the transition to adulthood for 1.5-generation Brazilians.

Matilda, who had medium brown skin and curly hair and believed that most people saw her as Latina, was one of the 80 percent of respondents who had her green card by age eighteen and asserted a secure Brazilian-American identity. Because she got her green card as a teenager, Matilda never faced formal legal barriers to productive wage labor as an adult. And despite not being able to pass as white in the US, Matilda, who was one of the few Brazilians who had grown up in a primarily Latino/a/x neighborhood, said that she had not experienced racial discrimination during childhood. ("Who would discriminate against me? The Colombians? Or Costa Ricans?" she scoffed.) But her experiences with racial discrimination changed as an adult when she began working in new areas with more white Americans, telling me that "older people, very traditional Americans," often discriminated against her at work.

Despite these experiences with racism, Matilda did not hesitate in telling me she identified as Brazilian-American. Notably absent from her identity discussions were conversations of discrimination she had experienced in her life, even when I probed. Instead she told me she chose a Brazilian-American identity because she felt connected to both cultures. On the one hand, she was very embedded in the Brazilian community in the Greater Boston area: she had married a Brazilian man, went to church with other Brazilians, spoke Portuguese on a daily basis, saw a Brazilian nutritionist, and preferred

Brazilian food and music. As a naturalized citizen, she also had the freedom of mobility (and had traveled back and forth between Brazil and the US). On the other hand, she saw herself as culturally American in important ways. Specifically, she saw herself as an American woman who rejected what she perceived as "chauvinistic" Brazilian gender norms, where "the woman does everything for the guy." For example, after she married her Brazilian husband, she said she tried to adhere to the ideal Brazilian "wife" role, before deciding she was not being true to herself. "I (picked up after him) for a long time, after we got married. But it's like, I did it in order to please him. I just wasn't being myself. (I was trying) to be Brazilian." Thus gender was particularly salient for Matilda when she thought of herself as "Brazilian-American."

Meanwhile, Henrique, who was of Italian heritage and white-passing, was one of the 25 percent of respondents who were still undocumented at age eighteen and who asserted a secure Brazilian-American identity. Expressing no ambivalence about his Brazilian-American identity, he told me he perceives himself as "half and half," explaining that "I know and I follow a lot of American culture . . . but I was born in Brazil, and I was there until I was nine. So I was raised there. I have a lot of Brazilian culture in me. But I am kind of American." He went on to specify that he prefers Brazilian food but American music.

Importantly, unlike other 1.5-generation Brazilians who were undocumented at age eighteen, the salience of illegality during the transition to adulthood was not as acute for him. He told me that while he felt bad for those who wanted to attend college and could not, he never aspired to go to college himself. Furthermore, as a dependent to a primary beneficiary for an adjustment in status, Henrique got his work permit in high school, allowing him to legally work. Thus the negative impacts of illegality were not as salient for him as they were for some of his undocumented peers.

To be sure, Henrique's assertion of a secure Brazilian-American identity was an exception among 1.5-generation Brazilians who were still undocumented at age eighteen. But he was not the only one. Gabriel, who had been racialized as Black, Hispanic, and Muslim in the US (see Chapter 1), experienced barriers due to illegality much more acutely than Henrique during the transition to adulthood. Two of the biggest ones had been: 1) his inability to apply to the US Military Academy at West Point due to his legal status (applicants must be US citizens) and 2) being detained on a trip to Puerto Rico (see

Chapter 1) due to his race and legal status.[10] Furthermore, he reported experiencing racism from Americans in his everyday life, including being called the N-word. Yet, like Henrique, Gabriel felt very culturally connected to both the US and Brazil. He especially felt connected to Brazilian culture through his church. He appreciated Brazilian music and enjoyed how Brazilians were more "easygoing" than Americans. At the same time, he told me, he valued Americans' "punctuality."

Despite the racism and barriers due to illegality he had faced, Gabriel also took a lot of pride in American society and believed the US was the best country in the world. For example, he described his mentality after 9/11.

> You could have airlifted me and dropped me off anywhere with a gun. I was ready for blood. And I think that's the general American consensus. How dare you try to attack America? This is, this is the place to be. The land of the free, home of the brave.

Gabriel's pride in the United States, combined with experiences being racialized as Black, was connected to his identity with the African American community.[11]

> I identify myself more with the African American community because I'm not white. You know what I mean? So, but ... but at the same time, I'm American. A lot of Hispanics, they never adopt being an American. You know, African Americans are American.

As discussed in the Introduction, race in the US has long operated on a Black-white binary, even as indigenous groups and other immigrant groups did not fit neatly into these racial categories. Today, this Black-white binary continues to matter, as immigrants from Asia and Latin America are often seen as "perpetual foreigners" even when they are second- or third-generation Americans (Chavez 2013; Ngai 2004). This history, combined with Gabriel's own experiences with racialization and illegality, shaped Gabriel's understanding of the status hierarchy in the US, his ethno-racial identity, and the boundary-work he engaged in between himself and Hispanic groups throughout our interviews (emphasizing how he chooses to "assimilate" and Hispanics do not).

Gabriel told me that he perceived African Americans as the third most influential and powerful group in the US—after white Americans and white Europeans—and ahead of Asian Americans, Latino/a/xs, and indigenous groups. He told me that African Americans, unlike these other groups, have "a strong voting base. They have established political leaders and figurehead. They've demonstrated power in the past. And they're Americans. They're citizens."[12] While Gabriel knows that he is not white due to his dark skin color, ethno-racially identifying as African American connects him to a group he is racialized to by others, a group he recognizes as American, and a group he perceives as relatively influential and powerful. Indeed, after being denied access to spaces like West Point due to his legal status, he places a premium on political citizenship and the rights it brings, especially the right to vote. And he sees African Americans as a powerful group in this regard.

Thus Gabriel's American identity—or in this case, his secure Brazilian-American identity—is closely connected to his ethno-racial identity. And as explored in the next section, this was also true for many of his white-passing peers. That is, for many, their ethno-racial and (non)American identities were inextricably linked. Specifically, for his white-passing peers who experienced a sense of twoness and rejected an American identity (or ambivalently identified as Brazilian-American), they largely did not racially identify as white in the US. In their minds, a white racial identity conveys citizenship, power, and privilege, things they did not have as an undocumented immigrant adults, underscoring the joining together of race, class, and (il)legality in the US in their minds.

ETHNO-RACIAL IDENTITIES: WHITE-PASSING, BUT NOT WHITE

Throughout the history of the US, a white racial identity has been synonymous with being an American. The dominant position of white Americans has been historically created and structurally perpetuated through slavery, settler colonialism, migration and citizenship laws, welfare state policies that have helped whites accrue generational wealth and power, and white ethnics' own boundary-work, which included locking Blacks out of unions (Chomsky 2018; Du Bois 1965; 1935; Hing 2004; Ngai 2004; Roediger 1991). When I talked to 1.5-generation Brazilians, regardless of their physical appearance and legal status, they were clear: "real Americans" were white American *citizens* with *social class privilege* in the US. For 1.5-generation undocumented, white-passing Brazilians, being white in the US is not only about skin color and other physical features or European ancestry. Instead, a white racial identity is also about being a US citizen, having opportunities in the labor market, and having access to social and civil dimensions of citizenship.

Furthermore, as we will see, many 1.5-generation Brazilians are also clear that white in the United States does *not* include immigrants from Latin America, especially not those who have ever experienced illegality. In this way, they perceive a geographic logic to whiteness in the US, a logic that excludes Latin American immigrants and underscores the complex ways in which race and nationality (among other factors) inform the "global color line" (Du Bois 1965). The US is not just a nation-state, but an empire state (King 2019) with a long history of political and economic interference in Latin America, where the US has extracted resources, overthrown governments, and racialized and exploited populations (Abrego 2014; Golash-Boza 2015; González 2000). Today's dominant discourse and framing of immigrants from Latin America as poor, undocumented, and brown (Chavez 2013) fits into this imperial logic.

Overall, 1.5-generation Brazilians had a hard time positioning themselves racially in the US. Indeed, the vast majority could not give a simple answer to how they ethno-racially identified. While Hispanic and Latino/a/x are technically defined as pan-ethnicities and not as racial groups, most Brazilians, like other groups from Latin America, *perceive* "Hispanic/ Latino/a/x" as a racial group (Hitlin, Brown, and Elder Jr. 2007). And as discussed in Chapter 1, most 1.5-generation Brazilians—especially (but not only) white-passing Brazilians—engage in boundary-work away from a Hispanic and Latino/a/x identity. Indeed, nearly 94 percent of white-passing Brazilians did not identify as Hispanic, while 72 percent of white-passing Brazilians refused to identify as Latino/a/x too.[13] Instead, 1.5-generation white-passing Brazilians often told me their race was "Brazilian" or refused to ethno-racially identify themselves at all.

All but a few 1.5-generation Brazilians told me that would have been considered white in Brazil. But, of the 37 respondents who could pass as white in the United States, only two *racially identified* as white in the US. Thus the vast majority, nearly 95 percent of those who could pass as white, did not identify as white in the United States. In their discussions about why they did not identify as white, they told me that whiteness is reserved for white Americans of European descent who are US citizens, whose family members did not migrate from Brazil (or other Latin American countries), and/or who have social class privilege in the US. In other words, race articulates with citizenship and class.

For example, Camila, who got her green card when she was in her early teens, emphasized that whiteness in the US excludes immigrants from Brazil. Camila has very light olive skin, light brown hair, and believes most people perceive her as Italian. Indeed, both sides of her family had migrated from Southern Europe to Brazil. But Camila does not consider herself white in the US because she is from Brazil. "My mom's side is Italian, my dad's side is Portuguese. So . . . but I don't consider myself white because I was born in Brazil. So, I'm not white."

Álvaro, who had been undocumented the first time we met but was a US citizen by the time I reinterviewed him, told me that he is white in Brazil and will mark Hispanic and white on forms, but does not *identify* as Hispanic nor as white. He explained that he cannot be white in the US since he was born in Latin America.

> I: So you're white in Brazil. How come you're not white here?
> R: I guess—because I was born in Latin America. And then, that was what they decided. If you were born in Latin America, you're not white. So you know what I mean?
> I: Who's "they" that decided?
> R: Well, I mean the forms. Like, the government, in terms of grouping people. Because they're the ones that come up [with] forms. At least for . . . especially like schools. They regulate the census, so they came up with it.

Álvaro's discussion of how "the government" decides your race through official forms, like the census, underscores the power of nation-states and institutions to dictate and construct the boundaries of race (Loveman 2014). Álvaro, who is of Portuguese descent, is rarely racialized as nonwhite in his daily interactions in the US. He speaks English without an accent and has light skin and soft, wavy, medium brown hair. But his understanding of himself as "not white" in the US is rooted in part in how the nation-state asks questions about race on official forms.[14]

Later in our conversation, Álvaro claimed that he would be white in the US if his ancestors had migrated directly from Portugal to the US without first settling in Brazil. "We would be white because of Europe," he told me. Helen Marrow (2003) has argued that "being Latino" has a racial, geographic, and linguistic logic. Here we see that Álvaro's understanding of being white in the US also has a geographic logic. That is, immigrants and their descendants need to migrate directly from Europe to the US, and *not* from Europe to Latin America to the United States. According to Álvaro, then, the geographic logic of whiteness in the US excludes immigrants who migrate from Latin America, even if their ancestry is European.

While Álvaro emphasizes a geographic logic of whiteness, Emílio, who is light-skinned with light brown hair and was undocumented when I met him, points to both the linguistic and geographic logics of race in the US. Emílio told me that most people, based on his physical appearance, think he is white until he starts talking. And once he speaks English with his Brazilian accent, people question his whiteness.

> There's a girl in my school. She always jokes around, because she's white. And the first day of school, I walked in, and she's like, "Oh yes, another white kid!" Just playing around. And I started talking, and she's like, "Oh, you're not white . . ." I'm like, "No, I'm Brazilian" . . . When I was in Brazil, we never had this thing like "Oh, he's white" or "He's Asian" or "He's Black." You know, everybody was Brazilian, and that's it. There's not a lot of difference. Even some people had—like, my grandparents were Italian. And just because they're Italian, I don't say I'm Italian. . . . But here, like, oh, their grandparents are Irish, then they say they are Irish. There's a lot of people who are characterized by their race and stuff. And . . . like, I would say that I was white. But then, when I got here, "Oh, you're Brazilian." I was like, "Okay." I guess white means that you're Caucasian. I don't know. I never really understood that.

While Emílio is white in Brazil, and his physical appearance marks him as white in the US, that changes for him in the US when he starts talking and his peers find out he is Brazilian. In this way, we can see how nonphysical social cues and scripts convey racial identities, including white identities, in the United States (Roth 2012; Saperstein and Penner 2012).

Emílio also underscores how 1.5-generation Brazilians sometimes assert "Brazilian" as their race on official forms—marking "other" and writing in "Brazilian." In this way, being Brazilian goes from being a national identity to an ethno-racial identity in the US (Margolis 2007). For Emílio, a Brazilian identity is preferable to racialized Hispanic identity, as he believes that Americans generally perceive Brazilians as better than Hispanics.

> I think . . . [being Brazilian is] not as bad as Hispanic. Because I think that Hispanic people are seen—when you say, "Oh, he's Spanish," all they think of is all immigrants and stuff. But when you say you're Brazilian, they don't really think that. I guess that when they think of . . . Brazil, they probably think of like, hot girls in bikinis, and Carnaval, and Amazon. That's mostly what they know. . . .

Stereotypes and assumptions about ethno-racial groups in the US vary across place and time (Dowling 2014; Menjívar 2021). But it is also true that different stereotypes of the same ethno-racial group can coexist. Indeed, I heard very different stereotypes of Brazilians from Americans during my fieldwork in the Greater Boston area. For example, when I told Americans in the area that I was doing research with Brazilians, some Americans' assumptions of Brazilians were as undocumented immigrants while others offered up similar stereotypes that Emílio asserted here—as fun-loving and sexual.[15]

Sabine, whom we met earlier in this chapter and who is white-passing, also does not identify as white.

> Race is just, like, a really strange thing to me. And this is why I said it is like, a social construct. Because—especially coming from another country where I was white, you know, like, coming here and being told, "You're not white—you're, you know, whatever you are." It just seems very trivial. Like, it doesn't really matter at the end of the day. But I don't think I would identify myself as white just because, you know, I'm an immigrant. [laughing] And even when I am a US citizen, does that change? Does that mean that I become white? Like, I don't think so. I still immigrated here from another country. . . . And I was from, you know, from *Brazil*. That makes me not white. Maybe. I don't know. It just makes me *feel* not white. . . . I don't feel that I would ever consider myself white in this country.

Here we see Sabine articulate how race is a social construct and that her own race changed from white to nonwhite when she migrated across international borders. Like other 1.5-generation Brazilians, Sabine connects her inability to identify as white in the US to her experiences as an immigrant from

Brazil. Indeed, in another part of our interview, she reiterated what Álvaro had said—that if she or her ancestors had migrated directly from Europe, she might consider herself white in the US.

Throughout the conversation, Sabine thoughtfully ruminated on race as a social construct and the complications of what, exactly, makes someone white. She was particularly struck by her own admission that she could pass as white in the US, but not *feel* white here. As discussed in Chapter 1, Sabine had crossed international borders without a passport and was let back in the US without issue. She understood her privilege in that instance as a function of her physical appearance, educational level, and nonaccented English. But ultimately, despite knowing she benefited from whiteness, she asserted that being white in the US means easy access to material opportunities and benefits, which she did not have for most of her life due to illegality. "Whiteness—it means, just more opportunities, you know? Or easier access. Or benefits too. If you want it, you could have more things. . . . It just means . . . easier access to certain things." Specifically, she articulated that these "things" included easier access to college, labor market opportunities, the freedom to travel internationally, and security from deportation.

Thus it was more than geography that made Sabine feel not white. It was also illegality *and* her family's class position in the US. Her experiences with illegality had kept her from (easily) accessing higher education, economic opportunities, and welfare benefits and from having a sense of security that she and her family members would not be deported. In other words, race, class, and illegality articulate together to configure her ethno-racial identity in the US in this historical conjuncture.

Pamela, who can pass as white in the winter, especially when she straightens her hair, also does not identify as white. Like Sabine, Pamela says that whiteness makes things "easier." In fact, Pamela notes that being born white makes you "normal" and "an American" and is the "best thing that could happen to you."

> The best thing that could ever happen is that you're born white. That's it. . . . Like you're white, you're good to go. Because you have—because when somebody looks at somebody that's not white . . . you go, "Oh, that person's definitely not American." [They're] going to think that they're dirty, or they smell, or they have twenty kids, or . . . you know? Things like that. And white people, you look at somebody, and you're like, "Oh, they're normal."

Like Sabine then, Pamela underscores how whiteness is a system of privileges that makes you "good to go" and brings social acceptance as an "American." Because Pamela was sometimes racialized as Latino/a/x, and because she had been legally excluded from American political citizenship and the social and civil rights it brings, she did not think of herself as white in the US. Instead, like Emílio, Pamela marked "other" and asserted "Brazilian" as her race on official forms.

Yet, as discussed in Chapter 3, Pamela also did not perceive race as static. Rather, she believed she could "become white" through marriage to a white American and having white children. In Brazil, she was white. In the US, she is not currently—but believes she could be in the future. In this way, she brings Brazilian racial logics into her understanding of gaining status in the American hierarchy.

CONCLUSION

We see in this chapter how being undocumented limits the wages of whiteness and presents a major barrier to belonging, even for those who have relative race and class privilege. Illegality during the transition to adulthood negatively impacts 1.5-generation Brazilians' internalized configurations of belonging as American, a finding that dovetails with previous research that finds that Latino/a/x millennials, first-generation immigrants from Latin America, and other undocumented 1.5-generation immigrants do not feel comfortable—or are ambivalent about identifying as American (Aranda, Vaquera, and Sousa-Rodriguez 2015; Flores-González 2017; Golash-Boza 2006; Joseph 2016; 2017). Indeed, most 1.5-generation Brazilians who are undocumented when they turn age eighteen ambivalently identify as a hyphenated Brazilian-American or reject an American identity altogether. In contrast, those who were able to adjust their status to lawful permanent resident by age eighteen were more likely to assert a secure Brazilian-American identity.

In this way, we see the increased salience of undocumented status after age eighteen, as 1.5-generation immigrants are more vulnerable to deportation, legally excluded from the labor market, and denied access to social welfare programs available to their similar-income peers (Gonzales 2011; Silver 2012).

And during the transition to—and experience of—young adulthood, undocumented 1.5-generation Brazilians become acutely aware of how they are not only excluded from formal political citizenship *but* social and civil elements of citizenship (Du Bois 1965; Marshall 1950). Furthermore, they also see just how dehumanized they are by white society—both its institutions and its people.

I argue that Du Bois's concept of double consciousness is particularly important for understanding their experiences. Like other racially and legally marginalized groups, 1.5-generation undocumented Brazilians express a sense of twoness. On the one hand, they often see themselves as culturally American. For women, this sense of being culturally American is tied to transnational dynamics and rooted in the intersection of gender, class, and the nation-state. On the other hand, undocumented 1.5-generation Brazilians understand that white Americans and its institutions perceive undocumented immigrants as "problems" to be exploited, detained, and/or deported. And because of this treatment, they do not see it as possible to fully embrace an American identity. Thus the 1.5-generation Brazilian case underscores how Du Bois's conception of the color line is a "spectrum of exclusion," where the articulation of race, class, nationality and legal status "shapes the extent to which people benefit from the full inclusion into the nation" (Du Bois 1965; Joseph and Golash-Boza 2021).

While most 1.5-generation Brazilians thought of themselves as white in Brazil—and their physical appearance allows them to (sometimes) pass as white in the US—they perceive a white racial identity in the US to be about more than skin color and ancestry. More specifically, they perceive a white racial identity in the US as connected to citizenship, economic privilege, and security. In contrast, as undocumented immigrants, they perceive themselves as being on the lowest rung of the legal status hierarchy. Furthermore, they understand "an undocumented status" to be racialized as nonwhite and stigmatized as poor and criminal (Chavez 2013; Menjívar 2021). Thus most white-passing Brazilians do not believe they can ethno-racially identify as white, even though they have often worked successfully to accrue some of whiteness's wages in the US. Like other groups in American society, then, we might argue that undocumented, white-passing 1.5-generation Brazilians are simultaneously positioned as white and nonwhite (Maghbouleh 2017; Moshin and Crosby 2018).

Importantly, 1.5-generation white-passing Brazilians racial identities differ from previous waves of *white* working-class ethnics who racially identified as white under Jim Crow segregation (Du Bois 1935; Roediger 1991). During that time period, white working-class men in the South had access to formal political citizenship—including the right to vote. And their votes were heavily courted. That's not the case for white-passing undocumented immigrants today. This is one reason why it's important to consider not just the articulation of race and class in the present day, but citizenship too.

CONCLUSION

"My life is nuts! It makes a good book, right!?" Elisabete, whose story opens this book, declared during our first interview. At the time, I was imagining a series of journal articles, not a book. Yet I agreed with her. Her life experiences, and those of the other 1.5-generation Brazilians I met, did make for a compelling and nuanced story. On the one hand, her position as an undocumented immigrant placed her at the bottom of the legal status hierarchy in the United States. But on the other, her ability to benefit from the wages of whiteness placed her near the top of the global, American, and Brazilian racial hierarchies. And it was clear that this privilege and marginalization—and the privilege and marginalization of many of her 1.5-generation Brazilian peers—hung together in complicated and untold ways. Illegality negatively impacted her material opportunities, her intimate relationships, and her sense of belonging. But whiteness served as a protective mechanism from vulnerability to detention and deportation and articulated with (il)legality and class as she navigated a gendered and racialized labor market.

When I began this book, the news outlets were certainly not covering stories about white-passing undocumented immigrants. But academic scholarship was not doing so either. Instead, nearly all the stories I read in the news and academic books were about immigrants from Mexico and Central America, most of whom cross the US-Mexico border clandestinely and who are racialized as nonwhite in the US. Their stories are clearly important, especially as immigrants from Mexico and Central America have historically made up the largest number of undocumented immigrants in the US. But the story of illegality in the United States is not a monolithic experience and varies by other social locations—as this book and work by other scholars demonstrate (Abrego 2014; Cho 2017; Enriquez 2017; 2019 2020; Herrera 2016; Patler 2014; Schmalzbauer 2014; Valdez and Golash-Boza 2020).

Indeed, a rising share of undocumented immigrants have been migrating from parts of the world other than Mexico and Central America, especially Asia, and overstaying visas. Between 2007 and 2017, during the years that I was conducting the research for this book, the percentage of newly arrived undocumented immigrants in the US (defined as being in the US for less than five years) not from Mexico or Central America increased from 37 percent to 63 percent—and the vast majority of these immigrants came on visas and overstayed (Lopez, Passel, and Cohn 2021). According to Warren and Kerwin (2017), in 2014, nearly two-thirds of recently arrived undocumented immigrants entered the country legally on a visa and overstayed. Due to the past and ongoing histories of colonialism and imperialism, visa overstayers, in comparison to those who enter without inspection, are disproportionately privileged in their home countries. And once in the US, this mode of entry stratifies their experiences with illegality and opportunities for shifts toward legal inclusion, with visa overstayers being privileged relative to those who entered without inspection (Aptekar and Hsin 2023; Cebulko 2018; López 2021).

Thus it behooves us to expand our scholarship on undocumented migration to account for and make sense of immigrants' varied experiences with illegality and what those experiences tell us about American society and the path forward for real social change. And as we expand our scholarship, immigration scholars will need to push beyond our dominant theoretical frameworks of assimilation and take seriously the critical insights of Black feminists and the Black Radical Tradition. We must critically account for the past and ongoing history of racial capitalism and the anti-Blackness and anti-indigeneity that undergird these systems. Furthermore, as I argue throughout the book, we must examine how race, class, and (il)legality join together *in* specifical historical conjunctures. A power-without-papers lens, rooted in an articulation framework, provides one path forward for considering how marginalization and power hang together, providing the flexibility to account for nuanced and varied immigrant experiences.

LESSONS OF POWER WITHOUT PAPERS FOR SCHOLARSHIP

Elisabete and other 1.5-generation Brazilians' lived experiences with illegality demonstrate that interlocking racial and social class inequalities are reproduced across borders, even for migrants who are denied full legal membership in the United States. Elisabete and other 1.5-generation Brazilians' ability to enter on tourist visas, bypassing the more dangerous route via the US-Mexico border, is a direct function of their racial and social class privilege in Brazil— and of US immigration policies that discriminate, both in the historical and contemporary eras, against low-income, racialized people in the Global South (Aptekar and Hsin 2023; Chomsky 2014; Hing 2004; Ngai 2004; Rosenberg 2022; Watson 2018). Importantly, this racial and class privilege in Brazil is born out of Brazil's own settler colonial history and nation-state building project, which has led to whites having disproportionate economic and political power and Blacks having the least (Bailey, Loveman, and Muniz 2013; Hernández 2012; Telles 2004).

Being middle-class and white in Brazil provided Elisabete and most other 1.5-generation Brazilians with the opportunity to migrate on visas and overstay, while race and class privilege join together with illegality to shape their other experiences once in the US, including the neighborhoods their parents' choose to settle in, the schools their parents send them to, the financial safety nets their parents provide for them, and the social networks their parents can tap into on their behalf. Indeed, in Chapter 2 we saw how 1.5-generation Brazilians' middle-class roots provide a financial safety net in the US as they navigate the difficult transition to adulthood, while in Chapters 1 and 2 we saw how whiteness provides powerful public, psychological, and material wages as they navigate public life and a racialized, classed, and gendered labor market. Although some 1.5-generation Brazilians who thought of themselves as white in Brazil are racially ambiguous in the US, many of them can successfully present as white, at least in some situations. Passing as white is a form of "legal passing" and can serve as a protective mechanism against the full deleterious impacts of being vulnerable, disposable laborers under neoliberal racial capitalism (García 2019). Of course, being undocumented is technically not a "visible" marker of one's identity, but (il)legality is racialized as Latino/a/x in the US context (Asad and Clair 2018; Chavez 2013; Menjívar 2021). And in this era of neoliberal racial capitalism, as hundreds of thousands of immigrants are deported each year and millions more are exploited in the labor market, strategic work toward whiteness and away from being racialized as Latino/a/x brings economic and social value.

Furthermore, because 1.5-generation Brazilians largely entered on tourist visas and overstayed, they are in better positions, relative to those who enter without inspection, to adjust their status to full citizenship in the US (Aptekar and Hsin 2023; Cebulko 2018; López 2021). Indeed, as mentioned in the Introduction, by the time I last interviewed respondents, 27 of the 43 respondents were lawful permanent residents or US citizens. And for those who are able to adjust their status, *power with papers*—that is, the joining together of citizenship, whiteness and Brazilian middle-class roots helps them navigate school, work, and daily public life in important ways.

These dynamics lay bare why immigration scholars of 1.5-generation undocumented immigrants must directly account for the ongoing power relations in structuring not only why people decide to migrate, but *how* nation-states receive them (that is, forcing them to cross the border or allowing for legal immigrant or nonimmigrant entry), and how immigrants and their children navigate the interlocking systems of oppression and domination they face. For far too long, the dominant assimilation frameworks have not critically wrestled with the interlocking systems of white supremacy and capitalism and the logics of anti-Blackness and anti-indigeneity that undergird them (Clergé 2014; 2019; Joseph and Golash-Boza 2021). While a segmented assimilation framework argues that race and legal status matter, it fails to critically examine how racism structurally created and maintained the United States' (and other nations') immigration and citizenship laws *and* the interconnected racial economies that migrants leave behind and confront in their new contexts.

Furthermore, the nuanced stories of power and marginalization in this book suggest there are limits to the master status framework, which has been the dominant lens explaining undocumented 1.5-generation immigrants' lives and which argues that illegality comes to overpower all other social locations in immigrants' lives as they age into adulthood (Gleeson and Gonzales 2012;

Gonzales 2016; Gonzales and Burciaga 2018; Gonzales and Ruszczyk 2021). To be sure, the master status lens has been important for illuminating the salience of illegality in young adults' lives. Indeed, even in the case of 1.5-generation Brazilians, we see how illegality sometimes trumps racial and class privilege in certain domains of their lives, limiting the wages of whiteness. For example, illegality clearly undermines their sense of belonging in US society while placing enormous obstacles to socioeconomic mobility, including limiting access to higher education and the highest-paying, highest-status jobs in a bifurcated racial economy.

At the same time, as we see throughout this book, other social locations—including gender, race, and class—shape experiences of illegality in profound ways (Abrego 2014; Cho 2017; Enriquez 2017; 2019; 2020; Herrera 2017; Patler 2014; Schmalzbauer 2014; Valdez and Golash-Boza 2020). Thus the power-without-papers lens builds off the call of scholars who call for more intersectional accounts of legal status as a source of stratification, paying attention to the interlocking structures of domination and oppression that shape their lives (Asad and Clair 2018; Enriquez 2017; 2020; García 2017; Herrera 2016; Valdez and Golash-Boza 2020). In so doing, power without papers also brings to the forefront the critical insights of the Black Radical Tradition, including the ways that white supremacy and anti-Blackness (and anti-indigeneity) have been—and continue to be—inextricably linked to the global racial economy and nation-state projects. These dynamics impact how and why people migrate as well as their incorporation experiences in their new host context.

A power-without-papers framework also specifically draws upon the conjunctural analysis of an articulation framework that necessitates that we account for how race, class, and (il)legality hang together in particular historical and geopolitical spaces that are embedded in local and global racialized social relations. I argue that this articulation lens allows for the *flexibility and nuance* to think about the work that race does for capitalism in particular conjunctures—in this case, how racially and class-privileged undocumented navigated this era of neoliberal racial capitalism as they came of age in Massachusetts in the 1990 and 2000s. In taking this lens, we can see how 1.5-generation Brazilians claim whiteness in particular ways, mobilize gender in certain ways, and lean into their economic and racial privilege when it assists them. More specifically, in Chapter 1, we see how *race is doing the work* of keeping white-passing 1.5-generation undocumented immigrants from fully uniting with other undocumented (and documented) immigrants from Latin America, as 1.5-generation Brazilians draw boundaries between themselves and other racialized immigrants, undercutting the sense of solidarity that movement scholars suggest is necessary for revolutionary collective mobilization against white supremacy and capitalism (Yazdiha 2021). Meanwhile, in Chapter 2, we can see *what race is doing for capitalist subjects* in this particular historical conjuncture—as racial privilege allows 1.5-generation Brazilians to avoid the most precarious jobs in the bifurcated racialized labor market. For example, as white-passing undocumented immigrants, they are often given front-of-house jobs in the restaurant industry and often promoted to managerial positions.

Yet, at other times in this book, we see that this racial and social class privilege is not always enough to overcome the negative impacts of illegality, especially with an expansive, hostile security apparatus targeting undocumented immigrants for detention and deportation (Golash-Boza 2011; 2015; Golash-Boza and Hondagneu-Sotelo 2013). Undocumented 1.5-generation Brazilians still know they are deportable, still experience blocks to higher education and exploitation in the workplace, and still feel a sense of stigma that negatively impacts their sense of belonging. Thus race, class, and citizenship articulate together in such a way that (il)legality circumscribes some of the benefits of whiteness even as whiteness serves as a protective mechanism against deportability.

Ultimately, then, a power-without-papers lens makes clear that we need to better understand how marginalization and power articulate together, the ways in which inequalities are reproduced across borders, and the ways in which immigrants themselves are agents in challenging and reifying these interlocking structures of domination and oppression (Bashi Treitler 2013; Roediger 1991). To be sure, passing as white is a protective strategy against the very real deleterious impacts of being racialized as nonwhite and being undocumented in the US. In a country built on white supremacy, it makes sense that 1.5-generation Brazilians would resist racial group membership with stigmatized Latino/a/xs (see Dowling 2014; Valdez 2011). And yet the anti-Blackness and anti-indigeneity in these efforts reify a global system of white supremacy that has been built on dispossessing indigenous groups of their lands and resources while enslaving Black people to accrue wealth (Bashi Treitler 2013).

Indeed, we see at times in this book how the logics of anti-Blackness and anti-indigeneity operate transnationally and shape how 1.5-generation Brazilians' navigate their transitions to adulthood. For example, boundary-making from Latino/a/x involves distancing themselves from racialized understandings of Latin American immigrants as looking "Mexican"—that is, having indigenous physical features, including brown skin, short stature, and dark black hair (Ortiz and Telles 2012). Furthermore, when some 1.5-generation Brazilians state that they "are not attracted" to Black partners romantically, we must analyze those comments through the anti-Black racial logics that are at play. This anti-Blackness is not only learned in the US. Rather, it existed in their own families' histories and has been passed down intergenerationally, only to be reinforced by their experiences with the particularities of white supremacy in the United States.

While the power-without-papers lens helps us move in important directions in accounting for the articulation of race, class, and (il)legality, it is clear that there are important underexplored gender and sexuality dynamics that also structure their experiences of power without papers. For example, many 1.5-generation Brazilian women could not discuss their identities without talking in depth about themselves as Americanized women and contrasting their experiences with Brazilian women they knew. Furthermore, they often sought out romantic partners they believed were Americanized and more willing to embrace their aspirations to pursue higher education and productive wage labor. I also did not do an adequate job attending to the role of sexuality in shaping their experiences, given that only one respondent did not identify as heterosexual. Thus we need future research to flesh out further how gender and sexuality shape "power without papers."

This study does not speak for all Brazilians' experiences in the Greater Boston area (or throughout the US). As I stated explicitly in the Introduction, the stories told in this book are the stories of 1.5-generation Brazilians who migrated as part of the *first* large wave of Brazilians to Massachusetts. We know that who migrates from a particular nation-state changes over time, and indeed, by 2007 scholars were already finding that the most recent arrivals were more likely to come via Mexico and were poorer and darker-skinned (Braga and Jouët-Pastré 2008). These racial and class differences between earlier and later arrivals to the Boston area were noted by some of my respondents too. Given that all of the 1.5-generation Brazilians I interviewed had migrated by 2001, there has been more than two decades of continued Brazilian migration to Massachusetts since the time my respondents arrived. And these later-arriving Brazilians are likely to have very different experiences than the Brazilians I interviewed due to their race and social class backgrounds in Brazil, their mode of entry, and the increasingly hostile immigration landscape in the US.

Furthermore, given that power without papers is rooted in an articulation framework that emphasizes how race, class, and (il)legality join together in specific geopolitical spaces in particular historical conjunctures, I do not claim that the specifics of the 1.5-generation Brazilian case would apply to other undocumented, white-passing immigrants in the present day. For example, we might expect that white-passing undocumented immigrants growing up and coming of age in the Trump and Biden eras would experience even more limits to their racial and class privilege, at least in certain domains. Flying internationally and slipping past the Border Patrol—as some of my respondents did in Chapter 1—might be particularly impossible in today's security era. Yet we might still anticipate that those undocumented immigrants with racial and social class privilege will be the ones who benefit from the very limited opportunities for adjustments in status. Thus power without papers suggests that scholars must consider how race, class, and illegality articulate together across borders to impact immigrants' lives in nuanced ways in particular historical conjunctures.

LESSONS OF POWER WITHOUT PAPERS FOR POLICY

Many scholars who study migration and illegality are united in their calls for policy changes, and many of these calls begin with advocating for pathways to citizenship for undocumented immigrants living in the United States. I echo these calls. But at the same time, I also draw upon the lessons from power without papers, pointing out the limitations of merely advocating for new citizenship policies.

Access to legal citizenship is extremely important in a global system of nation-states that allocate rights to citizens while excluding noncitizens from those rights. Without access to citizenship, immigrants—even those like the 1.5-generation Brazilians I interviewed who have some racial and class privilege—are vulnerable to workplace exploitation, detention, and deportation. They cannot vote and in many states cannot obtain a driver's license. And as seen in Chapter 4, they are vulnerable to feeling like social and legal outsiders, which negatively impacts their sense of belonging. Thus in a global system that divides lands into nation-states, we do need pathways to citizenship that open up opportunities for immigrants to become formal political members of the community.

In the absence of pathways to citizenship, DACA has been a lifeline. DACA has provided real tangible benefits to 1.5-generation Brazilians—especially with access to a work permit and a Social Security number for work purposes (Cebulko and Silver 2016; Gonzales, Terriquez, and Ruszczyk 2014; Patler 2018; Patler and Laster Pirtle 2018; Wong et al. 2019). But it's also true that DACA is a "crappy piece of duct tape," as Elisabete called it. It is temporary, uncertain, and leaves them short of full membership. In other words, it is a form of "liminal legality" (Abrego and Lakhani 2015; Burciaga and Malone 2011; Cebulko 2014; Cebulko and Silver 2016; Hamilton, Patler, and Savinar 2021; Roth 2019). And yet, getting rid of DACA will have devastating impacts for the nearly one million DACA beneficiaries and their family members. After all, it is not only DACA beneficiaries who directly benefit from their ability to lawfully work and their protection from deportation; it is their family members too—including, in some cases, their own US-citizen children (Enriquez 2020).

But a power-without-papers lens also underscores that merely advocating for pathways to full citizenship for undocumented immigrants is not enough to ensure full inclusion. Instead, calls for citizenship must critically attend to the sexism, racism, and classism embedded in most immigration policy proposals that reward immigrants framed as "deserving" and penalize others framed as "undeserving." Indeed, the "deserving" and "undeserving" framing in most proposed legislation by Congress over the past few decades would have disproportionately benefited the more privileged undocumented immigrants *as well as* those immigrants who conform to white middle-class norms and behaviors (see López 2021; Yukich 2013). Nearly all iterations of the Development, Relief, and Education for Alien Minors (DREAM) Act, which would provide pathways to citizenship for 1.5-generation immigrants—has eligibility requirements that would disproportionately benefit most of the relatively privileged 1.5-generation immigrants Brazilians I met. For example, one of the requirements is having "good moral character, " which excludes those with (most) criminal convictions, including any drug-related offenses. This disproportionately harms Black and brown immigrants, especially men, given the structural racism embedded in criminal and immigration enforcement practices (Golash-Boza 2011; 2015; Golash-Boza and Hondagneu-Sotelo 2013).

Furthermore, our calls for legislation to provide pathways to citizenship for all undocumented immigrants must be intersectional and work to ensure access not only to formal political citizenship, but the social and civic dimensions of citizenship too (Marshall 1950; Du Bois 1965). Indeed, we know that political citizenship has never ensured that racialized groups, LGBTQ+ folks, and women are treated as full members of society, entitled to full social and civic inclusion (Collins 1990; Crenshaw 1991; Du Bois 1965; 1935). Thus any call for pathways to formal citizenship must be deliberately intersectional and align itself with movements to end sexism, racism, classism, and homophobia in society.

Additionally, a power-without-papers lens reminds us that we must be careful about comprehensive immigration reform plans that pair pathways to citizenship with increased militarization of the border and further expansion of the internal enforcement apparatus. The interlocking systems of domination and oppression are not just a part of US society—but the global racial economy. Thus the intensification of border and internal enforcement will continue to further exacerbate the negative, and often deadly, impacts of US immigration and border policies on poorer Black and brown communities in the Global South, those who have been most harmed by settler colonialism and neoliberal racial capitalism (Golash-Boza 2015; Rosenberg 2022). Instead, as Golash Boza and Menjívar (2012) argue, we need to prioritize human rights at the center of our migration policies. We need to create opportunities for people to migrate across international borders, to *lawfully* enter new countries, and to be welcomed as members (see also Johnson 2007). This change will not come easily, especially in a the current political landscape, in which Trump-led Republicans have ratcheted up the racist anti-immigrant rhetoric and both Democrats and Republicans have implemented more hostile immigration policies, spending billions of dollars on internal and border enforcement. Thus to work toward these goals, we need to build strong coalitions for social change.

LESSONS OF POWER WITHOUT PAPERS FOR MOBILIZATION FOR SOCIAL CHANGE

While there are lots of components necessary for successful social change, some scholars argue that broad coalitions that put pressure on and challenge the nation-state are an important component (Almeida 2008; Perry and Edwards 2023). For example, Perry and Edwards (2023) find that the anti-imperial and antiracist Black Power movement in Trinidad and Tobago was composed of workers, marginalized youth, and civic leaders who successfully put pressure on the state to take a more active industrial approach that ultimately challenged the imperial and racial economic structures of society and improved social conditions. And yet forming broad coalitions for social change can be hard, especially if we are not honest about anti-Blackness and anti-indigeneity which undergirds the global racial economy. Indeed, as we saw in this book, 1.5-generation Brazilians often engage in boundary-work away from other marginalized groups. This not only undermines the potential for them to form a collective identity with marginalized others; it also keeps them from joining in a collective movement for revolutionary change (Cebulko 2013; Yazdiha 2021). Indeed, few of my respondents were active in the immigrants' rights or other social movements.

Thus one of the lessons of power without papers is that other relatively racially and class-privileged immigrant groups might be less likely to engage in broad movements for social change. Just as whiteness led white male workers away from collective solidarity with Blacks and other marginalized groups (Du Bois 1935; 2013) and whiteness led white women to ignore the plight of Black women and men during the US suffrage movement (Terborg-Penn 1998), whiteness and/or being middle-class can lead present-day immigrants away from solidarity movements.

And yet, importantly, building broad-based coalitions is not impossible. Some of my respondents, like Elisabete, Alexia, Sabine, and Marcus did critique white racism and did recognize their common struggles with other immigrants and racially marginalized groups. For example, as we saw in Chapter 3, Marcus wrote horror scripts that served as a metaphor of white society's racism toward "immigrant others." And in Chapter 4 we saw how Elisabete explicitly critiqued white institutional racism toward immigrants. While Elisabete, Alexia, Sabine, and Marcus were not active in solidarity movements when I met up with them, it is possible they could join in the future as one's political engagement can changes over the lifecourse. Indeed, we have some prominent examples of other relatively privileged undocumented immigrants eventually joining immigrant solidarity movements. Perhaps the most prominent of these examples is the Pulitzer Prize–winning journalist Jose Antonio Vargas, a Filipino-born American who "outed" himself in the *New York Times Magazine* in 2011 at age thirty (see Vargas 2011). For years, he concealed his illegality and built a successful career, working for the *Washington Post* and Huffington Post and writing a high-profile piece on Mark Zuckerberg for the *New Yorker*. But inspired by the courage and activism of undocumented young students, he wrote that he was "done running" in the *New York Times Magazine* piece. Since then, he has become a well-known immigraiton advocate, working to change the story on immigration through his organization, Define American.

To be clear, Latino/a/x and undocuqueer youth have been at the forefront of the struggle for young undocumented immigrants' rights (Gutirrez 2013). Yet the young undocumented immigrant movement is not a "Latino/a/x" only movement. Indeed, broader coalitions have formed and the movement includes Asian, Black, and formerly undocumented immigrants' voices (Escudero 2020; Nicholls 2013). Furthermore, Kevin Escudero (2020) demonstrates how organizers within the movement utilize an intersectional identity as a way to reflect the heterogeneity of unodcumented immigrant experiences and to and build coalitions with other movements. As the push for socially just immigration reform continues, we will need to build on the work of these activists who are deliberately taking an intersectional approach and building broader and more inclusive coalitions.

APPENDIX **REFLECTIONS ON METHODOLOGY**

OVERVIEW

I am not Brazilian. Nor am I an immigrant. Nor am I from the Boston area. I am a white American woman who grew up in the suburbs of Indianapolis, Indiana, multiple generations removed from the migration stories of my ancestors, who came to the United States from present-day Slovakia, Germany, France, and Ireland. Given these outsider positions, how did I get interested in researching the intersection of race, class, and illegality for Brazilian immigrants? And how did my positionality impact the research process?

These are important questions, the latter of which I have wrestled with over the past two decades as I recruited participants to engage in the study, sat down to listen to their stories, analyzed the data, and wrote up the findings. In traditional sociological circles, my lack of being Brazilian or an immigrant "insider" is a good thing—I cannot be accused of "me-search." And yet, being an outsider to the Brazilian and larger immigrant community can make some aspects of the research process more difficult, including what qualitative research books might call "gaining access to hard-to-reach populations" and "building rapport." But in addition to these practical and logistical concerns as an outsider, I was just as concerned with the ethical issues, especially given the intersection of my own educational, citizenship, class, and racial privilege as compared to many of my respondents. There is a long, problematic history of ethnographers and qualitative researchers going into "the field" in order to provide "expertise" about marginalized "others," reifying colonial, imperial, and other power dynamics and causing harm in the process (Bejarano et al. 2019)

Thus it was extremely important, at all stages of the research process, for me to critically reflect on how my outsider and insider statuses impacted the research project, a process known as *reflexivity*. This meant I needed to consider how my positionalities and perspectives influenced how I recruited participants, asked questions, analyzed the data, and wrote up the findings (Finlay 2002; Ide and Beddoe 2023). I also needed to consider how my outsider and insider statuses came together to shape the research process (Merriam et al. 2001).

To be sure, as I mentioned above, I was an outsider in many important ways. Not only am I not undocumented nor Brazilian, but I am white—and have never been perceived as anything other than white in my life no matter where in the world I have traveled. I am highly educated—I was working on my PhD when this project began and was an associate professor by the time it ended. I was born into a middle-class family who experienced upward mobility over time. But, despite these outsider statuses, I was also an insider in some important ways. First, I am a cisgender, heterosexual woman, as were the majority of the 1.5-generation Brazilians I interviewed. Furthermore, I was roughly the same age as the respondents when the research began. I was just twenty-six years old when I first moved to Boston, while some of my respondents were twenty-four when I first met them. At the time, I also wasn't married, didn't have children, and wasn't planning on any of these things in the near future. As the research continued for the next two decades, and I grew older and entered into new life-course rituals—getting engaged, getting married, having a child—many of my respondents were experiencing similar things.

Additionally, while I am not Brazilian or Brazilian-American, I do speak Portuguese (although not nearly as fluently as my respondents spoke English). I had also lived in Brazil for three months in the summer of 2005 and traveled to northeastern, southern, and southeastern Brazil, including the state of Minas Gerais, where many of the respondents were from. Importantly, I had lived in the Brazilian Amazon region for three months, a region of Brazil some of my respondents (and other Brazilians I met in Boston) often told me was "undeveloped' and "backwards," echoing long-standing racialized and stigmatized stereotypes of the Amazon that southern Brazilians articulate (Weinstein 2015). Indeed, many respondents were often incredulous that I had not only temporarily lived in the Brazilian Amazon, but had *enjoyed* my time there. At the end of the interviews, when I would ask them why they had agreed to do the interview with me, some respondents said that they were convinced I was open-minded and not a "judgmental person" if I lived in the Brazilian Amazon.

The fact that I was not Brazilian undoubtedly impacted the research process. So many Brazilian scholars have done amazing research with the Brazilian community—and I learned so much from their groundbreaking work, as detailed throughout this book (Beserra 2005; Braga and Jouët-Pastré 2008; De Biaggi 2001; Lima and Siqueira 2007; 2011; Margolis 1994; 2007; Martes 2011; 2011). To be sure, some potential respondents likely declined to do an interview with me because I was not Brazilian. And some of the 1.5-generation Brazilians I interviewed may have felt more comfortable with someone who had been Brazilian when researching their stories. Given my cultural outsider status, I did what I could to try to make respondents feel as comfortable as possible. Interestingly, for some respondents, my outsider status as a non-Brazilian was actually a good thing, at least in some ways. They often felt that first-generation Brazilians questioned their "Brazilianness" and told them they were too "Americanized." This was frustrating for them, as they often identified more as Brazilian than American given the legal exclusion they had experienced in the US. As a non-Brazilian, they did not worry that I would question the authenticity of their "Brazilianness." At the same time, my cultural familiarity with Brazil helped build a sense of rapport, as 1.5-generation Brazilians could discuss Brazilian foods, music, and customs with me. They felt more comfortable speaking English during interviews but could slip in and out of Portuguese during our conversations, especially when they wanted to use Brazilian expressions. One word that came up frequently—*saudades*—has no English translation. It conveys a deep sense of longing, nostalgia, and missing of people and places. Many respondents felt *saudades* for Brazil, a place they could not travel to due to their legal status.

But while they told me that they appreciated I was non-Brazilian because I could not judge their "Brazilianness," the process of reflexivity meant that I had to wonder: What did they hold back from telling me? And how might they have framed stories in particular ways, given my positionality as a white American? Did they say things to me as a white American that they would not have said to me if I were Black and/or Latino/a/x? Undoubtedly, the answer to all these questions is yes. And while I could not erase the power dynamics between us, I could take steps to critically think about these power dynamics *and* use my field notes from observations and conversations with others in the Brazilian community to critically analyze the interview data.

Part of this critical reflection took place after each interview as I jotted down notes about dynamics that emerged during the conversations, including questions that evoked laughter, tears, hesitation, or looks of discomfort. I also took notes after transcribing the interviews, considering statements and tones that I may have missed during the interview itself. During this critical reflection process, I could see that my positionalities had impacted the interview conversations in important ways. Indeed, had I been a Black American or Afro-Brazilian researcher—it is much less likely that 1.5-generation Brazilians would have been so explicitly anti-Black in their discussions with me. And if I had been a Latino/a/x researcher, they may not have been so open about their boundary-work away from being racialized as Latino/a/x. Importantly, while I certainly did most of the listening in the interviews, as the focus was on their experiences and perspectives, I also wanted the interviews to feel like a conversation. Thus, when anti-Blackness—or anti-Latino/a/x statements—emerged in an interview, I often did situate the racial stereotypes (or ability to migrate to the US on a tourist visa) in a larger structural picture. Sometimes this happened during the interview. Other times it was at the end of the interview.

It was evident during my memoing process that a real rapport had developed between my respondents and me, especially the ones who participated longitudinally in this project. Indeed, most respondents made highly critical or negative comments about white Americans and/or the American government. Sometimes they apologized—or otherwise indicated they hoped I would not take offense—for comments they made. For example, Sandra did not identify as an American due to her experiences with illegality and ended her animated discussion of not identifying as American by saying, "They don't deserve (interrupting me)—sorry, they don't deserve to have me as an American. No insult to you (the interviewer)." In this way she was conveying that she knew she was saying something that many white Americans would find offensive, but she felt comfortable enough sharing her critique with me and was hopeful I would not be too insulted.

Other times, as also seen in Chapter 4, respondents would portray white Americans as rich and spoiled and explicitly reference me in the conversation. For example, we see in Chapter 4 that Gabriela did not identify as white in the US. In her explanation, Gabriela explicitly brought me into her discussion. "American kids who don't care about school. Mommy and Daddy are paying. I'm not one of those. . . . So, white in the US is—one hundred percent white. American. That kind of life, yeah, you (to the interviewer) probably. (laughing) Not to offend you." Like Sandra, Gabriela was aware she was saying something that many white Americans would find offensive. But she was not too worried to share this sentiment with me.

I met Gabriela and Sandra early in my interviewing process and each participated longitudinally in this research. These comments were made in follow-up interviews, once rapport had been more firmly established, another benefit of longitudinal research. I was hyperaware from the beginning of the research process, however, that I needed to consider that some 1.5-generation Brazilians may not be so forthcoming, given my positionalities. This is one reason that semistructured interviews were important, as it provided freedom for me to ask questions in different ways depending on the dynamic emerging in the interview. It was also why fieldwork—including my field notes from observations and conversations with other Brazilians in the community—was so important.

During recruitment, I decided to ensure that respondents knew before they agreed to the interview who I was, my background, and why I was doing this project. This meant that I had the person who referred them to me—sometimes a Brazilian friend of mine, sometimes another respondent—explain who I was and what I was doing before I made contact with them. While I was not privy to those conversations, it was clear that most respondents knew before we walked into the interview that I was collaborating with local Brazilian nonprofits on a survey of Brazilians in the area and had lived in the Brazilian Amazon to do research.. For example, some respondents asked me about my experiences in the Amazon *before* we started the interview. Interestingly, most respondents were more curious about my previous experiences in the Amazon than they were about my work in the Brazilian community in Boston.

In the following sections, I examine further how all of these insider and outsider positions came together in nuanced ways to impact all stages of the research process. I begin with the why of this project, before diving into the how.

THE WHY: RESEARCH MOTIVATION

In my undergraduate courses, students often have a hard distinguishing between their motivating questions—or the "why" they want to study something—and their actual research questions—the specific questions guiding the research study. So here I want to make clear "my why" as it shaped my research process in important ways. Furthermore, in explaining "my why," I hope to provide some insight to aspiring researchers, especially undergraduate students, who might be thinking about their own "whys" for research.

The easy answer to the "why" is that I have always been motivated by human rights, social justice, and global issues. I have my mother to thank for this. I grew up in a conservative, wealthy, white suburb of Indianapolis but always felt like an outsider, especially due to our relatively lower social class. My mom was also a psychoanalyst and an activist, shaped by progressive Catholic ideas. Thus I grew up in a household that boycotted grapes in solidarity with United Farm Workers, spoke out against US involvement in Central America in the 1980s, and joined nuclear freeze protests during the Cold War. From a young age, then, I was interested in inequalities and the potential for social change. But, as the daughter of a psychoanalyst, I was also interested in people's own internal worlds and sense of belonging. In college I majored in psychology and minored in sociology.

But a motivation in human rights still does not explain why I chose this particular project. In truth, in the early years of graduate school, my original dissertation plan was to conduct fieldwork on internal migration in the Brazilian Amazon. I had worked as a research assistant for Dr. Leah VanWay, co-PI of the project "Amazonian Deforestation and the Structure of Households" alongside anthropologists Dr. Eduardo Brondizio and Dr. Emilio Moran. As part of the research assistantship, in the summer of 2005 I worked alongside other graduate and undergraduate students for three months in the Brazilian Amazon, collecting household survey data from farmers. I intended to return to the Amazon region for my dissertation fieldwork, but new events, new conversations, and new opportunities pushed me in a different direction, away from the Brazilian Amazon and to the Greater Boston area.

In the spring of 2006, large immigration protests took off around the country as immigrants' rights activists and allies decried US House bill HR 4437, the Border Protection, Antiterrorism, and Illegal Immigration Control Act (also known as the Sensenbrenner Bill), which would have criminalized undocumented immigrants and the actions of anyone who helped them enter or remain in the United States. As I watched the protests on TV, I thought back to a trip I had taken to Boston in 2004 for the Population Association of American conference. I had traveled there with my research colleagues and their families, including my dear friend Maria Fernanda (Mafer). Mafer was originally from Campinas, Brazil (in the state of São Paulo), and was living in Bloomington, Indiana, with her husband, Álvaro, who was one of my research colleagues. Everywhere Mafer and I went in Boston, we ran into Brazilians. It was during these interactions that Mafer and I learned that many were undocumented and that most did not see themselves as Latino/a/xs. So, as I watched groups of mostly Latino/a/x protestors take to the streets two years later in the spring of 2006, I wondered how many Brazilians in Boston—and their children—were engaged in the protests. Through conversations with my mentor, Dr. VanWey, I changed my dissertation focus from studying the lives of adult children migrants in the Brazilian Amazon to the lives of adult children of migrants to the Greater Boston area.

THE HOW: FIELDWORK, INTERVIEWS, AND RECRUITMENT

Overview

This study primarily draws upon interviews with 43 1.5-generation respondents, 23 of whom participated longitudinally, who were undocumented at some point in their lives. After securing IRB approval from Indiana University–Bloomington, I temporarily moved to Boston in the summer of 2006 for preliminary dissertation fieldwork, with the intention to move back out to the area for a longer period of time in January 2007.[1] The first wave of interviews for this book, from summer 2006 through spring 2008, come from this dissertation research. In truth, I only completed two interviews during the summer 2006 preliminary fieldwork. Thus the vast majority of the dissertation interviews came between January 2007 and April 2008. Given that I was particularly interested in how multiple categories of legal status shaped the lives of young adults for my dissertation, I interviewed both 1.5- *and* second-generation Brazilians during this first phase of research, including a handful of Brazilians who were attending local universities and were part of Brazilian student organizations. While the interviews with the second-generation Brazilians and 1.5-generation who had not experienced illegality are not the direct focus of this book, these additional interviews did provide important contextual insight into the stories of the 43 respondents. Indeed, some of the second-generation Brazilians were romantic partners of some of my respondents.

In 2009, I moved permanently to the Greater Boston region when I took a job as an assistant professor at Providence College in Providence, Rhode Island. While Providence is in a different state than Massachusetts, it's economic and cultural fabric is intertwined with Boston and the Bay State. Providence is one of the last spots on Boston commuter rail lines. The region's beloved New England Patriots play in Foxboro, halfway between Boston and Providence.

In 2011, two years after I moved to Providence, I began phase 2 of the project after securing IRB approval from my new institution, Providence College. This time, however, I was particularly interested in the experiences of those who were still undocumented at age eighteen and focused my efforts on follow-up interviews with 1.5-generation respondents from my dissertation fieldwork who had still been undocumented at that age. Then, in 2012, with the announcement of DACA, I expanded the recruitment process to include DACA beneficiaries whom I had not previously interviewed. In 2015 I began a third round of interviews. From 2011 to 2019 I caught up, both informally and in formal interviews, with 23 respondents.

Interview data was also supplemented with observations from fieldwork. In the spring of 2006, I was extremely fortunate to connect with Dr. Enrico Marcelli, who was then an assistant professor at the University of Massachusetts Boston and a Robert Wood Johnson Health & Society Scholar/Research Fellow at Harvard. He was beginning a collaborative project with Brazilian and Dominican community leaders to survey Brazilian and Dominican immigrants. In the summer of 2006, alongside other graduate students, I canvassed Boston-area neighborhoods for the upcoming survey. After canvassing,

I would take notes, writing down details about the housing structures, the green space, the restaurants, and the stores in these neighborhoods.

It was through Dr. Marcelli that I met several Brazilian community leaders, including Bernardo, who was the executive director of one of the local Brazilian nonprofit organizations, Brazilians United.[2] In the summer of 2006, Bernardo and I went out to lunch at a local Brazilian *churrascaria* (steakhouse) and I told him more about me and my project. He told me he appreciated that I had not approached him too formally, as if I were an "expert" wielding power over him and community members. For example, he appreciated that I had dressed casually (on the day I met him, I was wearing shorts, a tank top, and Havaianas flip-flops I had bought in Brazil, long before they became fashionable in the US). He also told me that I seemed to have a *jeitinho brasileiro*, or a "Brazilian spirit," about me. While this can take on a negative connotation when referring to corruption in Brazil, *jeitinho brasileiro* can also refer to a "Brazilian spirit" that is relaxed, flexible, and creative in dealing with life's complications. That afternoon, after our conversation at the *churrascaria*, he walked me over to a local business and introduced me to a young woman who agreed to do an interview with me later in the week. For the rest of the summer, when I was not canvassing neighborhoods or conducting interviews, I was often watching World Cup soccer games with Bernardo and other Brazilian community leaders, learning more about their inspiring work advocating for Brazilian—and all immigrants'—rights in the region.

In January 2007, I returned to Boston. Given that I had previous experience in nonprofit fundraising, Bernardo asked me to help plan the annual fundraising dinner for Brazilians United, or BU. I agreed, as I am committed to working as a publicly engaged scholar—giving back to the community in ways that draws on expertise I might have. BU was doing important work protecting and advocating for immigrants' rights and I became deeply committed to their mission. During my time at BU, I became fast friends with other young staffers, board members, and other Brazilian community leaders. Nearly all of these young people were Brazilian (although some were Portuguese) and were excited about my project, referring potential respondents. Meanwhile, Bernardo and I worked closely together, driving around the Greater Boston area, soliciting donations from local Brazilian businesses, immigration lawyers, and other community leaders. Through my work at BU, I also connected with other Brazilian community leaders and began serving as an intermittent grant consultant for another Brazilian nonprofit, once again using my fundraising background to assist with securing funds. Then, in the spring of 2007, I joined a recently formed committee that was focused on advocating for in-state tuition for undocumented students.

The insight I gained through my conversations with Brazilian small business owners, immigration attorneys, and other Brazilian and immigrant community leaders was invaluable for understanding dynamics in the Brazilian community, including Brazilians' experiences with illegality and adjusting statuses. In addition, my engagement in the Brazilian community helped me with recruitment, interview questionnaire design, and analysis.

Interview Recruitment

It was through my Brazilian networks in the Greater Boston area that I began participant recruitment. Bernardo was the first person to introduce me to respondents, but he was certainly not the only one. Indeed, several Brazilian community leaders and friends I made served as my entry points into the community, referring me to people in their extended families, churches, and occupational networks. Sometimes my Brazilian friends even recruited people they met while standing in line at the bank or grocery store.

To be eligible for participation in the initial study, respondents had to be eighteen or older, have been born in the US or migrated by age fifteen, and have at least one parent who identified as Brazilian.[3] I used a snowball sample, and at the end of each interview I would ask respondents if they knew of anyone else who might be interested in completing an interview. If they did know of someone, I asked them if they would feel comfortable reaching out to them to gauge interest or if they preferred that I directly contacted them. In almost all cases, they reached out to their contact first. If the person was interested, I would then reach out to them.

The interviews took place wherever respondents felt most comfortable. Often they chose to meet at their homes. At other times we met at their workplaces, their favorite bookstores, or their favorite restaurants. When I was living in Boston, I usually took public transportation or walked to the interview locations. Before and after each interview, I memoed, writing descriptions of the respondents, including their presentations of self as well as physical descriptions of their neighborhoods and their homes (or workplaces, favorite bookstores, etc.). It was during these walks that I continued to get a sense of the neighborhoods—the green spaces (or lack thereof), the proximity to public transportation, the restaurants and other stores nearby. I also memoed on my perception of the rapport during the interview.

My positionality undoubtedly impacted this recruitment process and likely skewed toward those who would feel comfortable speaking with a white American. Indeed, it's probably not an accident that most respondents who were still undocumented at age eighteen and agreed to do an interview with me were white-passing.[4] While research suggests that the first wave of Brazilians in the area are lighter-skinned than other Latin American and Caribbean groups, nearly 87 percent of the 1.5-generation immigrants I met were white-passing. A few participants told me they agreed to do this interview specifically because I was white and American and they were intrigued that someone like me would care enough to focus on their stories. Given that my focus is on "power without papers," and that whiteness is so underexplored in relation to the experiences of undocumented immigrants, overrepresentation of white-passing Brazilians was helpful for the analysis.[5]

Because of my engagement in the Brazilian community from 2006 to 2008, I often informally ran into respondents when I was out with Brazilian friends or working for Brazilians United. This contact with them continued on and off over the next fifteen years as some respondents reached out to me because they wanted to communicate significant events in their lives or they thought I might have valuable information to share about shifting immigration policies or names of reputable immigration attorneys. Sharing resources was one way I could give back to them in a meaningful way for their engagement in this project.

Asking Questions
Interviews were semistructured and the interview guide was designed by me. I had broad questions for each topic area, with probes under each question to ensure as much detail as possible. Because I wanted the interview to feel like a conversation, I let respondents speak at length about other important areas that emerged. While I certainly redirected conversations at times, I saw firsthand how important things can emerge when people tell their stories on their own terms and in their own way. If respondents seemed hesitant at times, I always reassured them that they could skip over certain conversations or not

elaborate. Informed consent is not something to only be done at the beginning of an interview; it is an ongoing process.

I conducted all the interviews myself. Topics covered their families' decisions to migrate, their memories of Brazil, their experiences with discrimination, their experiences with education and work, friendships and romance, political and civic engagement, and their ethno-racial and American identities. It quickly became apparent from my preliminary fieldwork, including the two interviews I did in summer 2006, that 1.5-generation Brazilians could not tell their stories without discussing illegality, including the gray areas of liminal legality that they and/or their family members experienced. Conversations about (il)legality often emerged when they described why they had not returned to Brazil to visit family members or when they talked about why they had never gotten a driver's license or gone to college straight after high school.

My fieldwork helped me to refine the interview guide—and to consider not only what questions to ask, but *how* to ask these questions, and the order in which to them. For example, race was a difficult topic for most Brazilians to discuss, sometimes even more difficult than discussions of (il)legality. But I learned quickly that one of the best ways to begin this conversation was to ask how they identified themselves ethno-racially on forms. Rather than shutting down conversations, respondents usually become animated, letting off big sighs or laughing or throwing their arms up in the air to begin a lengthy discussion about their frustrations with race, racial categories, and how to identify themselves racially in the United States. From there we would also talk about how they believed others perceived them on the street, the racial hierarchy in the US and in Brazil, and what they believed their race was in Brazil. Conversations about ethno-racial identity also emerged when I asked them if they identified as American and what it means to be "Brazilian" or "American." Some respondents would tell me that they could not be "American" since they were not white, even if they passed as white. It was during these conversations about American identity that I probed, pushing for deeper meanings on the identities they embraced, refused, or ambivalently accepted. This is when some respondents offered up that they were "Brazilian" "Brazilian-American" or an "Americanized Brazilian." Meanwhile, I asked about social class in a number of ways, including asking them to describe their lives and neighborhoods before they left, their parents' educational levels and occupations back in Brazil, and their own perceptions of their social class back in Brazil.

DATA ANALYSIS AND WRITING

All of the interviews were audio-recorded and transcribed at verbatim. While I transcribed most of the initial interviews for the first wave of data collection, I hired one undergraduate 1.5-generation Brazilian research assistant in Indiana to transcribe some of them. In later waves of data collection, I hired two other undergraduate transcriptionists.

Data analysis occurred throughout the research process, beginning with the memos I took following each interview, including a description of all themes and subthemes that emerged. These memos also included conversations I had with Brazilian community leaders and friends. Later I used Atlas TI, a qualitative data program, for coding the first wave of data interviews. During later stages of the project I switched to Dedoose, an alternative qualitative data program. I used my memos to help develop a list of codes and then, using the software programs, examined patterns in themes and trends for all interviews. As patterns emerged, I developed propositions and specifically sought out negative cases that might confirm or contradict these emerging propositions.

As previously mentioned, I asked about race and social class in a number of ways. Thus I used a number of indicators to operationalize race in the US and social class in Brazil. Given that race is a social construction, there is no "perfect" measure for categorizing someone's race. In Chapter 1, I focus on whether someone is white-passing, while in Chapter 4 I am interested in respondents' own understanding of their race in the US. Thus, given my analytical focus on whether or not someone could pass as white in the US in Chapter 1, I put respondents into one of two categories: white-passing or not-white-passing. I classified someone as "white-passing" if they told me during the interviews that other people on the street or in their daily interactions perceived them as European (usually this was Italian or Portuguese), or I classified them as such based on my own physical descriptions of them following our interactions and interviews. In Chapter 4, however, I used respondents' own self-reported racial identity in the US to classify someone as having a "white racial identity" or not.

Brazil has high levels of social inequality, with very few wealthy Brazilians and many more Brazilians living in poverty. The middle class in Brazil was much smaller in the 1980s (at the time my respondents began leaving Brazil) than it was in later decades due to the Brazilian government's policies under President Lula da Silva's first administration, which helped to reduce inequality, including programs like Bolsa Escola. The economic crisis of the 1980s also underscored how precariously close to economic insecurity many Brazilian middle-class families were, such that many felt compelled to migrate to the US. And yet, despite their families' precarious middle-class positions during the economic crisis, it was clear that all but one of my respondents did not come from "poor" families. Indeed, this one respondent was an outlier in several ways. Her family was poor, as her dad had been a coal miner in Brazil and she was the only respondent who crossed the border illegally with her family. Everyone else, however, provided at least one indicator that their family was middle-class.

Because respondents did not know their families' income back in Brazil, I instead used other indicators, including 1) descriptions of their Brazilian neighborhoods, 2) their parents' education level, 3) their parents' occupations back in Brazil, 4) private schooling in Brazil, and 5) what they believed their families' social class was in Brazil. In this way I used both traditional sociological indications of social class (educational level and occupation of parents), class consciousness indicators (what was your perception of your social class back in Brazil?), and other indicators (having a private school elementary education, living in gated communities or apartment buildings, having servants). Six respondents indicated that their families came from upper-middle-class backgrounds (had private school educations, lived in gated communities, had servants, or recognized their families as part of the upper-middle class) while one person indicated that her family was poor (as described in the previous paragraph). Everyone else was part of the Brazilian middle class (or lower middle class), as their parents had at least a high school education, or they reported their family's social class as middle-class, or they owned their own several businesses and properties in their hometowns.

While I did all the analysis myself prior to 2020, I had three undergraduate students—Christina Roca, Deborah Lopez, and Madison Cohen, who became research assistants in 2020—help me to analyze the data once again. Together we discussed themes that emerged around gender as we considered the experiences of "power without papers." Their insights were also particularly useful as we discussed gendered experiences with transitions out of high school. Furthermore, Christina and Deborah, both of whom come from

Central American families, had particularly important critical insights into the ways in which Brazilian experiences with the police and Border Patrol were very different from the experiences of immigrants they knew in their Central American communities in the US Northeast.

During the process of writing, I remained attentive to ethical issues, including confidentiality and risk. All respondents and the family members and friends they spoke of were given pseudonyms. I also chose to refer to all specific neighborhoods they lived in and schools they went to by pseudonyms.[6] While I have sometimes been encouraged to share specific demographic information for each respondent, I have decided to not do so, for confidentiality reasons. Not only do I want to protect respondents given their precarious legal status; I also want to protect them from stigma within the Brazilian community. Furthermore, there are times that I have left out specific details regarding how I made contact with a respondent or the specifics of a person's story in order to ensure their confidentiality. I am imperfect, as all humans are, and thus know that there is always room for growth. But in critically reflecting throughout this research process, I hope to have minimized as much risk for respondents and done justice to their experiences. To be sure, many of my respondents may have had relative "power" as compared to some of their peers. But it is also true that their lives in the US had been filled with pain and struggles, and their efforts at "legal passing" through constructing and presenting as white are a function of the ways in which white supremacy operates under neoliberal racial capitalism.

NOTES

Introduction

1. Elisabete and the names of all other respondents—and their friends and family members—are pseudonyms.

2. DACA is a discretionary policy that provides some undocumented young people who came to the US as children with temporary relief from deportation, renewable every two years. DACA also provides access to Social Security numbers for work purposes and work permits. Eligibility requirements included the following: being under age thirty-one and present in the US on June 15, 2012, living in the US for five years, and arrival in the US before age sixteen. Eligible recipients also must have no felony record and need to be in school or have completed at least a General Education Diploma (GED).

3. Trump's administration announced the termination of DACA in 2017. Republican governors and attorneys general led the charge against DACA. And in September 2023, Judge Andrew Hanen, a George W. Bush–appointed judge, ruled that DACA is unlawful. He continued, however, to stay the impact of the ruling for current program beneficiaries. At the time of this writing, this means that means that current DACA beneficiaries continue to have work authorization and protection from deportation and that the Biden administration can continue processing renewal applications. The Supreme Court, which will decide the ultimate fate of DACA, however, has grown increasingly conservative, jeopardizing its future.

4. At the time of writing, DACA was still in legal limbo. The courts had stopped the implementation of new applications, but renewals were still permitted.

5. As discussed in more detail in Chapter 3, Massachusetts did not provide in-state tuition to undocumented immigrants until August 2023. In 2007, the Board of Higher Education did allow those immigrants with work permits to pay in-state tuition rates.

And in 2012, after the passage of DACA, those with DACA—because of their work permits—were able to pay in-state rates.

6. Smith (2005) argues that children of immigrants' successes in the US—especially in school and work—helps to repay their parents' migration sacrifices.

7. Gender and sexuality are also important social locations shaping people's lived experiences. At times in this book, I examine how gender shaped how women and men navigate power without papers. Only one respondent openly identified as queer and all identified as cisgender.

8. Some scholars believe this unidirectional process would happen in a straight line, while others contended it would be "bumpy."

9. Stuart Hall never described himself as part of the Black Radical Tradition. But his work was committed to imagining postcolonial, postcapitalist, and postracist futures. As Sharad Chari (2017) argues, "Hall was never a self-described postsocialist' or 'postcolonial' thinker; he is rarely seen as canonical in postcolonial studies, nor was he a self-identified 'Black Marxist' or member of the 'Black Radical Tradition.' While not 'of' these schools, his work is legible precisely at their intersection."

10. I expand on these neoliberal policies later in this chapter and in Chapter 3.

11. As described later, whiteness is more expansive in Brazil than in the US, as someone who is nonwhite in the US may be seen as "legitimately white" in Brazil as the Brazilian system does not require "white racial purity" (Telles 2004). Capturing race in Brazil is hard (as it is elsewhere) and whether whites are a numerical majority or not has varied with the political projects of the Brazilian nation-state and how race is measured (Loveman 2014). Racial understandings have changed since the time that my respondents migrated to the US, and fewer people in Brazil identify as white today than did in the past.

12. I use *Latino/a/x* throughout the book, as *Latinx* is a newer and more gender-inclusive term. Polling among Latino/a/xs shows resistance to the term by those who identify as Hispanic or Latino/a, while some scholars contend that the polling is poorly done (see Yarin 2022 for a discussion). I use *Latino/a/x* to capture this complexity *except* when using direct quotes or when paraphrasing/writing in reference to Brazilians' own discussions. None of the Brazilians I met used *Latinx* and instead used *Latino* or *Latina*. They also used *Latino/a*, *Spanish*, and *Hispanic* interchangeably when describing other immigrants from Latin America. Thus at times I use *Hispanic* or *Latino/a* rather than *Latino/a/x* in this book, but only when using direct quotes or paraphrasing/referring to their discussions.

13. As explored in later chapters, even those who are not white-passing in the United States sometimes engaged in boundary work, drawing distinctions between themselves and other racialized groups, including emphasizing how they were classified as white in Brazil.

14. See Chapter 4 for a longer discussion of double consciousness.

15. The Illegal Immigration Reform and Immigrant Responsibility Act (IIRIRA) of 1996 put into place the three- and ten-year bars. Both bars to reentry are triggered once a person departs the United States. There are waivers of the three- and ten-year unlawful-presence bars for some people under some conditions, but the application

for these waivers became even more tenuous under the Trump administration. More details on this law are discussed in Chapters 1 and 3.

16. I lean heavily into Hall's articulation framework throughout this book. I am deeply indebted for the analytical contributions of intersectional scholars and acknowledge that the liberating work that Black and queer scholars of color have done that this book is not also doing.

17. Counting who is white and nonwhite has always been a political project, and today there is no agreed-upon "best way" to measure race in Brazil or to group Brazilians racially. See Bailey, Loveman, and Muniz (2013) for more.

18. European migration to Brazil was not limited to these three nations. Indeed, Germany in particular sent many migrants to Rio Grande du Sul.

19. Northeastern Brazilians are framed as traditional, "backwards," and nonwhite Other states also have articulated regional identities—those from Rio De Janeiro are known as "Cariocas," from Minas Gerais, "Mineiros," and from Rio Grande du Sul, "gauchos."

20. To be sure, Paulistas see everyone else—including Mineiros as "backwards." But as my own fieldwork revealed, identities are relative. For many Mineiros, it is the northeast and Amazon regions that they perceive as "backwards."

21. In general, the population of Brazil becomes much darker-skinned as one moves from the southernmost state of Brazil to the north (Telles 2004) and the requirements for whiteness are stricter in the south of Brazil than in the north (Monk 2016). As one moves from the south to the north, one's "racial" status can shift across these regions. The same person considered *pardo* (brown) in Salvador, Bahia (in the northeast), may be considered *preto* (Black) in a more southern state. Similarly, a person considered *pardo* (brown) in Curitiba, Paraná, may be considered *branco* (white) in Salvador, Bahia. Ultimately, then, as Monk (2016) reminds us, Brazil's color continuum is relational, and categorization depends on the particular phenotypes most prevalent in each region and the historical legacies of migration unique to each region.

22. Antimiscegenation laws targeted marriages between whites and nonwhites, including indigenous groups and Asians. But they mainly targeted marriages and relationships between whites and Blacks.

23. Overt racism never completely disappeared. And with the rise of Donald J. Trump, there has been more overt racist political discourse.

24. In this neoliberal era, the privatization of prisons and detention centers for mass incarceration and immigrant detention helps corporations turn massive profits while politicians can symbolically campaign on "getting tough" on marginalized groups who are dehumanized by the American public (Golash-Boza 2012).

25. Asad and Clair (2018) identify two different kinds of racial legal statuses that are racialized over time—criminal statuses (such as ex-felon status) and immigration statuses (undocumented statuses).

26. Working to accrue the wages of whiteness is not unique to the US. As discussed earlier and in Chapter 3, scholars also find that Brazilians worked the ethno-racial hierarchy to their advantage (Degler 1986; Osuji 2019; Twine 1998).

27. Please see the appendix for details on methodology, including how I navigated my positionality during the research process as a white American woman doing this research.

28. These other interviews, including all of the ones with second generation respondents, were part of the first stage of the project, which focused explicitly on how multiple categories of legal membership matter for incorporation. In later phases of data collection, the project became more explicitly focused on "power without papers."

29. All organizations are referred to by pseudonyms.

30. For example, in 2006, Boston mayor Thomas Menino (D) piloted Secure Communities, which allowed local police to detain immigrants for immigration violations after they had been stopped for other offenses (including traffic violations). But other towns were not participating. In 2014, the city council voted unanimously to deny further participation in Secure Community Agreements. Meanwhile, in 2006, then Governor Mitt Romney (R) signed a memorandum of agreement (MOA) between Massachusetts and US Immigration and Customs Enforcement (ICE) so that certain state troopers could enforce immigration laws. These MOAs are part of the 287(g) program that was added to the Immigration and Nationality (INA) in 1996 via the Illegal Immigration Reform and Immigrant Responsibility Act. The 287g program allows ICE to partner with state and local law enforcement agencies to enforce immigration laws. But in January 2007, Democratic governor Deval Patrick rescinded the agreement between Massachusetts and ICE.

31. Only one person identified as part of the LGBTQ+ community.

32. See the appendix for more information on how respondents discussed the Amazon. Many 1.5-generation Brazilians told me they felt comfortable doing the interview with me because I had lived in the Amazon for three months and enjoyed my time there. They believed that this was evidence that I was a nonjudgmental person.

33. Brazil is one of the most unequal nations in the world, and there is a smaller middle class there than in the US. See the appendix for more details.

34. A few respondents, since they had traveled at such young ages, were not certain of what visa they had when they entered the country. A handful of respondents, however, thought their parents may have entered on nonimmigrant religious visas, which enabled them to bring their dependents with them. The vast majority knew, however, they overstayed tourist visas.

35. Lawful permanent residents are entitled to some but not all of these rights and benefits. For example, lawful permanent residents are eligible for federal financial aid for college, but are ineligible to vote.

36. It is also possible that some of the respondents' families were able to secure counterfeit documents, and that their families never told them this. Indeed, Martes (2011) reports that in her travels to Governador Valadares, there were many travel agencies that financed tickets, had connections with visa and passport counterfeiting networks, would make bus rentals to transport people for interviews at the US consulate to obtain visas, and provided instructions for Brazilians when appearing for interviews at the consulate. In 1997, agents charged between 1,000 and 5,000 [[what currency]] per person for this service. The cost of the service could be paid in

installments, with candidates leaving agents a "a piece of real estate as collateral." But even in the 1990s, Brazilians born there had trouble obtaining US entry visas.

37. Brazilians usually did not have the necessary family connections to file family-based petitions, so they filed employment-based petitions.

38. Specifically, respondents ended up in liminal legality due to the implementation of Section 245i. If a petition for labor certification was approved, the beneficiary had to then wait for an immigrant visa number to become available (also known as waiting until the priority date was current). The beneficiary (my respondent's parent) also had to file both the Adjustment of Status (AOS) application and Employment Authorization Document (EAD). As I have described in previous work, "If the EAD was not adjudicated within ninety days, the beneficiary was eligible for an interim EAD that was granted at the local USCIS office. Then, if the AOS application was not adjudicated by the ninetieth day, the beneficiary—and the dependents—were entitled to an EAD (and Social Security card) for as long as the AOS application was pending. At this point, the immigrant (and the dependent) is no longer deportable on the basis of immigration status—but could still be deportable for criminal offenses" (Cebulko 2014, p. 150).

39. The appendix provides more information about the interview process, including how my positionality impacted the entire interview process, as well as more information on measuring race and social class.

40. As I detail in the appendix, I asked about race in multiple ways during the interview and wrote my own physical descriptions of respondents after interviews and informal interactions.

Chapter 1

1. Menjívar and Abrego (2012) argue that violence is inherent in the implementation of immigration laws, which are increasingly interconnected with criminal laws. This violence is normalized and cumulative over time, having harmful impacts on immigrants, even immigrants who are not the direct targets of these laws.

2. US Customs and Border Protection (CBP) is the federal agency that patrols the US border but claims a territorial reach far beyond the actual border. Indeed, the CBP can board vehicles and vessels and search for people without immigration documentation "within a reasonable distance from any external boundary of the United States" (land or water boundary). The federal government defines "a reasonable distance" as 100 air miles from any US boundary. Much of the Northeast—including all of Massachusetts—falls within this 100-mile border. See Castañeda (2019) for information on Border Patrol inspections along the US-Mexico border in Texas. The American Civil Liberties Union (2014) finds that Border Patrol officers routinely violate the constitutional rights of people in the US.

3. The police are only one law enforcement agency in the US. There is also the Border Patrol and ICE personnel, the latter of which operate in the interior of the US.

4. Ricardo's story of not being discriminated against in this instance dovetails with other research that demonstrates that lighter skin color among Latin American immigrants leads to lower reports of racial discrimination, especially from US-born whites (Marrow et al. 2022). To be sure, a lighter skin color does not mean that one may pass

as white, as color and race are two different things. Furthermore, how one is racially classified by themselves—and by others—is informed by other physical features and social cues, as discussed throughout this chapter.

5. See the appendix for further methodological details, including how I asked about race and ethnicity, how respondents' ethno-racially identified themselves, and how they believed others ethno-racially classified them.

6. Omi and Winant (2014) define racial projects as "simultaneously an interpretation, representation, or explanation of racial identities and meanings, and an effort to organize and distribute resources (economic, political, cultural) along particular racial lines" (125). Differing racial projects compete to become the dominant understanding about race, racial categories, and how they should play a role in society.

7. Passing as white works to protect against negative stereotypes for all nonwhite groups. But 1.5-generation Brazilians were most likely to be racially assigned as Latino/a/x by others if not assigned as white.

8. In using whiteness, I am referring to a system of privileges that accrue for individuals who are perceived as white and not for those racialized as nonwhite. Meanwhile, I use *white* to refer to a racial identity embraced and/or assigned to a particular individual. In this chapter, because I am largely referring to those who could pass a white, I am usually referring to those who report being "assigned" to a "white" racial identity by others. In contrast, Chapter 4 examines whether 1.5-generation Brazilians actually self-identify as white in the US.

9. During fieldwork, these supermodels were often named to me by Brazilians, both respondents as well as my Brazilian coworkers and friends. But the sexualization of Brazilian women is not unique to Boston nor time period. Indeed, Beserra (2008) demonstrates how they have existed at least since Portuguese-born, Brazilian singer Carmen Miranda came to the US in 1939. Miranda was stereotypes as mixed-race and sexually available and gained fame for her cultural appropriation of Afro-Brazilian inspired music.

10. See the appendix for methodological details on how I classified Brazilians as white-passing.

11. I use pseudonyms for all towns respondents report living in to help protect their anonymity. I name, however, specific spaces in Boston they avoided since that does not threaten their confidentiality.

12. Dorchester and Roxbury are not pseudonyms because they are the names of the neighborhoods his family avoided. As previously noted, using the names of these neighborhoods his family avoided does not threaten Álvaro's confidentiality.

13. Throughout the conversations, Gabriela used *Hispanic*, *Latino*, and *Mexican* interchangeably.

14. Marta, like many respondents, often used *Spanish* and *Hispanic* and *Latino/a/x* interchangeably.

15. Local immigration lawyers told me that the US government had made it more difficult for Brazilians to get a tourist visa to come to the US, not only because of 9/11, but because the government realized that many Brazilians—like Fausto's

family—were overstaying visas. Furthermore, as Brazilians started going through Mexico, the US put pressure on Mexico to restrict their migration. In turn, Mexico began requiring Brazilians to get tourist visas to arrive there, further making that journey a challenge.

16. Danilo, saw himself as closer to the "invaders" than the "white wannabees" given that he migrated at age 11 and could not pass as white.

17. While this chapter focuses on how 1.5-generation Brazilians navigate deportability and work to accrue the wages of whiteness, Chapter 4 examines their sense of belonging in society, including their ethno-racial identities. Thus, see Chapter 4 for more details on how 1.5-generation Brazilians ethno-racially identified.

Chapter 2

1. See the Introduction for more information on DACA.

2. There are a few states that have made state public aid available. Massachusetts finally did so in August 2023.

3. In August 2023, Massachusetts became the twenty-fourth state to offer in-state tuition for undocumented students. Additionally, at the same time, Massachusetts began to offer state financial aid.

4. Only 3 of the 43 respondents knew about SIM. All three had been active with organization, with some meeting with Massachusetts state representatives.

5. Leila had a bachelor's degree as she navigated the labor market. Meanwhile, Gabriela was working and piecing together night classes at extension programs after she graduated high school, while Bianca did not go to college in the US.

6. See Asad (2023) for more information on each of these options. My respondents reported working under the books and providing ITIN numbers. The US Department of the Treasury created ITIN numbers in 1996 so that foreign nationals without social security numbers would be in compliance with tax laws. The ITIN is a nine digit number, but it is not a Social Security number and does not provide work authorization. To receive an ITIN, a person needs to provide at least two documents verifying proof of age and identity. Importantly, the IRS does not report those who use ITIN numbers to file taxes to immigration authorities. Yet there can still be negative consequences for immigration from using them (Asad 2023). Many immigrants—both those lawfully present and those not lawfully present—may have ITIN numbers, and the American Immigration Council (2022) reports that the IRS reports that 4.4 million ITIN filers paid over $5.5 billion in payroll and Medicare taxes in 2015.

7. The passage of the Immigration and Control Act (IRCA) in 1986 set the groundwork for contemporary work-site enforcement laws. Specifically, this act implemented the use of I-9 forms as a way for employers to verify the eligibility of their employees to legally work in the US and set up a system of civil and criminal penalties known as "employer sanctions." In 2007, President George W. Bush renamed the entire program "E-verify."

8. The order did not take effect until September 8, 2009.

9. As of 2013, nineteen other states mandated that all or some employers use it.

Chapter 3

1. See the Introduction and Chapter 1 for more details on the ten-year bars to reentry.
2. Black men and Asian women are the most likely to marry outside of their race (Wang 2012).
3. Whites are much less likely to live in multigenerational households than Asian, Black, and Hispanic families (Cohn et al. 2022). Thus, in nonwhite families, grandparents, aunts, and uncles may act as important caretakers and guardians, but they are ineligible to sponsor a family members for citizenship. Furthermore, this law also discriminates against households in which the parents are not married.
4. In some cases, those who entered without inspection can file a waiver to the bar to reentry. However, while this option may be available for some spouses, it is not available to those seeking a petition through a sibling.
5. Bread and Bagels is a pseudonym.
6. Elisabete told me that she believed Keith was denied a visa because the US government believed his motivation for a student visa was fraudulent due to his marriage to Elisabete, a DACA recipient.
7. LGBTQ+ relationships were recognized for immigration purposes in 2013.
8. Importantly, some Brazilians are naturalized and/or US born citizens. Thus, dating and marrying someone who is Brazilian does not necessarily cut off access to citizenship.

Chapter 4

1. As discussed in Chapter 1, 1.5-generation Brazilians often did believe that Brazilians in the Greater Boston area were seen more positively than other Latin American immigrants, especially due to their relatively lighter skin color. At the same time, however, they were acutely aware of the larger narrative about undocumented immigrants as racialized Latino/a/x others and how many everyday Americans did not know the difference between Brazilians and other immigrants from Latin America. Thus, these ideas and thoughts coexisted and shaped their boundary work and identification.
2. Given that race and ethnicity have some overlap, I use ethno-racial identities to capture the overlap in these identities. For example, Gabriela asserts "Brazilian" as her racial identity—thereby asserting her national origin group, which some might call an ethnic group because of Brazilians' shared history and culture, as her racial identity in the US. I use racial identity, however, when referring to "white racial identity."
3. See the appendix for more details on methodology. I often began the conversations about race and American identities during our interviews by asking them about how they mark their race on forms. This question led to exasperated sighs and animated conversations about race, racial identities, and feelings of (not) being American, underscoring the ways in which identifying as American is connected to race and racism in the US.
4. Please see the appendix for details on how I engaged respondents in a discussion of their American and ethno-racial identities.

5. Given that there were only six respondents who could not pass as white, I do not break this table down by race.

6. Please see the appendix for details on how I engaged respondents in a discussion of their American and ethno-racial identities.

7. As described in Chapter 2, Leila's own Brazilian middle-class roots had provided her family with a financial safety net that allowed her to overcome legal and financial barriers in the US to attend a four-year college.

8. Both of these respondents asserted a Brazilian identity.

9. Like other respondents, Alexia conflated white and American, using the two interchangeably.

10. The United States Military Academy at West Point does allow up to sixty international cadets—from certain eligible countries—to study there at any given time. Gabriel, however, was already living in the US.

11. Gabriel has been racialized as Black, Hispanic, and Muslim in the United States. How he was racialized depended on how he was wearing his hair, what he was wearing, who he is with, and what language he was speaking (see Chapter 1).

12. Gabriel was not alone in articulating this emphasis on African American power in the US—as it resonated with 1.5-generation Brazilians who contrasted it with what they perceived as the absence of such power for Black Brazilians. In some ways, this perspective was likely shaped by the timing of their migration—as they had left Brazil in the 1980s and '90s, largely before the Brazilian state's formal reckoning with ongoing systemic racism through policies such as affirmative action. In other words, in Brazil they had seen less evidence that Black Brazilians had been able to impact institutional change.

13. This was often expressed when I asked them how they identified themselves on official forms. They often sighed or exclaimed that they never knew how to fill them out. This would then launch long discussions about race. Some respondents were more open to *Latino/a/x* than *Hispanic* because they perceive *Latino/a/x* as being from Latin America rather than about speaking the Spanish language. However, most told me that in the minds of Americans, *Hispanic* and *Latino/a/x* mean the same thing, and they reject being categories with Spanish-speaking immigrants from Latin America.

14. The US government first asks about whether someone identifies ethnically as Hispanic/Latino/a, before asking questions about race. This was confusing to Brazilians—and they believed the government was trying to get them to mark "Hispanic/Latino/a" even if they did not personally identify as such. See Telles (2018) for more on Latino/a/xs, race, and the census.

15. See Chapter 1 for further discussion of Brazilians' understandings of stereotypes of Brazilians in the US.

Appendix

1. I first received IRB approval for this study while at Indiana University. I later received IRB approval from Providence College when I became a professor there.

2. Both Bernardo and Brazilians United are pseudonyms.

3. In the second stage of the study (and thereafter), second-generation respondents were no longer eligible for the study. Thus respondents had to be over the age eighteen, have migrated to the US from Brazil by age fifteen, and still have been undocumented by age eighteen.

4. To be sure, some referrals declined to participate. I spoke with ten people on the phone who considered doing the interview (and who met eligibility requirements), who ultimately declined to participate. They did not give a reason, but it would not be surprising that my positionalities as white and American, during a time of rising anti-immigrant hostility, kept some of them from participating. While I know that some of those who declined included both undocumented immigrants and green card holders, I do not know the race or class of those who declined.

5. It's also possible that my respondents were representative of the first wave of 1.5-generation Brazilians to the area. Survey data of skin color often corresponds with one moment in time. But many Brazilians I met told me how much their skin color changes seasonally. Furthermore, Marcelli and colleagues' (2008) research included many Brazilians who migrated after 2001, and thus likely included poorer and darker-skinned participants than respondents in my study.

6. As previously mentioned, I refer to spaces they avoided by their real names (for example, how they avoided Dorchester and Roxbury), since these comments did not jeopardize a respondent's confidentiality.

REFERENCES

Abrego, Leisy. 2008. "Legitimacy, Social Identity, and the Mobilization of Law: The Effects of Assembly Bill 540 on Undocumented Students in California." *Law & Social Inquiry* 33(3):709–34. doi: 10.1111/j.1747-4469.2008.00119.x.

Abrego, Leisy. 2014. *Sacrificing Families: Navigating Laws, Labor, and Love Across Borders*. Stanford, CA: Stanford University Press.

Abrego, Leisy J. 2011. "Legal Consciousness of Undocumented Latinos: Fear and Stigma as Barriers to Claims-Making for First- and 1.5-Generation Immigrants." *Law & Society Review* 45(2):337–70. doi: https://doi.org/10.1111/j.1540-5893.2011.00435.x.

Abrego, Leisy J., and Sarah M. Lakhani. 2015. "Incomplete Inclusion: Legal Violence and Immigrants in Liminal Legal Statuses." *Law & Policy* 37(4):265–93. doi: 10.1111/lapo.12039.

Abrego, Leisy Janet. 2006. "'I Can't Go to College Because I Don't Have Papers': Incorporation Patterns of Latino Undocumented Youth." *Latino Studies* 4(3):212–31. doi: 10.1057/palgrave.lst.8600200.

Alba, Richard D. 1985. *Italian Americans: Into the Twilight of Ethnicity*. Englewood Cliffs, NJ: Prentice-Hall.

Alba, Richard, and Victor Nee. 2005. *Remaking the American Mainstream: Assimilation and Contemporary Immigration*. Cambridge, MA: Harvard University Press.

Alexander, Karl, Doris Entwisle, and Linda Olson. 2014. *The Long Shadow: Family Background, Disadvantaged Urban Youth, and the Transition to Adulthood*. 1st ed. New York: Russell Sage Foundation.

Alexander, Michelle. 2012. *The New Jim Crow: Mass Incarceration in the Age of Colorblindness*. New York: New Press.

Almeida, Paul. 2008. "The Sequencing of Success: Organizing Templates and Neoliberal Policy Outcomes." *Mobilization: An International Quarterly* 13(2):165–87. doi: 10.17813/maiq.13.2.cl74r52765281005.

Amaral, Ernesto Friedrich, and Wilson Fusco. 2005. *Shaping Brazil: The Role of International Migration*. Washington, DC: Migration Policy Institute.

American Civil Liberties Union. 2014. "The Constitution in the 100-Mile Border Zone." Retrieved April 5, 2024 (https://www.aclu.org/documents/constitution-100-mile-border-zone).

American Immigration Council. 2016. "The Three- and Ten-Year Bars: How New Rules Expand Eligibility for Waivers." *American Immigration Council*. Retrieved September 4, 2022 (https://www.americanimmigrationcouncil.org/research/three-and-ten-year-bars).

American Immigration Council. 2022. "The Facts About the Individual Taxpayer Identification Number (ITIN)." *American Immigration Council*. Retrieved September 25, 2023 (https://www.americanimmigrationcouncil.org/research/facts-about-individual-taxpayer-identification-number-itin).

Andrews, George Reid. 1996. "Brazilian Racial Democracy, 1900–90: An American Counterpoint." *Journal of Contemporary History* 31(3):483–507. doi: 10.1177/002200949603100303.

Aptekar, Sofya, and Amy Hsin. 2023. "Stratified Entry into Illegality: How Immigration Policy Shapes Being Undocumented." *Social Forces* 102(1):45–62. doi: 10.1093/sf/soac125.

Aranda, Elizabeth, Elizabeth Vaquera, and Isabel Sousa-Rodriguez. 2015. "Personal and Cultural Trauma and the Ambivalent National Identities of Undocumented Young Adults in the USA." *Journal of Intercultural Studies* 36:1–20. doi: 10.1080/07256868.2015.1072906.

Armenta, Amada. 2017. "Racializing Crimmigration: Structural Racism, Colorblindness, and the Institutional Production of Immigrant Criminality." *Sociology of Race and Ethnicity* 3(1):82–95. doi: 10.1177/2332649216648714.

Arnett, Jeffrey Jensen. 2004. *Emerging Adulthood: The Winding Road from the Late Teens through the Twenties*. New York: Oxford University Press.

Asad, Asad L. 2020. "On the Radar: System Embeddedness and Latin American Immigrants' Perceived Risk of Deportation." *Law & Society Review* 54(1):133–67. doi: 10.1111/lasr.12460.

Asad, Asad L. 2023. *Engage and Evade: How Latino Immigrant Families Manage Surveillance in Everyday Life*. Princeton, NJ: Princeton University Press.

Asad, Asad L., and Matthew Clair. 2018. "Racialized Legal Status as a Social Determinant of Health." *Social Science & Medicine* 199:19–28. doi: 10.1016/j.socscimed.2017.03.010.

Bailey, Stanley R., Fabrício Fialho, and Michelle Peria. 2018. "Support for Race-Targeted Affirmative Action in Brazil." *Ethnicities* 18(6):765–98. doi: 10.1177/1468796814567787.

Bailey, Stanley R., Mara Loveman, and Jeronimo O. Muniz. 2013. "Measures of 'Race' and the Analysis of Racial Inequality in Brazil." *Social Science Research* 42(1):106–19. doi: 10.1016/j.ssresearch.2012.06.006.

Bany, James A., Belinda Robnett, and Cynthia Feliciano. 2014. "Gendered Black Exclusion: The Persistence of Racial Stereotypes Among Daters." *Race and Social Problems* 6(3):201–13. doi: 10.1007/s12552-014-9122-5.

Bashi Treitler, Vilna. 2013. *The Ethnic Project: Transforming Racial Fiction into Ethnic Factions.* Stanford, CA: Stanford University Press.

Batlan, Felice. 2020. "'She Was Surprised and Furious': Expatriation, Suffrage, Immigration and the Fragility of Women's Citizenship, 1907–1940." *Stanford Journal of Civil Rights and Civil Liberties* 15:315–49.

Bejarano, Carolina Alonso, Lucia López Juárez, Mirian A. Mijangos García, and Daniel M. Goldstein. 2019. *Decolonizing Ethnography: Undocumented Immigrants and New Directions in Social Science.* Durham, NC: Duke University Press.

Bertrand, Marianne, and Sendhil Mullainathan. 2004. "Are Emily and Greg More Employable Than Lakisha and Jamal? A Field Experiment on Labor Market Discrimination." *American Economic Review* 94(4):991–1013. doi: 10.1257/0002828042002561.

Beserra, Bernadete. 2005. "From Brazilians to Latinos? Racialization and Latinidad in the Making of Brazilian Carnival in Los Angeles." *Latino Studies* 3(1):53–75. doi: 10.1057/palgrave.lst.8600131.

Beserra, Bernadette. 2008. "In the Shadow of Carmen Miranda and the Carnival: Brazilian Immigrant Women in Los Angeles." Pp. 57–79 in *Becoming Brazuca: Brazilian Immigration to the United States*, edited by C. Jouët-Pastré and L. J. Braga. Cambridge, MA: Harvard University Press.

Blau, Peter M., Carolyn Beeker, and Kevin M. Fitzpatrick. 1984. "Intersecting Social Affiliations and Intermarriage*." *Social Forces* 62(3):585–606. doi: 10.1093/sf/62.3.585.

Bonilla-Silva, Eduardo. 2017. *Racism without Racists: Color-Blind Racism and the Persistence of Racial Inequality in America.* 5th ed. Lanham, MD: Rowman & Littlefield.

Boston Planning & Development Agency Research Division. 2017. *Brazilians in Boston.* Boston.

Braga, Leticia J., and Clémence Jouët-Pastré. 2008. "Introduction: Interdisciplinary Perspectives on Becoming Brazuca." Pp. 1–21 in *Becoming Brazuca: Brazilian Immigration to the United States., Cambridge Studies in Comparative Politics*, edited by C. Jouët-Pastré and L. J. Braga. Cambridge, MA: Harvard University Press.

Branch, Enobong. 2011. *Opportunity Denied: Limiting Black Women to Devalued Work.* New Brunswick, NJ: Rutgers University Press.

Brodkin, Karen. 1998. *How Jews Became White Folks and What That Says about Race in America.* New Brunswick, NJ: Rutgers University Press.

Brown, Hana E. 2011. "Refugees, Rights, and Race: How Legal Status Shapes Liberian Immigrants' Relationship with the State." *Social Problems* 58(1):144–63. doi: 10.1525/sp.2011.58.1.144.

Burciaga Edelina M., and Aaron Malone. 2021. " Intensified Liminal Legality: The Impact of the DACA Rescission for Undocumented Young Adults in Colorado." *Law & Social Inquiry*: 46(4):1092-1114. doi:10.1017/lsi.2021.8

Calavita, Kitty. 2007. "Immigration Law, Race, and Identity." *Annual Review of Law and Social Science* 3(1):1–20. doi: 10.1146/annurev.lawsocsci.3.081806.112745.

Caldwell, Beth C. 2019. *Deported Americans: Life After Deportation to Mexico.* Durham, NC: Duke University Press.

Carter, Prudence L. 2007. *Keepin' It Real: School Success Beyond Black and White.* Oxford and New York: Oxford University Press.

Castañeda, Heide. 2019. *Borders of Belonging: Struggle and Solidarity in Mixed-Status Immigrant Families.* Stanford, CA: Stanford University Press.

Castillo, Mariano. 2012. "Rising Brazil Tackles Immigration Question." *CNN.* Retrieved October 23, 2023 (https://www.cnn.com/2012/01/28/world/americas/brazil-immigration/index.html).

Cebulko, Kara. 2014. "Documented, Undocumented, and Liminally Legal: Legal Status During the Transition to Adulthood for 1.5-Generation Brazilian Immigrants." *Sociological Quarterly* 55(1):143–67. doi: https://doi.org/10.1111/tsq.12045.

Cebulko, Kara. 2016. "Marrying for Papers? From Economically Strategic to Normative and Relational Dimensions of the Transition to Adulthood for Unauthorized 1.5-Generation Brazilians." *Sociological Perspectives* 59(4):760–75. doi: 10.1177/0731121415611684.

Cebulko, Kara. 2018. "Privilege without Papers: Intersecting Inequalities among 1.5-Generation Brazilians in Massachusetts." *Ethnicities* 18(2):225–41. doi: 10.1177/1468796817752562.

Cebulko, Kara. 2021. "Becoming White in a White Supremacist State: The Public and Psychological Wages of Whiteness for Undocumented 1.5-generation Brazilians." *Social Sciences* 10(5): 184. doi: 10.3390/socsci10050184.

Cebulko, Kara B. 2013. *Documented, Undocumented, and Something Else: The Incorporation of Children of Brazilian Immigrants.* El Paso, TX: LFB Scholarly Publishing.

Cebulko, Kara, and Alexis Silver. 2016. "Navigating DACA in Hospitable and Hostile States: State Responses and Access to Membership in the Wake of Deferred Action for Childhood Arrivals." *American Behavioral Scientist* 60(13):1553–74. doi: 10.1177/0002764216664942.

Chappetta, Kelsey, and Joan Barth. 2022. "Interracial Dating: A Closer Look at Race and Gender Differences in Heterosexual Dating Preferences." *Sexuality & Culture* 26(3):1060–73. doi: 10.1007/s12119-021-09931-9.

Chari, Sharad. 2017. "Three Moments of Stuart Hall in South Africa: Postcolonial-Postsocialist Marxisms of the Future." *Critical Sociology* 43(6):831–45. doi: 10.1177/0896920515620475.

Chavez, Leo R. 2013. *The Latino Threat: Constructing Immigrants, Citizens, and the Nation.* Second. Stanford: Stanford University Press.

Childs, Erica Chito. 2005. "Looking behind the Stereotypes of the 'Angry Black Woman': An Exploration of Black Women's Responses to Interracial Relationships on JSTOR." *Gender and Society* 19(4):544–61.

Cho, Esther Yoona. 2017. "Revisiting Ethnic Niches: A Comparative Analysis of the Labor Market Experiences of Asian and Latino Undocumented Young Adults." *RSF: The Russell Sage Foundation Journal of the Social Sciences* 3(4):97–115. doi: 10.7758/RSF.2017.3.4.06.

Chomsky, Aviva. 2014. *Undocumented: How Immigration Became Illegal.* Boston: Beacon Press.

Chomsky, Aviva. 2018. *"They Take Our Jobs!" and 20 Other Myths about Immigration.* Expanded edition. Boston: Beacon Press.

Christie, Nils. 1986. "The Ideal Victim." Pp. 17–30 in *From Crime Policy to Victim Policy*, edited by E. A. Fattah. London: Palgrave Macmillan.

Clarno, Andy, and Salim Vally. 2023. "The Context of Struggle: Racial Capitalism and Political Praxis in South Africa." *Ethnic and Racial Studies* 46(16):3425–47. doi: 10.1080/01419870.2022.2143239.

Clergé, Orly. 2014. "Toward a Minority Culture of Mobility: Immigrant Integration into the African-American Middle Class." *Sociology Compass* 8(10):1167–82. doi: 10.1111/soc4.12201.

Clergé, Orly. 2019. *The New Noir: Race, Identity, & Diaspora in Black Suburbia*. Berkeley: University of California Press.

Cohambee River Collective. 1977. "A Black Feminist Statement." Pp. 231–40 in *Words of Fire: An Anthology of African-American Feminist Thought*, edited by B. Guy-Sheftall. New York: New Press.

Cohn, D'Vera, Juliana Menasce Horowitz, Rachel Minkin, Richard Fry, and Kiley Hurst. 2022. *The Demographics of Multigenerational Households*. Washington, DC.

Collins, Patricia Hill. 1990. *Black Feminist Thought: Knowledge, Consciousness, and the Politics of Empowerment*. Boston: Unwin Hyman.

Collins, Patricia Hill. 2015. "Intersectionality's Definitional Dilemmas." *Annual Review of Sociology* 41(1):1–20. doi: 10.1146/annurev-soc-073014-112142.

Cook-Martín, David, and David Fitz Gerald. 2010. "Liberalism and the Limits of Inclusion: Race and Immigration Law in the Americas, 1850–2000." *Journal of Interdisciplinary History* 41(1):7–25.

Coontz, Stephanie. 2006. *Marriage, a History: How Love Conquered Marriage*. New York: Penguin Random House.

Cornell, Stephen, and Douglas Hartman. 2006. *Ethnicity and Race: Making Identities in a Changing World*. Thousand Oaks, CA: Sage Publications.

Coutin, Susan. 1993. *The Culture of Protest: Religious Activism and the US Sanctuary Movement*. Boulder, CO: Westview Press.

Cox, Oliver Cromwell. 1948. *Caste, Class, and Race*. New York: Modern Reader.

Crenshaw, Kimberlé. 1991. "Mapping the Margins: Intersectionality, Identity Politics, and Violence against Women of Color." *Stanford Law Review* 43(6):1241–99. doi: 10.2307/1229039.

Crutchfield, Jandel, Latocia Keyes, Maya Williams, and Danielle R. Eugene. 2022. "A Scoping Review of Colorism in Schools: Academic, Social, and Emotional Experiences of Students of Color." *Social Sciences* 11 (1): 15. https://doi.org/10.3390/socsci11010015.

Dalto, Fabiano Abranches Silva. 2019. "Brazilian Financial Crisis in the 1980s: Historical Precedent of an Economy Governed by Financial Interests." *Revista de Economia Contemporânea* 23:e192332. doi: 10.1590/198055272332.

DeBiaggi, Sylvia Duarte Dantas. 2001. *Changing Gender Roles: Brazilian Immigrant Families in the US*. New York: LFB Scholarly LLC.

De Genova, Nicholas P. 2002. "Migrant 'Illegality' and Deportability in Everyday Life." *Annual Review of Anthropology* 31(1):419–47. doi: 10.1146/annurev.anthro.31.040402.085432.

Degler, Carl N. 1986. *Neither Black nor White: Slavery and Race Relations in Brazil and the United States*. Madison: University of Wisconsin Press.

Donato, Rubén, and Jarrod Hanson. 2012. "Legally White, Socially 'Mexican': The Politics of De Jure and De Facto School Segregation in the American Southwest." *Harvard Educational Review* 82(2):202–25. doi: 10.17763/haer.82.2.a562315u72355106.

Dowling, Julie A. 2014. *Mexican Americans and the Question of Race.* Reprint. Austin: University of Texas Press.

Dreby, Joanna. 2015. *Everyday Illegal: When Policies Undermine Immigrant Families.* 1st ed. Oakland: University of California Press.

Du Bois, W. E. B. 1899. *The Philadelphia Negro: A Social Study.* Philadelphia: Ginn.

Du Bois, W. E. B. 1935. *Black Reconstruction in America, 1860–1880.* New York: Atheneum.

Du Bois, W. E. B. 1965. *The Souls of Black Folk.* London: Longman, Green.

Du Bois, W. E. B. 2013. "The Black Man and the Unions." Pp. 97–100 in *Capitalism vs. Collectivism: The Colonial Era to 1945.* New Brunswick, NJ: Routledge.

Edin, Kathryn, and Maria Kefalas. 2011. *Promises I Can Keep: Why Poor Women Put Motherhood before Marriage.* Berkeley: University of California Press.

Enriquez, Laura. 2011. "'Because We Feel the Pressure and We Also Feel the Support': Examining the Educational Success of Undocumented Immigrant Latina/o Students." *Harvard Educational Review* 81(3):476–500. doi: 10.17763/haer.81.3.w7k703q050143762.

Enriquez, Laura E. 2017. "A 'Master Status' or the 'Final Straw'? Assessing the Role of Immigration Status in Latino Undocumented Youths' Pathways out of School." *Journal of Ethnic and Migration Studies* 43(9):1526–43. doi: 10.1080/1369183X.2016.1235483.

Enriquez, Laura E. 2019. "Border Hopping Mexicans, Law-Abiding Asians, and Racialized Illegality: Analyzing Undocumented College Students' Experiences through a Relational Lens." *Relational Formations of Race: Theory, Method and Practice.* edited by N. Molina, D. Martinez HoSang, and R.A. Gutiérrez. Berkeley: University of California Press.

Enriquez, Laura E. 2020. *Of Love and Papers: How Immigration Policy Affects Romance and Family.* Berkeley: University of California Press.

Enriquez, Laura E., and Daniel Millán. 2019. "Situational Triggers and Protective Locations: Conceptualising the Salience of Deportability in Everyday Life." *Journal of Ethnic and Migration Studies* 0(0):1–20. doi: 10.1080/1369183X.2019.1694877.

Epp, Charles R., Steven Maynard-Moody, and Donald P. Haider-Markel. 2014. *Pulled Over: How Police Stops Define Race and Citizenship.* Chicago: University of Chicago Press.

Escudero, Kevin. 2020. *Organizing While Undocumented: Immigrant Youth's Political Activism Under the Law.* New York: New York University Press.

Feagin, Joe R. 2020. *The White Racial Frame: Centuries of Racial Framing and Counter-Framing.* 3rd ed. New York: Routledge.

Feagin, Joe R., and Melvin P. Sikes. 1994. *Living with Racism: The Black Middle-Class Experience.* Boston: Beacon Press.

Feliciano Cynthia, Rennie Lee, and Belinda Robnett. 2011. "Racial Boundaries among Latinos: Evidence from Internet Daters' Racial Preferences." *Social Problems* 58:189–212.

Ferber, Abby L. 1999. *White Man Falling: Race, Gender, and White Supremacy*. Lanham, MD: Rowman & Littlefield.
Finlay, Linda. 2002. "'Outing' the Researcher: The Provenance, Process, and Practice of Reflexivity." *Qualitative Health Research* 12(4):531–45. doi: 10.1177/104973202129120052.
FitzGerald, David Scott, and David Cook-Martín. 2014. *Culling the Masses: The Democratic Origins of Racist Immigration Policy in the Americas*. Cambridge, MA: Harvard University Press.
Flores-González, Nilda. 2017. *Citizens but Not Americans: Race and Belonging among Latino Millennials*. New York: New York University Press.
Fox, Cybelle. 2012. *Three Worlds of Relief: Race, Immigration, and the American Welfare State from the Progressive Era to the New Deal*. Princeton, NJ: Princeton University Press.
Francis, Dania V., and William A. Darity. 2021. "Separate and Unequal Under One Roof: How the Legacy of Racialized Tracking Perpetuates Within-School Segregation." *RSF: The Russell Sage Foundation Journal of the Social Sciences* 7(1):187–202. doi: 10.7758/rsf.2021.7.1.11.
French, Jan Hoffman. 2013. "Rethinking Police Violence in Brazil: Unmasking the Public Secret of Race." *Latin American Politics and Society* 55(4):161–81. doi: 10.1111/j.1548-2456.2013.00212.x.
Fresnoza-Flot, Asuncion. 2022. "Multiform Transmission and Belonging: Buddhist Social Spaces of Thai Migrant Women in Belgium." *Advances in Southeast Asian Studies* 15(2). doi: 10.14764/10.ASEAS-0079.
Fresnoza-Flot, Asuncion, and Laura Merla. 2018. "'Global Householding' in Mixed Families: The Case of Thai Migrant Women in Belgium." Pp. 23–37 in *Making Multicultural Families in Europe: Gender and Intergenerational Relations, Palgrave Macmillan Studies in Family and Intimate Life*, edited by I. Crespi, S. Giada Meda, and L. Merla. Cham, Switzerland: Springer International.
Freyre, Gilberto. 1986. *The Masters and the Slaves [Casa-Grande and Senzala]*. Berkeley: University of California Press.
Fujita, Dennis Minoru, Felipe Scassi Salvador, Giselle Pacífico Sartori Damião, Gerusa Maria Figueiredo, and Luiz Henrique da Silva Nali. 2019. "Increase of Immigrants in Emerging Countries: Free Public Healthcare and Vaccination as Preventive Measures in Brazil." *Cadernos de Saúde Pública* 35:e00228118. doi: 10.1590/0102-311X00228118.
Furstenberg, Frank F. 2010. "On a New Schedule: Transitions to Adulthood and Family Change." *Future of Children* 20(1):67–87.
Gans, Herbert J. 1979. "Symbolic Ethnicity: The Future of Ethnic Groups and Cultures in America*." *Ethnic and Racial Studies* 2(1):1–20. doi: 10.1080/01419870.1979.9993248.
García, Angela S. 2019. *Legal Passing: Navigating Undocumented Life and Local Immigration Law*. Berkeley: University of California Press.
García, San Juanita. 2017. "Racializing 'Illegality': An Intersectional Approach to Understanding How Mexican-Origin Women Navigate an Anti-Immigrant Climate." *Sociology of Race and Ethnicity* 3(4):474–90. doi: 10.1177/2332649217713315.

García, San Juanita. 2018. "Living a Deportation Threat: Anticipatory Stressors Confronted by Undocumented Mexican Immigrant Women." *Race and Social Problems* 10(3):221–34. doi: 10.1007/s12552-018-9244-2.

Garner, Steve, and Saher Selod. 2015. "The Racialization of Muslims: Empirical Studies of Islamophobia." *Critical Sociology* 41(1):9–19. doi: 10.1177/0896920514531606.

Garraio, Júlia. 2019. "Framing Sexual Violence in Portuguese Colonialism: On Some Practices of Contemporary Cultural Representation and Remembrance." *Violence Against Women* 25(13):1558–77. doi: 10.1177/1077801219869547.

Gelatt, Julia, Devlin Hanson, Heather Koball, Carl Hedman, Chris Hayes, and Rolf Pendall. 2015. *How Immigrants Are Reshaping Residential Segregation*. Washington DC: Urban Institute.

Gilbert, Keon L, and Rayshawn Ray. 2016. "Why Police Kill Black Males with Impunity: Applying Public Health Critical Race Praxis (PHCRP) to Address the Determinants of Policing Behaviors and "Justifiable" Homicides in the USA." *Journal of Urban Health* (1): 122-140 doi: 10.1007/s11524-015-0005-x.

Gleeson, Shannon. 2010. "Labor Rights for All? The Role of Undocumented Immigrant Status for Worker Claims Making." *Law & Social Inquiry* 35(03):561–602. doi: 10.1111/j.1747-4469.2010.01196.x.

Gleeson, Shannon, and Roberto G. Gonzales. 2012. "When Do Papers Matter? An Institutional Analysis of Undocumented Life in the United States." *International Migration* 50(4):1–19. doi: https://doi.org/10.1111/j.1468-2435.2011.00726.x.

Goffman, Erving. 1959. *The Presentation of Self in Everyday Life*. 1st edition. New York: Anchor.

Golash-Boza, Tanya. 2006. "Dropping the Hyphen? Becoming Latino(a)-American through Racialized Assimilation." *Social Forces* 85(1):27–55.

Golash-Boza, Tanya, and Pierrette Hondagneu-Sotelo. 2013. "Latino Immigrant Men and the Deportation Crisis: A Gendered Racial Removal Program." *Latino Studies* 11(3):271–92. doi: 10.1057/lst.2013.14.

Golash-Boza, Tanya Maria. 2011. *Immigration Nation: Raids, Detentions, and Deportations in Post-9/11 America*. Boulder, CO: Paradigm.

Golash-Boza, Tanya Maria. 2015. *Deported: Immigrant Policing, Disposable Labor and Global Capitalism*. New York: New York University Press.

Golash-Boza, Tanya, and Cecilia Menjívar. 2012. "Causes and Consequences of International Migration: Sociological Evidence for the Right to Mobility." *International Journal of Human Rights* 16(8):1213–27. doi: 10.1080/13642987.2012.727802.

Goldstein, Donna. 1999. "'Interracial' Sex and Racial Democracy in Brazil: Twin Concepts?" *American Anthropologist* 101(3):563–78. doi: 10.1525/aa.1999.101.3.563.

Gomberg-Muñoz, Ruth. 2016. *Becoming Legal: Immigration Law and Mixed-Status Families*. Oxford: Oxford University Press.

Gonzales, Roberto G. 2010. "On the Wrong Side of the Tracks: Understanding the Effects of School Structure and Social Capital in the Educational Pursuits of Undocumented Immigrant Students." *Peabody Journal of Education* 85(4):469–85. doi: 10.1080/0161956X.2010.518039.

Gonzales, Roberto G. 2011. "Learning to Be Illegal: Undocumented Youth and Shifting Legal Contexts in the Transition to Adulthood." *American Sociological Review* 76(4):602–19. doi: 10.1177/0003122411411901.

Gonzales, Roberto G. 2012. "In Spite of the Odds: Undocumented Immigrant Youth, School Networks, and College Success." Pp. 253–74 in *The Immigrant Paradox in Children and Adolescents: Is Becoming American a Developmental Risk?* Washington, DC: American Psychological Association.

Gonzales, Roberto G. 2016. *Lives in Limbo: Undocumented and Coming of Age in America*. Oakland: University of California Press.

Gonzales, Roberto G., and Edelina Burciaga. 2018. "Segmented Pathways of Illegality: Reconciling the Coexistence of Master and Auxiliary Statuses in the Experiences of 1.5-Generation Undocumented Young Adults." *Ethnicities* 18(2):178–91. doi: https://doi.org/10.1177/1468796818767176.

Gonzales, Roberto G., and Ariel G. Ruiz. 2014. "Dreaming beyond the Fields: Undocumented Youth, Rural Realities and a Constellation of Disadvantage." *Latino Studies* 12(2):194–216. doi: 10.1057/lst.2014.23.

Gonzales, Roberto G., and Stephen P. Ruszczyk. 2021. "The Legal Status Divide among the Children of Immigrants." *Daedalus* 150(2):135–49. doi: 10.1162/daed_a_01851.

Gonzales, Roberto G., Veronica Terriquez, and Stephen P. Ruszczyk. 2014. "Becoming DACAmented: Assessing the Short-Term Benefits of Deferred Action for Childhood Arrivals (DACA)." *American Behavioral Scientist* 58(14):1852–72. doi: 10.1177/0002764214550288.

González, Juan. 2000. *Harvest of Empire: A History of Latinos in America*. London: Penguin Books.

Goza, Franklin. 1994. "Brazilian Immigration to North America." *International Migration Review* 28(1):136–52. doi: 10.1177/019791839402800107.

Greenman, Emily, and Matthew Hall. 2013. "Legal Status and Educational Transitions for Mexican and Central American Immigrant Youth." *Social Forces* 91(4):1475–98. doi: 10.1093/sf/sot040.

Groes, Christian, and Fernandez. 2018. "Intimate Mobilities: Sexual Economies, Marriage and Migration in a Disparate World." in *Intimate Mobilities*. Berghahn Books.

Gutiérrez, David G. 1995. *Walls and Mirrors: Mexican Americans, Mexican Immigrants, and the Politics of Ethnicity*. Berkeley: University of California Press.

Gutirrez, Jorge. 2013. "I Am Undocuqueer: New Strategies for Alliance Building for the LGBTQ and Immigrant Rights Movements." Huffington Post. Retrieved October 21, 2023 (https://www.huffpost.com/entry/i-am-undocuqueer_b_2521339).

Hacker, Karen, Jocelyn Chu, Carolyn Leung, Robert Marra, Alex Pirie, Mohamed Brahimi, Margaret English, Joshua Beckmann, Dolores Acevedo-Garcia, and Robert P. Marlin. 2011. "The Impact of Immigration and Customs Enforcement on Immigrant Health: Perceptions of Immigrants in Everett, Massachusetts, USA." *Social Science & Medicine* 73(4):586–94. doi: 10.1016/j.socscimed.2011.06.007.

Hall, Stuart. 1980. "Race, Articulation, and Societies Structured in Dominance." Pp. 305–45 in *Sociological Theories: Race and Colonialism*, edited by UNESCO. Paris: UNESCO.

Hamad, Ruby. 2019. *White Tears, Brown Scars: How White Feminism Betrays Women of Color*. Melbourne: Melbourne University Press.

Hamilton, Erin R., Caitlin Patler, and Robin Savinar. 2021. "Transition into Liminal Legality: DACA's Mixed Impacts on Education and Employment among Young Adult Immigrants in California." *Social Problems* 68(3):675–95. doi: 10.1093/socpro/spaa016.

Haney López, Ian. 1996. *White by Law: The Legal Construction of Race*. New York: New York University Press.

Haney López, Ian F. Haney. 1994. "The Social Construction of Race: Some Observations on Illusion, Fabrication, and Choice." *Harvard Civil Rights–Civil Liberties Law Review* 29:1.

Harris, Cheryl I. 1993. "Whiteness as Property." *Harvard Law Review*. Retrieved October 15, 2023 (https://harvardlawreview.org/print/no-volume/whiteness-as-property/).

Harris, David R., and Hiromi Ono. 2005. "How Many Interracial Marriages Would There Be If All Groups Were of Equal Size in All Places? A New Look at National Estimates of Interracial Marriage." *Social Science Research* 34(1):236–51. doi: 10.1016/j.ssresearch.2004.01.002.

Harris, Tina M., and Pamela J. Kalbfleisch. 2000. "Interracial Dating: The Implications of Race for Initiating a Romantic Relationship." *Howard Journal of Communications* 11(1):49–64. doi: 10.1080/106461700246715.

Harvey, David. 2003. *The New Imperialism*. Oxford: Oxford University Press.

Headley, Andrea M., and James E. Wright II. 2020. "Is Representation Enough? Racial Disparities in Levels of Force and Arrests by Police." *Public Administration Review* 80(6):1051–62. doi: 10.1111/puar.13225.

Hernández, Tanya Katerí. 2012. *Racial Subordination in Latin America: The Role of the State, Customary Law, and the New Civil Rights Response*. Cambridge: Cambridge University Press.

Herrera, Juan. 2016. "Racialized Illegality: The Regulation of Informal Labor and Space." *Latino Studies* 14(3):320–43. doi: 10.1057/s41276-016-0007-1.

Hing, Bill Ong. 2004. *Defining America Through Immigration Policy*. Chicago: Temple University Press.

Hitlin, Steven, J. Scott Brown, and Glen H. Elder Jr. 2007. "Measuring Latinos: Racial vs. Ethnic Classification and Self-Understandings." *Social Forces* 86(2):587–611. doi: 10.1093/sf/86.2.587.

hooks, bell. 1981. *Ain't I a Woman: Black Women and Feminism*. Boston: South End Press.

Ide, Yayoi, and Liz Beddoe. 2023. "Challenging Perspectives: Reflexivity as a Critical Approach to Qualitative Social Work Research." *Qualitative Social Work* 14733250231173522. doi: 10.1177/14733250231173522.

Ignatiev, Noel. 1995. *How the Irish Became White*. New York: Routledge.
Ikemura Amaral, Aiko. 2022. "Neither Natives nor Nationals in Brazil: The 'Indianisation' of Bolivian Migrants in the City of São Paulo." *Bulletin of Latin American Research* 41(1):53–68. doi: 10.1111/blar.13287.
Itzigsohn, José, and Karida L. Brown. 2020. *The Sociology of W. E. B. Du Bois*. New York: New York University Press.
Jayaraman, Saru. 2011. "Restaurants and Race: Discrimination and Disparity in the Food Service Sector." *Race, Poverty & the Environment* 18(1):7–9.
Jimenez, Anthony M. 2021. "The Legal Violence of Care: Navigating the US Health Care System While Undocumented and Illegible." *Social Science & Medicine* 270:113676. doi: 10.1016/j.socscimed.2021.113676.
Johnson, Kevin R. 2007. *Opening the Floodgates: Why America Needs to Rethink Its Borders and Immigration Law*. New York: New York University Press.
Jordan-Zachery, Julia S. 2007. "Am I a Black Woman or a Woman Who Is Black? A Few Thoughts on the Meaning of Intersectionality." *Politics & Gender* 3(2):254–63. doi: 10.1017/S1743923X07000074.
Joseph, Tiffany D. 2015. *Race on the Move: Brazilian Migrants and the Global Reconstruction of Race*. 1st ed. Stanford, CA: Stanford University Press.
Joseph, Tiffany D. 2016. "What Health Care Reform Means for Immigrants: Comparing the Affordable Care Act and Massachusetts Health Reforms." *Journal of Health Politics, Policy and Law* 41(1):101–16. doi: 10.1215/03616878-3445632.
Joseph, Tiffany D. 2017. "Falling through the Coverage Cracks: How Documentation Status Minimizes Immigrants' Access to Health Care." *Journal of Health Politics, Policy and Law* 42(5):961–84. doi: 10.1215/03616878-3940495.
Joseph, Tiffany, and Tanya Golash-Boza. 2021. "Double Consciousness in the 21st Century: Du Boisian Theory and the Problem of Racialized Legal Status." *Social Sciences* 10(9):345. doi: 10.3390/socsci10090345.
Kasinitz, Philip, Mary C. Waters, John H. Mollenkopf, and Jennifer Holdaway. 2008. *Inheriting the City: The Children of Immigrants Come of Age*. New York: Russell Sage Foundation.
Kefalas, Maria J., Frank F. Furstenberg, Patrick J. Carr, and Laura Napolitano. 2011. "'Marriage Is More Than Being Together': The Meaning of Marriage for Young Adults." *Journal of Family Issues* 32(7):845–75. doi: 10.1177/0192513X10397277.
King, Katrina Quisumbing. 2019. "Recentering US Empire: A Structural Perspective on the Color Line." *Sociology of Race and Ethnicity* 5(1):11–25. doi: 10.1177/2332649218761977.
Lamont, Michèle, and Virág Molnár. 2002. "The Study of Boundaries in the Social Sciences." *Annual Review of Sociology* 28(1):167–95. doi: 10.1146/annurev.soc.28.110601.141107.
Lima, Alvaro, and Carlos Siqueira. 2007. "Brazilians in the US and Massachusetts: A Demographic and Economic Profile." *Gastón Institute Publications*.
Lima, Alvaro, and Carlos Siqueira. 2011. "Socio-Economic Profile of Brazilian Businesses in Allston-Brighton." *Gastón Institute Publications*.

Lima, Marcia, and Ian Prates. 2019. "Racial Inequalities in Brazil: A Persistent Challenge." Pp. 113–34 in *Paths of Inequality in Brazil: A Half-Century of Changes*, edited by M. Arretche. Cham, Switzerland: Springer International.

Logan, John R., and Charles Zhang. 2010. "Global Neighborhoods: New Pathways to Diversity and Separation." *American Journal of Sociology* 115(4):1069–1109. doi: 10.1086/649498.

López, Jane Lilly. 2021. *Unauthorized Love: Mixed-Citizenship Couples Negotiating Intimacy, Immigration, and the State*. Stanford, CA: Stanford University Press.

Lopez, Mark Hugo, Jeffrey S. Passel, and D'vera Cohn. 2021. *Key Facts about the Changing US Unauthorized Immigrant Population*. Washington, DC: Pew Research Center.

Loveman, Mara. 2014. *National Colors: Racial Classification and the State in Latin America*. Oxford: Oxford University Press.

Loveman, Mara, Jeronimo O. Muniz, and Stanley R. Bailey. 2012. "Brazil in Black and White? Race Categories, the Census, and the Study of Inequality." *Ethnic and Racial Studies* 35(8):1466–83. doi: 10.1080/01419870.2011.607503.

Maghbouleh, Neda. 2017. *The Limits of Whiteness: Iranian Americans and the Everyday Politics of Race*. Stanford, CA: Stanford University Press.

Marcelli, Enrico, Louisa Holmes, David Estella, Fausto da Rocha, Phillip Granberry, and Orfeu Buxton. 2008. "(In)Visible (Im)Migrants: The Health and Socioeconomic Integration of Brazilians in Metropolitan Boston."

Marcelli, Enrico, Louisa Holmes, Magalis Troncoso, Phillip Granberry, and Orfeu Buxton. 2008. "Permanently Temporary? The Health and Socioeconomic Integration of Dominicans in Metropolitan Boston."

Margolis, Maxine. 1994. *Little Brazil: An Ethnography of Brazilian Immigrants in New York City*. Princeton, NJ: Princeton University Press.

Margolis, Maxine. 2007. "Becoming Brazucas: Brazilian Identity in the United States."." Pp. 213–30 in *The Other Latinos: Central and South Americans in the United States*, edited by J. L. Falconi and J. A. Mazzotti. Cambridge, MA: Harvard University Press.

Marrow, Helen. 2003. "To Be or Not to Be (Hispanic or Latino): Brazilian Racial and Ethnic Identity in the United States." *Ethnicities* 3(4):427–64.

Marrow, Helen B., Dina G. Okamoto, Melissa J. García, Muna Adem, and Linda R. Tropp. 2022. "Skin Tone and Mexicans' Perceptions of Discrimination in New Immigrant Destinations." *Social Psychology Quarterly* 85(4):374–85. doi: 10.1177/01902725221128387.

Marshall, Thomas H. 1950. *Citizenship and Social Class*. Vol. 11. New York: Cambridge University Press.

Martes, Ana Cristina Braga. 2000. *Brasileiros Now Stados Unidos: Un Estudo Sobre Imigrantes Em Massachusetts*. São Paulo: Paz e Terra.

Martes, Ana Cristina Braga. 2011. *New Immigrants, New Land: A Study of Brazilians in Massachusetts*. Illustrated edition. Gainesville: University Press of Florida.

Martinez, Lisa M., and Debora M. Ortega. 2019. "Dreams Deterred: The Collateral Consequences Of Localized Immigration Policies On Undocumented Latinos In Colorado." *Law & Policy* 41(1): 120-141. https://doi.org/10.1111/lapo.12118.

Marx, Anthony W. 1997. *Making Race and Nation: A Comparison of South Africa, the United States, and Brazil*. Cambridge: Cambridge University Press.

Massey, Douglas S. 2007. *Categorically Unequal: The American Stratification System*. New York: Russell Sage Foundation.

Massey, Douglas S. 2012. *The New Latino Underclass: Immigration Enforcement as a Race-Making Institution*. Stanford, CA: Stanford Center on Poverty and Inequality.

Massey, Douglas S., and Karen A. Pren. 2012. "Unintended Consequences of US Immigration Policy: Explaining the Post-1965 Surge from Latin America." *Population and Development Review* 38(1):1–29.

Massey, Douglas S., and Magaly R. Sánchez. 2010. *Brokered Boundaries: Creating Immigrant Identity in Anti-Immigrant Times*. New York: Russell Sage Foundation.

McDonald, Daniel Lee. 2014. "The City of Minas: The Founding of Belo Horizonte, Brazil and Modernity in the First Republic, 1889–1897 (Masters Theses. 32.)."

McDonnell, Judith, and Cileine de Lourenço. 2009. "You're Brazilian, Right? What Kind of Brazilian Are You? The Racialization of Brazilian Immigrant Women." *Ethnic and Racial Studies* 32(2):239–56. doi: 10.1080/01419870802361328.

Menjívar, Cecilia. 2006. "Liminal Legality: Salvadoran and Guatemalan Immigrants' Lives in the United States." *American Journal of Sociology* 111(4):999–1037. doi: 10.1086/499509.

Menjívar, Cecilia. 2021. "The Racialization of 'Illegality.'" *Daedalus* 150(2):91–105. doi: 10.1162/daed_a_01848.

Menjívar, Cecilia, and Leisy Abrego. 2012. "Legal Violence: Immigration Law and the Lives of Central American Immigrants." *American Journal of Sociology* 117(5):1380–1421. doi: 10.1086/663575.

Merriam, Sharan B., Juanita Johnson-Bailey, Ming-Yeh Lee, Youngwha Kee, Gabo Ntseane, and Mazanah Muhamad. 2001. "Power and Positionality: Negotiating Insider/Outsider Status Within and Across Cultures." *International Journal of Lifelong Education* 20(5):405–16. doi: 10.1080/02601370120490.

Mineo, Liz. 2007. "Report Says Mass. Brazilians Lead Nation." *State Journal-Register*.

Molinsky, Andrew. 2007. "Cross-Cultural Code-Switching: The Psychological Challenges of Adapting Behavior in Foreign Cultural Interactions." *Academy of Management Review* 32(2):622–40.

Monk, Ellis P., Jr. 2016. "The Consequences of 'Race and Color' in Brazil." *Social Problems* 63(3):413–30. doi: 10.1093/socpro/spw014.

Moshin, Jamie, and Richard Benjamin Crosby. 2018. "Liminally White: Jews, Mormons, and Whiteness." *Communication, Culture and Critique* 11(3):436–54. doi: 10.1093/ccc/tcy009.

Mountz, Alison, Richard Wright, Ines Miyares, and Adrian J. Bailey. 2002. "Lives in Limbo: Temporary Protected Status and Immigrant Identities." *Global Networks* 2(4):335–56. doi: 10.1111/1471-0374.00044.

Muñoz, Carolina Bank. 2011. *Transnational Tortillas: Race, Gender and Shop-Floor Politics in Mexico and the United States*. Ithaca, NY: Cornell University Press.

Muro, Jazmin A., and Lisa M. Martinez. 2018. "Is Love Colorblind?: Racial Blind Spots And Latinas' Romantic Relationships." *Sociology of Race and Ethnicity*. 4(4), 527-540. https://doi-org.providence.idm.oclc.org/10.1177/2332649217748428

Negrón-Gonzales, Genevieve. 2011. "The Making & Unmaking of Common Sense: Undocumented Latino Youth & Political Consciousness." PhD thesis, University of California, Berkeley, CA.

Ngai, Mae. 2004. *Impossible Subjects: Illegal Aliens and the Making of Modern America*. Princeton, NJ: Princeton University Press.

Nicholls, Walter J. 2013. *The DREAMers: How the Undocumented Youth Movement Transformed the Immigrant Rights Debate*. Stanford, CA: Stanford University Press.

Nobles, Melissa. 2000. *Shades of Citizenship: Race and the Census in Modern Politics*. Stanford, CA: Stanford University Press.

Omi, Michael, and Howard Winant. 2014. *Racial Formation in the United States*. 3rd ed. New York: Routledge.

Orfield, Gary, Daniel Losen, Johanna Wald, and Christopher B. Swanson. 2004. *Losing Our Future: How Minority Youth Are Being Left Behind by the Graduation Rate Crisis*. Harvard Education Publishing Group, Cambridge, MA 02138.

Ortiz, Vilma, and Edward Telles. 2012. "Racial Identity and Racial Treatment of Mexican Americans." *Race and Social Problems* 4(1):41–56. doi: 10.1007/s12552-012-9064-8.

Osgood, D. Wayne, E. Michael Foster, Constance Flanagan, and Gretchen R, eds. 2007. *On Your Own without a Net: The Transition to Adulthood for Vulnerable Populations*. Chicago: University of Chicago Press.

Osuji, Chinyere K. 2019. *Boundaries of Love: Interracial Marriage and the Meaning of Race*. New York: New York University Press.

Pande, Amrita. 2021. "'Mix or Match?': Transnational Fertility Industry and White Desirability." *Medical Anthropology* 40(4):335–47. doi: 10.1080/01459740.2021.1877289.

Pascoe, Peggy. 2009. *What Comes Naturally: Miscegenation Law and the Making of Race in America*. Oxford and New York: Oxford University Press.

Patler, Caitlin. 2014. "Racialized Illegality: The Convergence of Race and Legal Status among Black, Latino and Asian-American Undocumented Young Adults." Pp. 93–113 in *Scholars and Southern Californian Immigrants in Dialogue: New Conversations in Public Sociology*, edited by V. Carty, R. Luévano, and T. Woldemikael. Lanham, MD: Lexington Books.

Patler, Caitlin. 2018. "Citizen Advantage, Undocumented Disadvantage, or Both? The Comparative Educational Outcomes of Second and 1.5-Generation Latino Young Adults." *International Migration Review* 52(4):1080–1110. doi: 10.1111/imre.12347.

Patler, Caitlin, and Whitney Laster Pirtle. 2018. "From Undocumented to Lawfully Present: Do Changes to Legal Status Impact Psychological Wellbeing among Latino Immigrant Young Adults?" *Social Science & Medicine* 199:39–48. doi: 10.1016/j.socscimed.2017.03.009.

Paulle, Bowen. 2013. *Toxic Schools: High-Poverty Education in New York and Amsterdam*. Chicago: University of Chicago Press.

Perry, Keston K., and Zophia Edwards. 2023. "'Power to the People!' The Catalytic Role of the Black Power Movement in Trinidad and Tobago's Industrialization." *Social Science History* 1–27. doi: 10.1017/ssh.2023.15.

Pila, Daniela. 2016. "'I'm Not Good Enough for Anyone': Legal Status and the Dating Lives of Undocumented Young Adults." *Sociological Forum* 31(1):138–58. doi: https://doi.org/10.1111/socf.12237.

Pleck, J. 1995. "The Gender Role Strain Paradigm: An Update." Pp. 11–32 in *A New Psychology of Men*, edited by R. F. Levant and W. S. Pollack. New York: Basic Books.

Portes, Alejandro, and Rubén G. Rumbaut. 2001. *Legacies: The Story of the Immigrant Second Generation*. Berkeley: University of California Press.

Portes, Alejandro, and Min Zhou. 1993. "The New Second Generation: Segmented Assimilation and Its Variants." *Annals of the American Academy of Political and Social Science* 530(1):74–96. doi://10.1177/0002716293530001006.

Pyke, Karen D., and Denise L. Johnson. 2003. "Asian American Women and Racialized Femininities: 'Doing' Gender across Cultural Worlds." *Gender and Society* 17(1):33–53.

Ramos, Dandara, Emanuelle Góes, Joilda Nery, and Osiyallê Rodrigues. 2022. "Violence, Structural Racism, and Their Relation to Health Outcomes of Black Brazilian Youth." Pp. 53–66 in *Racism and Human Development*, edited by L. Dutra-Thomé, D. F. Rabelo, D. Ramos, and E. F. Góes. Cham, Switzerland: Springer International.

Ray, Ranita. 2017. *The Making of a Teenage Service Class: Poverty and Mobility in an American City*. 1st ed. Oakland: University of California Press.

Ray, Rashawn. 2020. "Bad Apples Come from Rotten Trees in Policing." *Brookings*. Retrieved September 5, 2022 (https://www.brookings.edu/blog/how-we-rise/2020/05/30/bad-apples-come-from-rotten-trees-in-policing/).

Restaurant Opportunities Center United. 2015. *Ending Jim Crow in America's Restaurants: Racial and Gender Occupational Segregation in the Restaurant Industry*. New York: ROC United.

Rincón, Alejandra. 2008. *Undocumented Immigrants and Higher Education: Si Se Puede!* El Paso, TX: LFB Scholarly Publishing.

Robinson, Cedric J. 2000. *Black Marxism: The Making of the Black Radical Tradition*. Chapel Hill: University of North Carolina Press.

Roediger, David. 1991. *The Wages of Whiteness: Race and the Making of the American Working Class*. London: Verso.

Romero, Mary. 2006. "Racial Profiling and Immigration Law Enforcement: Rounding Up of Usual Suspects in the Latino Community." *Critical Sociology* 32(2–3):447–73. doi: 10.1163/156916306777835376.

Romero, Mary, and Marwah Serag. 2005. "Violation of Latino Civil Rights Resulting from INS and Local Police's Use of Race, Culture and Class Profiling: The Case of the Chandler Roundup in Arizona." *Cleveland. State Law Review* (52):75–96.

Rosenberg, Andrew S. 2022. *Undesirable Immigrants: Why Racism Persists in International Migration*. Princeton, NJ: Princeton University Press.

Roth, Benjamin J. 2019. "The Double Bind of DACA: Exploring the Legal Violence of Liminal Status for Undocumented Youth." *Ethnic and Racial Studies* 42(15):2548–65. doi: 10.1080/01419870.2018.1540790.

Roth, Wendy. 2012. *Race Migrations: Latinos, and the Cultural Transformation of Race*. 1st ed. Stanford, CA: Stanford University Press.

Rouse, Roger. 1992. "Making Sense of Settlement: Class Transformation, Cultural Struggle, and Transnationalism among Mexican Migrants in the United States." in *Towards a Transnational Perspective on Migration: Race, Class, Ethnicity, and Nationalism Reconsidered*, edited by N. Glick-Schiller, L. Basch, and C. Blanc-Szanton. New York: New York Academy of Sciences.

Rumbaut, Rubén G. 2008. "Reaping What You Sow: Immigration, Youth, and Reactive Ethnicity." *Applied Developmental Science* 12(2):108–11. doi: 10.1080/10888690801997341.

Sanchez, Casey. 2008. "Massachusetts Brothers Lead Nativist Crusade Against Brazilian Immigrants in Boston Suburb." *Southern Poverty Law Center*. Retrieved October 16, 2023 (https://www.splcenter.org/fighting-hate/intelligence-report/2008/massachusetts-brothers-lead-nativist-crusade-against-brazilian-immigrants-boston-suburb).

Sánchez, Bernadette, Yesenia Garcia-Murillo, Lidia Y. Monjaras-Gaytan, Kay Thursby, Grevelin Ulerio, Wendy de los Reyes, Ida R. Salusky, and Claudio S. Rivera. 2022. "Everyday Acts of Resistance: Mexican, Undocumented Immigrant Children and Adolescents Navigating Oppression With Mentor Support." *Journal of Research on Adolescence* 32 (2): 398–416. https://doi.org/10.1111/jora.12755.

Sansone, Livio. 2003. *Blackness Without Ethnicity: Constructing Race in Brazil*. Houndmills: Palgrave Macmillan.

dos Santos, Sales Augusto. 2002. "Historical Roots of the 'Whitening' of Brazil." *Latin American Perspectives* 29(1):61–82. doi: 10.1177/0094582X0202900104.

Saperstein, Aliya, and Andrew M. Penner. 2012. "Racial Fluidity and Inequality in the United States." *American Journal of Sociology* 118(3):676–727. doi: 10.1086/667722.

Schmalzbauer, Leah. 2014. *The Last Best Place? Gender, Family, and Migration in the New West*. 1st ed. Stanford, CA: Stanford University Press.

Schwartzman, Luisa Farah. 2007. "Does Money Whiten? Intergenerational Changes in Racial Classification in Brazil." *American Sociological Review* 72(6):940–63. doi: 10.1177/000312240707200605.

Selod, Saher. 2018. *Forever Suspect: Racialized Surveillance of Muslim Americans in the War on Terror*. New Brunswick, NJ: Rutgers University Press.

Shah, Khushbu, and Juweek Adolphe. 2019. "400 Years since Slavery: A Timeline of American History." *Guardian*, August 16.

Sheriff, Robin E. 2001. *Dreaming Equality: Color, Race, and Racism in Urban Brazil*. Piscataway, NJ: Rutgers University Press.

Silva, Nelson do Valle. 1994. "Uma Nota Sobre 'raça Social' No Brasil." *Estudos Afro-Asiáticos* 26:67–80.

Silver, Alexis. 2012. "Aging into Exclusion and Social Transparency: Undocumented Immigrant Youth and the Transition to Adulthood." *Latino Studies* 10(4):499–522. doi: 10.1057/lst.2012.41.

Silver, Alexis M. 2018a. "Displaced at 'Home': 1.5-Generation Immigrants Navigating Membership after Returning to Mexico." *Ethnicities* 18(2):208–24. doi: 10.1177/1468796817752560.

Silver, Alexis M. 2018b. *Shifting Boundaries: Immigrant Youth Negotiating National, State, and Small-Town Politics*. Stanford, CA: Stanford University Press.

Siqueira, Carlos Eduardo, and Thiago Jansen. 2008. "Updating Demographic, Geographic, and Occupational Data on Brazilians in Massachusetts." Pp. 105–24 in *Becoming Brazuca: Brazilian Immigration to the United States*, edited by C. Jouët-Pastré and L. J. Braga. Cambridge, MA: Harvard University Press.

Skidmore, Thomas E. 1992. *Black into White: Race and Nationality in Brazilian Thought*. Durham, NC: Duke University Press.

Smedley, Brian D., Adrienne Y. Stith, Lois Colburn, Clyde H. Evans, and Institute of Medicine (US). 2001. "Inequality in Teaching and Schooling: How Opportunity Is Rationed to Students of Color in America." in *The Right Thing to Do, the Smart Thing to Do: Enhancing Diversity in the Health Professions: Summary of the Symposium on Diversity in Health Professions in Honor of Herbert W. Nickens, M.D.* National Academies Press.

Smith, Robert. 2005. *Mexican New York: Transnational Lives of New Immigrants*.

Sommers, Benjamin D., Meredith Roberts Tomasi, Katherine Swartz, and Arnold M. Epstein. 2012. "Reasons for the Wide Variation in Medicaid Participation Rates Among States Hold Lessons for Coverage Expansion in 2014." *Health Affairs* 31(5):909–19. doi: 10.1377/hlthaff.2011.0977.

Suárez-Orozco, Carola, Marcelo Suárez-Orozco, and Irina Todorova. 2008. *Learning a New Land: Immigrant Students in American Society*. Cambridge, MA: Harvard University Press.

Telles, Edward. 2018. "Latinos, Race, and the US Census." *Annals of the American Academy of Political and Social Science* 677(1):153–64. doi: 10.1177/0002716218766463.

Telles, Edward E. 2002. "Racial Ambiguity among the Brazilian Population." *Ethnic and Racial Studies* 25(3):415–41. doi: 10.1080/01419870252932133.

Telles, Edward E. 2004. *Race in Another America: The Significance of Skin Color in Brazil*. Princeton, NJ: Princeton University Press.

Telles, Edward, René D. Flores, and Fernando Urrea-Giraldo. 2015. "Pigmentocracies: Educational Inequality, Skin Color and Census Ethnoracial Identification in Eight Latin American Countries." *Research in Social Stratification and Mobility* 40:39–58. doi: 10.1016/j.rssm.2015.02.002.

Terborg-Penn, Rosalyn. 1998. *African American Women in the Struggle for the Vote, 1850–1920*. Bloomington: Indiana University Press.

Terriquez, Veronica. 2014. "Trapped in the Working Class? Prospects for the Intergenerational (Im)Mobility of Latino Youth." *Sociological Inquiry* 84(3):382–411. doi: https://doi.org/10.1111/soin.12042.

Twine, France Winddance. 1998. *Racism in a Racial Democracy: The Maintenance of White Supremacy in Brazil*. New Brunswick, NJ: Rutgers University Press.

UNHR. 2022. "Brazil: UN Experts Decry Acts of Racialised Police Brutality." *OHCHR*. Retrieved October 16, 2023 (https://www.ohchr.org/en/press-releases/2022/07/brazil-un-experts-decry-acts-racialised-police-brutality).

United States Citizenship and Immigration Services. 2022. "Unlawful Presence and Inadmissibility | USCIS." Retrieved September 4, 2022 (https://www.uscis.gov/laws-and-policy/other-resources/unlawful-presence-and-inadmissibility).

Urry, John. 2007. *Mobilities*. Malden, MA: Policy Press.

Valdez, Zulema. 2011. *The New Entrepreneurs: How Race, Class, and Gender Shape American Enterprise*. Stanford, CA: Stanford University Press.

Valdez, Zulema, and Tanya Golash-Boza. 2020. "Master Status or Intersectional Identity? Undocumented Students' Sense of Belonging on a College Campus." *Identities* 27(4):481–99. doi: 10.1080/1070289X.2018.1534452.

Vargas, Jose Antonio. 2011. "My Life as an Undocumented Immigrant." *New York Times Magazine*.

Vasquez-Tokos, Jessica. 2017. *Marriage Vows and Racial Choices*. New York: Russell Sage Foundation.

Villazor, Rose Cuison. 2011. "The Other Loving: Uncovering the Federal Government's Racial Regulation of Marriage." *New York University Law Review* 86:1395–1400.

Wald, Johanna, and Daniel J. Losen. 2003. "Defining and Redirecting a School-to-Prison Pipeline." *New Directions for Youth Development* 2003(99):9–15. doi: 10.1002/yd.51.

Wang, Wendy. 2012. *The Rise of Intermarriage: Rates, Characteristics Vary by Race and Gender*. Washington, DC: Pew Research Center.

Wanzo, Rebecca. 2008. "The Era of Lost (White) Girls: On Body and Event." *Differences* 19(2):99–126. doi: 10.1215/10407391-2008-005.

Warren, Robert, and Donald Kerwin. 2017. "The 2,000 Mile Wall in Search of a Purpose: Since 2007 Visa Overstays Have Outnumbered Undocumented Border Crossers by a Half Million—Robert Warren, Donald Kerwin, 2017." *Journal on Migration and Human Security* 5(1):124–37. doi: https://doi-org.providence.idm.oclc.org/10.1177/233150241700500107.

Waters, Mary C. 2001. *Black Identities: West Indian Immigrant Dreams and American Realities*. Cambridge, MA: Russell Sage Foundation Books at Harvard University Press.

Watson, Jake. 2018. "Family Ideation, Immigration, and the Racial State: Explaining Divergent Family Reunification Policies in Britain and the US." *Ethnic and Racial Studies* 41(2):324–42. doi: 10.1080/01419870.2017.1324169.

Weinstein, Barbara. 2015. *The Color of Modernity: São Paulo and the Making of Race and Nation in Brazil*. Durham, NC: Duke University Press.

Willen, Sarah S. 2007. "Toward a Critical Phenomenology of 'Illegality': State Power, Criminalization, and Abjectivity among Undocumented Migrant Workers in Tel Aviv, Israel." *International Migration* 45(3):8–38. doi: 10.1111/j.1468-2435.2007.00409.x.

Wilson, Eli Revelle Yano. 2020. *Front of the House, Back of the House: Race and Inequality in the Lives of Restaurant Workers*. New York: New York University Press.

Winant, Howard. 2004. *The New Politics of Race: Globalism, Difference, Justice*. Minneapolis: University of Minnesota Press.

Wong, Tom K., Sanaa Abrar, Claudia Flores, Tom Jawetz, Ignacia Rodriguez Kmec, Greisa Martinez Rosas, Holly Straut-Eppsteiner, and Philip E. Wolgin. 2019. "DACA Recipients' Livelihoods, Families, and Sense of Security Are at Stake This November." *Center for American Progress*. Retrieved January 6, 2021 (https://www.americanprogress.org/issues/immigration/news/2019/09/19/474636/daca-recipients-livelihoods-families-sense-security-stake-november/).

Yarin, Sophie. 2022. "If Hispanics Hate the Term 'Latinx', Why Is It Still Used?" *Boston University*. Retrieved October 23, 2023 (https://www.bu.edu/articles/2022/why-is-latinx-still-used-if-hispanics-hate-the-term/).

Yazdiha, Hajar. 2021. "Toward a Du Boisian Framework of Immigration Incorporation: Racialized Contexts, Relational Identities, and Muslim American Collective Action." *Social Problems* 68(2):300–320. doi: https://doi.org/10.1093/socpro/spaa058.

Yoshikawa, Hirokazu. 2011. *Immigrants Raising Citizens: Undocumented Parents and Their Young Children*. New York: Russell Sage Foundation.

Yukich, Grace. 2013. "Constructing the Model Immigrant: Movement Strategy and Immigrant Deservingness in the New Sanctuary Movement." *Social Problems* 60(3):302–20. doi: 10.1525/sp.2013.60.3.302.

Zamora, Lazaro. 2013. *E-Verify Brief History and Overview: Bipartisan Policy Center*. Washington, DC: Bipartisan Policy Center.

Zhou, Min. 1997. "Segmented Assimilation: Issues, Controversies, and Recent Research on the New Second Generation." *International Migration Review* 31(4):975–1008. doi: 10.1177/019791839703100408.

Zong, Jie, and Jeanne Batalova. 2019. "How Many Unauthorized Immigrants Graduate from US High Schools Annually?" *Migrationpolicy.org*. Retrieved January 2, 2021 (https://www.migrationpolicy.org/research/unauthorized-immigrants-graduate-us-high-schools).

INDEX

Abrego, Leisy, 11, 195n1
activism, 7, 14, 31, 174, 181
adjustment of status (AOS), 35, 36, 88, 99, 108, 117, 195n38
affirmative action, 19, 199n12
Africa, 7, 23, 25, 103
African Americans, 25, 127, 128, 153; Brazilian ancestry, 129; power of, 154, 199n12; stigmatized, 136. *See also* Black Americans
Africans, 20; enslaved, 18, 19
Afro-Brazilians, 19, 110, 127, 128, 178, 196n9
Afro-Caribbeans, 23, 27, 57
Alexander, Michelle, 25
Amazon, Brazil's, 16–17t, 33, 158, 176, 177, 179–81, 193n20, 194n32
ambivalence about identification, 38, 132, 138, 139, 140–47, 140t, 151, 152, 154, 160
America, Northeastern, 41, 189, 195n2
American society, 3, 5, 26, 138, 153, 161, 164; domination/oppression system in, 172; ethno-racial hierarchy in, 43; excludes undocumented immigrants, 146, 151; insiders in, 70; marrying for love in, 122; racial uplift in, 57; reactive ethnicity owing to, 133–34; romance in, 102; sense of belonging in, 45, 167; standard of living in, 135
American South, 16–17t, 24, 26
American Southwest, 23
Americanization, 5, 177; dating preferences, 125, 126; identifying as American and, 135, 142, 145, 149, 150, 169, 186
anti-Blackness, 131, 168, 178; in Brazil vs. US, 16–17t; of Brazilian immigrants, 105; *mineiro* identity, 21; mulatto escape hatch, 110; operates transnationally, 169; in romantic preferences, 124, 126–30; undergirds global racial economy, 173; in undocumented migration scholarship, 164; in US immigration history, 26; white supremacy and capitalism, 8, 166, 167
anti-indigeneity, 7, 164, 166, 167, 168, 169, 173. *See also* indigenous groups
antimiscegenation laws, 24, 107, 110, 193n22. *See also* interracial marriage
Arabs, 46, 49
Aranda, Elizabeth, 138

221

arrest, 11, 28, 41, 44, 47, 97, 142, 143. *See also* detention; incarceration
articulation framework, 5, 164, 167, 170, 193n16
Asia, 7, 16–17t, 23, 25, 55, 122, 126, 153, 164
Asians, 2, 56, 153, 157, 174, 198n3; in antimiscegenation laws, 193n22; Chinese, 23, 27, 28, 57; dating, 124, 127; Japanese, 107; Koreans, 89; marrying outside race, 198n2; migrants, 20
assimilation, 7, 13, 26, 135, 136, 153, 164, 166

back of house jobs, 76, 92, 93
Bahia, Brazil, 193n21
Bany, James, 127
barriers, 152; to belonging, 38, 160; financial, 11, 38, 41, 77–81, 87, 90, 146, 199n7; to socioeconomic mobility, 28; to status change, 8; to work, 2, 13, 75, 151
barriers to education, 2, 4, 13, 38, 41, 73, 75, 82; financial, 11, 77–81, 87, 90, 100, 146, 199n7; informational, 100; legal, 11, 77–81, 87, 90, 199n7
Bashi Treitler, Vilna, 27, 57
beauty, 16–17t, 47, 50, 67, 69, 127, 129. *See also* physical features
belonging, sense of, 180; American identity and, 135, 136; in American society, 45, 167; barriers to, 38, 160; government's treatment of immigrants hinders, 149, 150; illegality hinders, 5, 28, 39, 163; outsider status, 171; passing as white does not lead to, 10; power without papers and, 7, 132; stigma hinders, 168
Biden, Joe, 170; processes DACA applications, 191n3
Black Americans, 3, 24, 127, 137, 178. *See also* African Americans
Black feminists, 14, 164
Black Radical Tradition, 7, 14, 18, 164, 167, 192n9

Black space, 54–56
Blackness, 22, 23, 26, 27. *See also* anti-Blackness
Black/white binary, 16–17t, 153
blue-collar jobs, 9, 76, 95, 101
Board of Higher Education, 78, 81, 191n5
Bolivians, 16–17t, 19
Bolsa Escola (program), 188
Bonilla-Silva, Eduardo, 24
bootstrap narrative, 16–17t, 22
Border Patrol, 40, 41, 44, 46, 47, 170, 189, 195n2, 195n3. *See also* immigration enforcement
Border Protection, Antiterrorism, and Illegal Immigration Control Act, 181
boundary-making, 43, 56–62, 169
boundary-work, 37, 62, 153, 154, 155, 173, 178, 192n13
Brazil: Amazon, 16–17t, 33, 158, 176, 177, 179–81, 193n20, 194n32; Bahia, 193n21; Curitiba, 193n21; Espirito Santo, 33, 34t; Governador Valadares, 29, 194n36; Minas Gerais, 21, 29, 33, 34t, 176, 193n19; Paraiba, 34t; Parana, 34t, 193n21; Rio de Janeiro, 33, 34t, 69, 87, 193n19; Rio Grande du Sul, 193n19; Salvador, 193n21; Santa Catarina, 33, 34t; São Paulo, 20, 21, 33, 34t, 181
Brazilian elites, 18, 19, 20, 110
Brazilian-American identities, 139, 160; affirming, 151–54; ambivalent, 140–47
Brazilianness, 177
Brondizio, Eduardo, 180
Brown, Karida, 137
Brown space, 54–56
Burciaga, Edelina, 14
Bush, George W., 92, 191n3, 197n7

California, 14, 30, 42, 74, 78, 81, 89, 95
Canada/Canadians, 35, 46, 59, 113, 114, 115
Caribbean immigrants, 23, 25, 27, 57, 69, 185
Central America/Central Americans, 14, 109, 122, 163, 164, 180, 189

character, 61, 172
Chari, Sharad, 192n9
Chavez, Leo, 3, 4, 26
Childs, Erica Chito, 127
Chinese, 23, 27, 28, 57
Chinese Exclusion Act, 23
Cho, Esther, 89, 90
citizenship policies, 16, 19, 170. *See also* immigration policies
Civil War, US, 23, 24
class, poor, 20, 33, 188; in Brazil, 34t; European immigrants of, 22; in Greater Boston area, 54; illegality conflated with, 139; immigration patterns of, 58, 61, 169, 200n5; immigration/border laws/policies' effects on, 109, 172; Latin American immigrants framed as, 155; public and psychological wages of whiteness for, 45; resource access, 15; Southern white workers, 27; stigmatization of, 134, 161. *See also* poverty
class, upper-middle, 3, 34t, 61, 72, 73, 74, 108, 188. *See also* wealth
classed hierarchy, 76
classed labor market, 91, 92, 165
classed status, 136
classed stereotypes of illegality, 56
classism, 59, 61, 171, 172
Clergé, Orly, 7
coalitions for social change, 39, 172, 173, 174
co-ethnic niches, 89–91, 100
collective identity, 43, 62, 173
college degree, 9, 76, 85, 91, 92, 94, 145. *See also* higher education; postsecondary education
Collins, Patricia Hill, 15
color line, 137, 155, 161
color-blind ideology, 16–17t, 22, 24, 25, 55, 61
colorism, 83
Congress, US, 135, 171; Chinese Exclusion Act, 23; Defense of Marriage Act, 106; Expatriation Act, 106; Hart-Celler Act, 25; Illegal Immigration Reform and Immigrant Responsibility Act (IIRIRA), 108, 181, 192n15, 194n30; Immigration and Nationality Act (INA), 36, 108–9, 194n30; Immigration Marriage Fraud Amendment (IMFA), 108; Immigration Reform and Control Act (IRCA), 92, 197n7; Legal Immigration Family Equity (LIFE) Act, 36
constructing whiteness, 6, 28, 43, 63, 71, 75; gendered, 74; legal passing and, 51–54, 70
Cook-Martin, David, 18
courtship, 109, 111–13, 115. *See also* romantic partnerships/relationships
Crenshaw, Kimberlé, 14
criminalization, 24, 25, 107, 181
Crutchfield, Jandel, 83
Curitiba, Brazil, 193n21
Customs and Border Protection (CBP), 195n2. *See also* Border Patrol

da Silva, Lula, 188
DACA (Deferred Action for Childhood Arrivals), 65, 88, 115, 118, 148, 182; affects education financing, 31, 191–92n5; benefits of, 84; DACAmented, 13, 27, 74, 141; driver's license, 111; eligibility for, 114, 191n2; implementation of, 32; liminal legality of, 35, 96, 142, 171; precarity of, 1–3; status, 191n4; stratifies, 11–13; Trump terminates, 64, 191n3; work permits, 50, 87
data analysis, 175, 176, 178, 187–89
data collection, 31–37, 180, 181, 182, 194n28. *See also* fieldwork
Defense of Marriage Act, 106
Degler, Carl, 21, 110
dehumanization, 137, 150, 161, 193n24
Democrats, 172, 194n30
Department of Homeland Security (DHS), 149

deportability, 39, 65, 143, 168; immigration status and, 12, 195n38; under neoliberal capitalism, 25, 37, 43, 70; passing as white reduces, 44, 66, 71

detention, 11, 28, 40, 47, 49, 62, 163, 168, 171, 193n24. *See also* arrest; incarceration

Development, Relief, and Education for Alien Minors (DREAM) Act, 171

discrimination, 37, 41, 51, 97, 140, 150, 186; in immigration laws/policies, 23, 25, 108, 165, 198n3; racial, 16–17t, 18, 24, 96, 151, 195n4

disposable workforce, 9, 16–17t, 25, 44, 165

domination/dominance, 172; global systems of, 5, 10; in higher paid jobs, 95; intersectionality and, 14; passing as white and, 42; penalty and privilege in, 15; power without papers and, 6–8; in restaurant jobs, 92, 93, 94; in romantic relationships, 126; structures of, 166, 167, 168; white, 16–17t, 154; of white men, 127. *See also* oppression

Dominicans, 28, 29, 30, 87, 182

double consciousness, 10, 38, 137, 138, 161. *See also* twoness

Dowling, Julie, 5

DREAMer movement, 62, 73, 81; Development, Relief, and Education for Alien Minors (DREAM) Act, 171

driver's license, 3, 41, 43, 52, 89, 115, 144, 186; ability to obtain, 171; adjustment of status provides access to, 88; DACA provides access to, 12, 65, 111; Massachusetts, 46, 53

Du Bois, W. E. B., 10, 26, 27, 45, 136, 137, 144, 150, 161

Eastern Europeans, 16–17t, 20, 23
economic uplift, 45
elites, 16–17t, 26, 79, 81; Brazilian, 18, 20, 110; economic, 19, 20; US, 20
embranquecimento, 110
employment authorization, 12, 36, 195n38

employment authorization card. *See* work permits

Enriquez, Laura, 11, 14, 43, 44, 105, 109, 114, 122

Escudero, Kevin, 14, 174

Espirito Santo, Brazil, 33, 34t

ethnic projects, 27

ethnicity, 133, 198n2; articulation of, 134, 138; intersection with legal status, 136

ethno-racial identities, 134, 135, 138, 153, 154–60, 186, 196n8, 197n17, 198n2

Eurocentrism, 69, 83

Europe, 55, 103, 122, 134, 157, 159; colonizers, 8, 18, 154; Eastern Europeans, 16–17t, 20, 23; European physical features, 83, 105, 110, 127, 129; immigrants, 22; migration from to Brazil, 21; Southern Europeans, 16–17t, 20, 23, 42, 92, 94, 156

E-verify, 87, 92, 101, 197n7

EWI. *See* inspection

Expatriation Act, 106

exploitation, 8, 10, 18, 136, 155, 161; economic, 26; workplace, 25, 27, 77, 87, 97–100, 101, 166, 168, 171

family formation, 38, 105, 106, 107, 111, 114

family reunification, 25, 105, 108, 109, 117

Feagin, Joe, 49

federal student grants/loans, 2, 4, 11, 12, 78, 135, 144. *See also* financial aid (for college)

feelings of belonging. *See* sense of belonging

feelings of desirability, 38, 105, 109, 112, 130

Feliciano, Cynthia, 127

feminism, 19, 105, 126; Black feminists, 14, 164

fieldwork, 28, 31, 32, 33, 66, 78, 158, 179, 180, 181–87. *See also* data collection

financial aid (for college), 2, 80, 85, 194n35, 197n3. *See also* federal student grants/loans; tuition

financial safety nets, 4, 77, 79, 85, 86, 87–89, 165, 199n7
first-generation Brazilians, 9, 27, 30, 54, 62, 126, 135, 177
first-generation immigrants, 160
Fitzgerald, David, 18
Flores-González, Nilda, 140
for-profit organizations, 89–91
Franklin, Benjamin, 26
Freyre, Gilberto, 18–19
front of house jobs, 76, 92, 94, 168

García, Angela, 5, 42, 43
gender/sexuality, 169, 188, 192n7; LGBTQ+ people, 172, 194n31
genocide, 18
geographic logic, 155, 157
Global North, 29, 76, 78
global racial capitalism, 18, 19, 25
global racial economy, 5, 8, 13, 27, 69, 75, 167, 172, 173
global racialized social relations, 15, 167
Global South, 76, 108, 124, 165, 172
Goffman, Erving, 42
Golash-Boza, Tanya, 7, 9, 14, 25, 69, 70, 137, 140, 172
Gonzales, Roberto, 2, 13, 14, 63, 74
Governador Valadares, Brazil, 29, 194n36
Great Britain, 96, 113, 115
green cards, 200n4; from adjustment-of-status application, 36; American identity, 140, 147, 151; college and, 85, 99; deportation and, 40, 48, 49, 104; *Green Card*, 117; lawful permanent residents, 12; marrying for, 120; obtaining, 61, 82, 83, 133; of respondents, 34t; stigma and, 51; white identity, 156

Haitians, 16–17t, 19
Hall, Stuart, 8, 15, 192n9, 193n16
Hanen, Andrew, 191n3
Haney López, Ian, 23, 108
Harris, Cheryl, 42

Hart-Celler Act, 25
health care, 16–17t, 22
heteronormativity, 106
hierarchies: American, 160; Brazilian racial, 163; ethno-racial, 7, 27, 28, 43, 71, 128, 129, 193n26; gendered, 76; global racialized economic, 8; immigration status, 161; legal status, 163; occupational, 89; race/class, 16–17t, 42, 76, 110, 186; racial/economic, 5, 6, 136; social/economic, 19; status, 26, 153
higher education, 100, 169; access to, 13, 76, 78, 159, 167; affirmative action quotas in, 19; barriers to, 11, 81–82, 102, 168; cost of, 31; DACA effects on, 1; expands dating pools, 122; interruptions to, 38, 77, 79, 83–85; power without papers shapes, 75, 87. *See also* postsecondary education
homophobia, 172
hooks, bell, 107
hostility, 32, 119; in immigration enforcement, 9, 67; in immigration laws, 5, 12, 77, 130, 172; information vacuum on navigating, 81; of labor market, 87; toward immigrants, 25, 42, 92, 99, 168, 170, 200n4
housing, 16–17t, 19, 22, 33, 54, 66, 183
human rights, 172, 180

I-9 forms, 92, 197n7
identities of 1.5-generation Brazilians, 140t
Illegal Immigration Reform and Immigrant Responsibility Act (IIRIRA), 108, 181, 192n15, 194n30
illegality, 170; classed stereotypes of, 56; concealing, 51–54, 62, 63–64, 71, 74; hinders sense of belonging, 5, 28, 39, 163; racial/class privilege articulates with, 39, 75, 77; racialized, 7, 15, 42, 43; salience of, 77–85, 139, 152, 160, 167; stigma of, 104, 113, 147; in systems of power, 14–16; wages of whiteness limited by, 38, 132, 160, 167

immigrants, children of, 6, 16–17t, 30, 31, 136, 181, 192n6; post-1935, 13
immigrants' rights, 173, 174, 181, 183
Immigration and Customs Enforcement (ICE), 3, 41, 66, 67, 194n30, 195n3. *See also* immigration enforcement
Immigration and Nationality Act (INA), 36, 108–9, 194n30
immigration enforcement, 11, 15, 43, 44, 62, 68, 70, 71, 172; encounters with, 45–49; hostility in, 9, 67; in workplace, 92, 197n7. *See also* Border Patrol; Immigration and Customs Enforcement (ICE); law enforcement
immigration laws, 25, 164; affect romantic experiences, 104–6, 111, 113–15, 120, 130; Chinese Exclusion Act, 23; discrimination in, 23, 25, 108, 165, 198n3; on family reunification, 109, 117; Hart-Celler Act, 25; hostility in, 5, 12, 77, 130, 172; Illegal Immigration Reform and Immigrant Responsibility Act (IIRIRA), 108, 181, 192n15, 194n30; Immigration and Nationality Act (INA), 36, 108–9, 194n30; Immigration Marriage Fraud Amendment (IMFA), 108; Immigration Reform and Control Act (IRCA), 92, 197n7; Legal Immigration Family Equity (LIFE) Act, 36; legal violence of, 11, 40, 44, 195n1; prevents travel, 97; whiteness and, 46, 47
immigration lawyers, 31, 32, 36, 183, 196n15
Immigration Marriage Fraud Amendment (IMFA), 108
immigration officers, 15, 40, 65
immigration policies, 59, 68, 165, 171, 172, 185
immigration reform, 172, 174
Immigration Reform and Control Act (IRCA), 92, 197n7
immigration status, 52, 64; college opportunities affected by, 4, 77; deportability and, 195n38; hierarchies, 161; identity and, 74, 144; lawful permanent residency and, 82; legal, 12, 13, 38; racialized, 6, 139, 149–50, 193n25; romantic relationships affected by, 104, 113, 118; travel hinders, 177
imperialism, 7, 18, 25, 155, 164; economic structures, 173; power dynamics, 176
incarceration, 22, 24, 25, 48, 49, 78, 97, 143, 193n24. *See also* arrest
indigenous groups, 153; anti-indigeneity, 7, 164, 166, 167, 168, 169, 173; domination over, 15; genocide of, 18; marginalization of, 16–17t; physical features of, 3; racial intermixing with, 110, 193n22; racialization as, 26, 33; removal/enslavement of, 8; violence against, 19
Individual Tax Identification Number (ITIN), 86, 197n6
inequalities, 111–21, 136, 168, 180, 188; race/class, 19, 21, 35, 38, 105, 165; social, 187
information vacuum, 81–83
insider status, 70, 175, 176, 180. *See also* outsider status
inspection, 48, 195n2; entry without, 9, 33, 35, 59, 109, 164, 166, 198n4
in-state tuition, 12, 31, 81, 100, 135; in Massachusetts, 2, 11, 73, 78, 191n5, 197n3
internal enforcement, 92, 172
interracial marriage, 16–17t, 107, 110, 129. *See also* antimiscegenation laws
intersectionality, 14–15, 136, 167, 172, 174
Ireland, 22, 175
Irish immigrants, 16–17t, 57, 95, 157; Irish threat, 26
Italians, 54, 57, 59, 103, 152, 156, 157, 187
Italy, 20, 22
Itzigsohn, José, 137

jail. *See* incarceration
Japanese women, 107
Jim Crow laws, 16–17t, 18, 24, 25, 45, 162
Joseph, Tiffany, 7, 131, 137

INDEX   227

Kerwin, Donald, 164
Koreans, 89

LatCrit, 14, 15
Latino Threat Narrative, 4
law enforcement, 41, 43, 97, 194n30, 195n3. *See also* Border Patrol; Immigration and Customs Enforcement (ICE); immigration enforcement
legal (political) citizenship, 5, 135, 137, 141–43, 154, 160–62, 170, 172
legal exclusion, 5, 119, 133, 139, 147, 148, 149, 177
Legal Immigration Family Equity (LIFE) Act, 36
legal inclusion, 86, 96, 164
legal passing, 5, 37, 42, 43, 51–54, 70, 165, 189
legal violence, 11, 40, 44
legalization (of immigrants), 75, 101, 103, 106, 109, 130; relationships, 117–21
LGBTQ+ people, 172, 194n31
Lima, Álvaro, 89
liminal legality, 59, 82, 84, 186; adjustment-of-status application leads to, 46; affects education choices, 78, 79, 85; affects travel, 83; DACA leads to, 12, 35, 96, 142, 171; precariousness of, 88; respondent statistics, 34t; Section 245i of Immigration and Nationality Act led to, 195n38
low-wage jobs, 9, 28, 76, 86, 90, 100

machismo, 125, 126. *See also* patriarchy
Marcelli, Enrico, 182, 183, 200n5
marginalization, 10, 43, 70, 77, 173, 176, 193n24; of Black and indigenous groups, 16–17t; of Brazilian immigrants, 6; legal, 51, 121, 138, 161; power without papers, 69, 135, 163; power works with, 8, 15, 165, 166, 168; racial, 78, 173; under racial capitalism, 44
Margolis, Maxine, 30
marriage markets, 122–24

marriage myths, 117–22
Marrow, Helen, 30, 157
marrying for papers, 38, 101, 103–6, 117–21, 130
Marshall, T. H., 135, 144
Martes, Ana Cristina Braga, 29, 194n36
Marxism, 18, 192n9
Maryland, 107
Massachusetts, 66, 74, 133, 195n2; barriers to college in, 38, 100; Brazilian immigrant's coming of age in, 8, 33, 167; Brazilian migration to, 5, 20, 21, 28–31, 169, 170; Brazilians' self-employment rate in, 89; driver's licenses, 46, 53; E-Verify in, 92; immigrant student financial aid, 197n2; immigrant students' needs and rights in, 32; information vacuum in, 81; legal, financial, and institutional hurdles in, 85; partnership with ICE, 194n30; school quality in, 72; in-state tuition, 2, 11, 73, 78, 191n5, 197n3; Student Immigrant Movement (SIM), 197n4; University of Massachusetts Boston, 79, 182
master status, 2, 7, 13, 14, 70, 71, 140, 166, 167
Menino, Thomas, 194n30
Menjívar, Cecilia, 11, 172, 195n11
methodology, 31–37, 175–89
Mexican-American War, 24
Mexicans, 14, 23, 24, 25–26, 27, 57, 59, 60; 1.5-generation, 89, 122; deportees, 68; immigrants in California, 42, 74, 95
Mexico, 197n15; Hart-Celler Act, 25; immigrants from, 109, 163, 164; immigration route through, 8, 61, 62, 165, 169, 188; inspection via, 33, 35, 59; migration from encouraged, 24. *See also* US-Mexico border
Middle East, 122
Millán, Daniel, 43, 44
Minas Gerais, Brazil, 21, 29, 33, 34t, 176, 193n19

mineiro, 21, 193n19, 193n20
Miranda, Carmen, 196n9
miscegenation, 16–17t, 24, 107, 110, 193n22
mixed-race, 16–17t, 128, 129, 196n9
mobility, 152; blocked, 38, 84, 86, 94; downward, 4, 37, 73, 94, 131; geographic, 56; socioeconomic, 9, 28, 71, 167; upward, 7, 85, 110, 124, 136, 176
Monk, Ellis, 21, 193n21
Moran, Emilio, 180
Morrison, Toni, 140
mulatto escape hatch, 16–17t, 21, 110
Muslims, 36, 48, 129, 152, 199n11

Nabuco, Joaquim, 20
nationality, 6, 7, 38, 101, 105, 113, 137, 140, 155, 161
nation-state building, 5, 14–15, 165; power without papers in, 18–26; US, 22–26
naturalization, 23, 115, 143, 152, 198n7
neoliberal agenda, 9
neoliberal capitalism, 137, 166, 167, 172; deportability under, 25, 37, 43, 70; passing as white in, 42; undocumented immigrant workers under, 16–17t, 40, 45, 165; white supremacy under, 189
neoliberal economic changes, 77, 85, 106
neoliberal policies, 8, 29, 69, 76, 78
neoliberal racial economy, 9, 16, 75, 100, 101
neoliberal restructuring, 25
neoliberalism, 27, 193n24
New York, 46
9/11 attacks, 49, 58, 62, 68, 92, 153, 196n15
nonprofit organizations, 32, 88, 89–91, 93, 100, 179, 183, 184
norms: of Black and Brown underclass (in assimilation theories), 7; cultural, 12, 13, 122, 124–26; dating, 112, 116; gendered, 106, 111, 124–26, 131, 139, 152; social, 108; white middle-class, 171

oppression, 5–8, 10, 14, 15, 124, 166–68, 172. *See also* domination/dominance
Osuji, Chinyere, 57, 110, 129
outsider status, 57, 70, 112, 141, 175–77, 180; legal, 171. *See also* insider status

Paraiba, Brazil, 34t
Parana, Brazil, 34t, 193n21
passing as white: constructing whiteness, 52; deportability, 44, 66, 71; domination/dominance and, 42; identity and, 5, 134, 136; as legal-passing strategy, 37, 43, 165; negative stereotypes, 196n7; sense of belonging, 10; white wannabes, 62; work opportunities, 94, 168. *See also* legal passing
patriarchy, 14–15, 103, 105, 106, 107, 108, 125, 126, 139
Patrick, Deval, 194n30
permanent residency/status, 36, 82, 119, 166, 194n35; American identity, 133, 144, 160; deportability of, 12; green cards, 12; immigration laws affecting, 108; on pathway to citizenship, 101; respondent statistics, 35; rights/benefits of, 75, 77, 78, 83, 194n35
petitions, 116; employment-based, 36, 195n37; family-based, 195n37, 198n4; for labor certification, 195n38; for spouses, 109
Philadelphia, 27
physical features, 134, 154–55; in court racial decisions, 23; European, 83, 105, 110, 127, 129; of indigenous groups, 3; looking Mexican, 169; race determined by, 51, 196n4; for white-passing, 36, 54; for whites, 45. *See also* beauty; skin color
police brutality, 3, 16–17t
Portugal, 19, 20, 43, 156; colonization, 5, 16–17t, 19, 110

Portuguese descent, 41, 52, 60, 134, 183, 187, 196n9; Boston communities, 54, 90; identifying as white, 156; Massachusetts communities, 29

Portuguese language, 55, 83, 90, 150, 151, 176, 177; passing as white, 57, 70; racialized as Latino/a/x when speaking, 9; socioeconomic/racial status, 27

positionalities, 37, 175, 176, 178, 179, 185, 200n4

postsecondary education, 71, 75, 77, 78, 79, 81, 100. *See also* college degree; higher education

poverty, 26, 27, 30, 72, 87, 92, 109, 187. *See also* class, poor; wealth

power systems. *See* systems of power

power without papers, 6–10, 185, 194n28; 1.5-generation Brazilians' lives shaped by, 37, 44; deportability experiences shaped by, 43; of first wave of Brazilian immigrants, 30; gender/sexuality, 169, 188, 192n7; higher education and labor market shaped by, 75, 87; in immigration reform, 171, 172, 173; marriage markets and, 122–24; in nation-state building, 18–26; postsecondary transitions shaped by, 71; power/privilege and marginalization, 69, 135, 163–64, 168; race, class, and illegality, 170; race and racial positioning, 16; rights, 136; romantic relationships shaped by, 38, 105, 130; sense of belonging, 132; white supremacy and anti-Blackness, 167; work opportunities shaped by, 91

precarity/precariousness, 188; of DACA, 1–3, 12; hostile US laws cause, 5; legal status, 45, 48, 113, 114, 142, 189; of liminal legality, 88; of undocumented status, 39; of work, 28, 76, 168

prison. *See* incarceration

private schools, 13, 33, 73, 79, 80, 188

protective mechanisms, 6, 37, 43, 44, 70, 163, 165, 168

psychological wages of whiteness, 71, 131; confidence as, 48, 67, 68; of exploited white workers, 10, 26, 27; of legal-passing Brazilians, 37, 45, 46; protections from stigma, detention, and deportation, 62; respect as, 53. *See also* public wages of whiteness

public schools, 13, 80, 91

public wages of whiteness, 10, 45, 48, 50, 51, 67. *See also* psychological wages of whiteness

Puerto Rico/Puerto Ricans, 48, 128, 143, 152

queerness, 14, 174, 192n7, 193n16

racial capitalism, 167, 172; 1.5-generation Brazilians in, 7; anti-Blackness and anti-indigeneity in, 164; deportability under, 37, 43; global, 18–22; low wages in, 45; middle-class Brazilian immigration, 9; migration, nation-state building, and, 22–26; passing as white in, 42, 70; privilege and marginalization work together under, 44; racialized, compliant workers under, 40; racialized people's subjectivity in, 137; reaping benefits of, 16; romantic partner preferences in, 131; white supremacy operates under, 189; work toward whiteness in, 166

racial democracy, 16–17t, 18, 19, 21, 22

racial discrimination, 16–17t, 18, 24, 96, 151, 195n4

racial dynamics, 45–51, 128

racial economy, 10, 26–28, 30, 35, 37, 58, 87, 166. *See also* global racial economy; neoliberal racial economy

racial identification, 5, 134, 135, 139, 154, 155, 161, 162, 196n5

racial ideologies, 15, 16–17t, 19, 129

racial logics, 57, 110, 111, 129, 131, 160, 169

racial preferences, 110, 111, 121, 126–30, 131

racial projects, 5, 26, 42, 131, 196n6

racial solidarity, 10, 27, 37, 43, 180; of Blacks, 173; immigrant, 174; of whites, 49–51
racial status, 27, 105, 128, 129, 193n21
racial strategies, 42
racial uplift, 27, 57, 58, 128, 129
racial/class privilege, 35, 175; in Brazil, 165; of Brazilian immigrants, 9, 167, 168; deportation experiences shaped by, 37; financial safety nets provided by, 86; illegality articulates with, 39, 75, 77; with legal marginalization, 51; overstaying visa, 109; power without papers, 173; of "real Americans," 154; school experience affected by, 83; socioeconomic mobility and, 71; transitioning out of postsecondary education, 100; of undocumented immigrants, 28, 170; wages of whiteness and, 160; white identity and, 156
racialized legal status, 7, 15, 42, 43, 137, 147
reactive ethnicity, 134
"real" Americans, 16–17t, 45, 47, 134, 154
"real" Brazilians, 16–17t
recruitment, 175, 176, 179, 181–87
reentry, 12, 36, 67, 68, 69, 71, 104, 109, 192n15, 198n4
reflexivity, 176, 177
Republicans, 1, 172, 191n3
research process, 175–77, 179–80, 187, 189
respondent statistics, 34t
rights, 12, 24; of Black Americans, 137, 154; civil, 105, 135, 136, 139, 160; human, 172, 180; of immigrants, 32, 76, 173, 174, 181, 183; of lawful permanent residents, 194n35; legal, 148; political, 105, 135, 136, 139, 160; social, 6, 105, 135, 136, 160; stripping, 25, 27; of US citizens, 35, 139, 144, 170, 195n2
Rio de Janeiro, Brazil, 33, 34t, 69, 87, 193n19
Rio Grande du Sul, Brazil, 193n19
Robertson, Cedric, 18

Robnett, Belinda, 127
romantic love, 38, 102, 103, 105, 106, 121
romantic partnerships/relationships, 31, 37, 106, 109–11, 120–24, 127, 129, 132, 169, 182; domination/dominance in, 126; immigration status affects, 118; with non-US citizens, 113–15; power without papers shapes, 38, 105, 130
romantic preferences, 110, 111, 121, 124, 126, 127, 128, 131
Romero, Mary, 15
Romney, Mitt, 194n30
Roth, Wendy, 42

Salvador, Brazil, 193n21
Santa Catarina, Brazil, 33, 34t
São Paulo, Brazil, 20, 21, 24t, 33, 181
saudades, 177
schooling, 12, 16–17t, 33, 73, 75, 77, 79, 86; Brazil, 188; postsecondary, 100; US, 143
Schwartzman, Luisa, 21, 57
second-generation Brazilians, 31, 123, 182, 200n3
second-generation immigrants, 126, 136
Section 245i (of Immigration and Nationality Act), 36, 99, 195n38
Secure Communities, 194n30
segregation, 14, 18, 24, 45, 54, 78, 83, 122, 162
self-employment, 87, 89
sense of belonging. *See* belonging, sense of
Sensenbrenner Bill, 181
settler colonialism, 16–17t, 154, 165, 172
situational triggers, 44, 47, 64–66, 71
skin color, 42; of Brazilians vs. other Latin Americans, 198n1; changes seasonally, 200n5; courts use to make racial decisions, 23; of Hispanics, 60; in interracial unions, 16–17t; in racial discrimination, 96, 195n4; for white identity, 21, 134, 154, 161. *See also* physical features

slavery, 23, 24, 25, 137, 154, 168; of Africans, 18, 19; in Brazil, 20; in Brazil vs. US, 16–17t; of indigenous groups, 8; racial laws, 107
Smith, Robert C., 4, 192n6
social change, 39, 164, 172, 173–74, 180
social citizenship, 137
social cues, 52, 53, 70, 157, 196n4
social locations, 6, 13, 14, 100, 164, 166, 167, 192n7
social meanings, 37, 43, 45, 51
Social Security number, 36, 41, 91, 95, 116, 117, 197n6; adjustment of status provides access to, 88, 195n38; DACA provides access to, 1, 12, 35, 171, 191n2
social uplift, 129
socialization, 12, 13, 28, 100, 143
socioeconomic mobility/opportunities, 9, 28, 39, 71, 101, 167
socioeconomic status, 27
solidarity, 62, 168, 173, 174
Sousa-Rodriguez, Isabel, 138
Southern Europeans, 16–17t, 20, 23, 42, 92, 94, 156
Spain, 20
stereotypes, 42, 60, 196n9; alpha male, 112; of the Amazon, 177; in Brazil, 32; classed, 56; of ethno-racial groups, 158; gendered, 47; of Latino/a/x immigrants, 58; racial, 178; of undocumented immigrants, 131; of white-passing Brazilians, 62, 196n7
stigma, 21, 37, 47, 62, 63, 64, 68, 69, 82, 130; of Blackness, 110; in Brazilian community, 189; of illegality, 104, 113, 147; of interracial relationships, 107; of undocumented immigrants, 168
stigmatization, 8, 16–17t, 20, 33, 39, 42, 43, 56–62, 82; of African American underclass, 136; job related, 76, 92, 93; of Latino/a/xs, 168; as poor/criminals, 134, 161; status in the US, 132; stereotypes of the Amazon, 177; of undocumented immigrants, 80, 138, 149

strategic work toward whiteness, 51–62, 166
stratification, 5, 10, 23, 70, 89, 137, 164, 167; of educational transition, 77–85; legal status as source of, 11–14
Student Immigrant Movement (SIM), 81, 197n4
student visa, 2, 115, 198n6
Supreme Court, 23; on DACA, 1, 191n3; Defense of Marriage Act repeal (2013), 106; *Loving v. Virginia* (1967), 24, 107; *Plyler v. Doe* (1982), 12, 78
systemic racism, 5, 16–17t, 19, 62, 199n12
systems of power, 6, 51, 106, 108, 122; illegality in, 14–16

Texas, 1, 30, 78, 81, 195n2
Thirteenth Amendment, 24
tourist visas, 196–97n15; entering US on, 5, 8, 16, 29, 35, 61, 73, 165, 166, 178; overstaying, 9, 194n34
transitions, educational, 77–85
Transportation Security Administration (TSA), 49
trauma, 66, 138
Treaty of Guadalupe Hidalgo, 24
Trinidad and Tobago, 173
Trump, Donald, 13, 32, 64, 167, 170, 172, 191n3, 193n15, 193n23
tuition, 4, 13, 77, 80. *See also* financial aid (for college)
tuition, in-state, 2, 11, 12, 31, 73, 78, 81, 100, 135, 184; Massachusetts offers for undocumented students, 191n5, 197n3
Twine, France, 110, 129
twoness, 137–41, 140t, 147, 148, 150, 151, 154, 161. *See also* double consciousness

undocumented status, 3, 4, 14, 73, 87, 95, 101, 121, 147; after age 18, 13, 160; prevents travel, 114; racialization of, 161, 193n25
undocumented students, 2, 63, 73, 81, 184, 197n3

undocumented workers, 16–17t, 29, 44, 59, 80
undocumented youth, 4, 11–14, 31, 73, 78, 81, 85, 100, 121
unlawful presence time, 12, 37, 69
US Citizenship and Immigration Services (USCIS), 149, 195n38
US-Mexico border, 35, 58, 163, 165, 195n2. *See also* Mexico

Valdez, Zulema, 14
VanWay, Leah, 180
Vaquera, Elizabeth, 138
Vargas, Jose Antonio, 174
Vasquez-Tokos, Jessica, 123, 124
Venezuelans, 16–17t, 19
Villazor, Rose Cuison, 107
violence, 15, 195n1; legal, 11, 40, 44; racial, 18, 19; sexual, 107
visa overstay, 46, 59, 194n34; Brazilian immigration trends, 29, 35, 73, 196–97n15; immigration laws privilege, 117, 164; marriage and, 115; presents fewer barriers to status adjustment, 9, 109, 166; race and class privilege permit, 165; under racial capitalism, 9; undocumented immigrants vs., 67

wage labor, 73, 85, 87–89, 145, 151, 169
wages of whiteness, 163, 197n17; in Brazil, 193n26; Europeans benefited from, 22; illegality limits, 38, 132, 160, 167; physical, cultural, and social cues, 52; racial dynamics that enable, 45–51; self-constructions, 71; travel, 67, 68; for undocumented, 28; white identity, 134, 135; for white-passing Brazilian immigrants, 27. *See also* psychological wages of whiteness; public wages of whiteness
wealth, 23, 56, 108, 109, 168, 180; in Brazil, 20, 29, 33, 187; of European colonizers, 8, 18, 154; pre-migration, 4; of whites vs. nonwhites, 16–17t, 21. *See also* class, upper-middle
West Point, Military Academy at, 152, 154, 199n10
white racial identity, 139, 154, 155, 161, 187
white racial purity, 16–17t, 104, 107, 110, 192n11
white space, 54–56, 71
white supremacy: in Brazil, 110, 169; capitalism interlocks with, 6, 7, 42, 166; constructing whiteness sustains, 28; double consciousness and, 10; housing, education, and health effects of, 19; *mineiro* identity, 21; mobilization against, 168; under neoliberal racial capitalism, 189; power without papers and, 167; shapes immigration laws, 106; US built on, 13, 16, 22, 124; violence against women and, 14
whiteness, limits of, 10, 62–69. *See also* constructing whiteness; passing as white; wages of whiteness
whitening, 16, 19, 20, 110, 129, 131; by money, 21, 33, 57
white-passing. *See* passing as white
work permits, 2, 13, 36, 77, 84–89, 91, 94, 95, 117; college attendance and, 81; DACA provides, 1, 50, 171, 191n2; eligibility for, 41, 152; liminal legality, 35; needed for job opportunities, 100; in-state tuition rates, 31, 78, 191–92n5

ARTICULATIONS   STUDIES IN RACE,
                IMMIGRATION,
                AND CAPITALISM

EDITORS
Cedric de Leon
Pawan Dhingra

Change is afoot in sociology and related fields. Motivated by mounting social inequality and the latest groundbreaking research, a new generation of scholars is pushing for a more synthetic and empirically rigorous approach to race, immigration, and capitalism. This book series seeks work at the intersection of these three fields. The series is a space to push forward a positive research agenda that articulates immigration, race, and capitalism together as overlapping systems that are experienced in people's everyday lives. Such studies will allow us to offer more nuanced analyses on topics such as immigrant assimilation, the pervasiveness of white supremacy, and the governing economic structures that surround all forms of discrimination. With an emphasis on sociological and qualitative work, the series will also be interested in interdisciplinary work across the social sciences and humanities, with a range of methodological approaches.

Language Brokers: Children of Immigrants Translating Inequality and Belonging for Their Families
HYEYOUNG KWON   2024

The authorized representative in the EU for product safety and compliance is:
Mare Nostrum Group B.V.
Mauritskade 21D
1091 GC Amsterdam
The Netherlands
Email address: gpsr@mare-nostrum.co.uk

KVK chamber of commerce number: 96249943

The authorized representative in the EU for product safety and compliance is:
Mare Nostrum Group
B.V Doelen 72
4831 GR Breda
The Netherlands

www.ingramcontent.com/pod-product-compliance
Lightning Source LLC
Chambersburg PA
CBHW031808220426
43662CB00007B/570